"*Dragon Ride* is the most exciting modern mission book I have ever read. It is a lively narration of how God used a former atheist to reach atheists and others in one of the greatest mission fields in the world—China. It is realistic but positive, a God-centered, and God-empowered view of outreach work that will rekindle the desire to reach the 'unreachable'. Pastors, youth leaders, teachers, parents, and Christian apologists will profit greatly from the techniques learned from three decades of on-the-job experience."

Norman Geisler, Ph.D.
Professor, theologian, philosopher, and apologist
Co-founder of Veritas Evangelical Seminary
Co-founder of Southern Evangelical Seminary
Author and co-author of more than 100 books, including
I Don't Have Enough Faith to Be an Atheist

"I loved this book! It became an instant favorite. Grace lets us in on her beautiful journey and enables the reader to experience her honest doubts, difficult questions and even her frustration with God, only to see his faithful plan and provision unfold. Too many times when we hear, "The Lord works all things together for good" we don't really understand it or even necessarily believe it. This book makes that promise come alive as we repeatedly see God's sovereign and wise hand at work, even through the most difficult of circumstances. The writing is raw, honest, and inspiring. It will imr--- -y-one who reads it."

Brent Maxwell
Pastor, The Door, Three Rivers, OR

D1502755

"Buckle your seat belts for an adventure at ~~~~~~ ~~~~~ ~~~~ ~~g~) and in multiple dimensions! I could not put it down. Grace, the author and guide to this adventure, has chosen vignette after vignette to immerse you into the 'not-for-the-faint-of-heart' challenges and realities of living and working in China and following a God-given north star. And, the adventure is made even more vivid because it is told with truth, grit, wit, wisdom, and heart. Yet it gets better than that because of Grace's blessed awareness of physical, spiritual, cultural, and biblical contexts. Grace's battle-tested journey—and the journeys of those she loves—are on view. You'll be boldly encouraged and inspired to answer God's call for your own life."

Dr. Benjamin K. Homan
President, Langham Partnership (formerly John Stott Ministries)

i

"As an American pastor I've always dreamt of spending time in a far-away culture as a gospel carrier … But the reality is that I probably never will. And yet, after reading *Dragon Ride*, I feel that I have. I feel as though I've been a missionary in China without ever stepping foot on its soil. Every fear, tear, struggle, adjustment, joy, relationship, conversation, and gospel triumph recorded here became mine. Honest, sincere, human, and accessible. I found this work extremely easy to pick up and hard to put down. But what inspired me the most was the gospel-centered intentionality and heart of Grace. She was a woman, a wife, and a mother on mission, to the glory of God. I will be putting this book in the hands of everyone in our church, that we, too, may be diligently committed to tell the good news of him who saves all people everywhere. Evangelistically inspiring!"

David Thompson
Pastor, The Door, Three Rivers, OR

"Having lived for 20 years in China, one observes a range of people who come and go. Some, and rightfully so, are there for only a brief season, know little of the people and culture, and leave with an interesting life experience. A very few others integrate into the culture and become vital contributors to the expansion of God's kingdom in that great land. The Jacobs are most definitely in the latter category. Observing their lives and ministry was one of the great privileges of our life in Asia."

Tom Lowder, Th.M., Ph.D.

"This is a beautifully written story of a courageous American woman who, along with her husband and two sons, made her home in China for 29 years. It describes her unsettling journey as a young person through atheism, and then traces her extraordinary life in coming to know and love the Lord Jesus Christ. Why should any of us pay the cost of being an authentic follower of Jesus? *Dragon Ride* shows us that a lifetime of overcoming hurts and obstacles in loving obedience to Jesus is never a waste, but is a doorway to the most fruitful, adventurous, and meaningful life possible. This amazing, life-changing story of one who gave up everything for the sake of giving voice to Christ's culture-embracing love beautifully illustrates the words of Jesus when he said 'For whoever wishes to save his life will lose it, but whoever loses his life for My sake and the gospel's will save it.'" (Mark 8:35, NASB)

David Ewert
Pastor Emeritus, New Hope Church, Winston, OR
Ministry Resource, Emmanuel Reformed Church, Castleton, NY

"I never imagined I'd see God moving in a Communist country like China until I got to know Grace and Justin. They worked underground, secretly sharing God's grace in Jesus Christ. *Dragon Ride* is an inspiring story of God's call, his equipping, and his faithfulness to carry out the task."

Jim Cashwell
Area Director, Charlotte/Knoxville
Joni and Friends International Disability Ministry

"This is a thrilling account of the grace of God demonstrated in the lives of humble servants who were called to a seemingly impossible assignment in China. Justin and Grace Jacob shine with the beauty of Jesus when facing danger, stress, illness, persecution, trials, and spiritual warfare."

Dr. John H Munro
Senior Pastor, Calvary Church, Charlotte, NC

"*Dragon Ride* is a front row seat to the challenges and joys experienced by missionaries in Mainland China. Each story presents a gripping adventure, full of intrigue, often in dangerous situations charged with cross-cultural nuances and divine interventions. You will laugh and be inspired as you witness this bold family live out their faith."

Brenden Bridges
Pastor, Richvale Evangelical Free Church, Richvale, CA

"*Dragon Ride* is a well-written and insightful look into the lives of missionaries serving in a creative access country. It is filled with true life experiences shared in an easy-to-read short story format. I also found the author's candid honesty about her personal challenges refreshing, particularly as they demonstrate what God can accomplish through fallible human beings who obey God's directions and courageously follow him. In short, an inspiring book."

Dr. Jim Isaacson
Pastor, Portland Avenue Evangelical Free Church, Tacoma, WA

"Walking in the Spirit, maximizing your spiritual giftedness, the normal Christian life—*Dragon Ride* paints a picture of all the adventure, heartache, and joy of living this kind of life. I enjoyed every chapter!"

Pat Foutz
President, Transform
Pastor, Redemption Fellowship, Tukwila, WA

DRAGON RIDE

True Stories of Adventure, Miracles, and Evangelism from China

Grace Jacob

This book is dedicated to

Ben, Carmen, Charlotte & David

I love you.

I am praying and waiting.

AUTHOR'S NOTE

The stories in *Dragon Ride* are true. I have recreated events, locales, and conversations to the best of my memory. I also referred to my notes, letters, and photographs, and I asked others who were present.

To protect our Chinese friends, the names of most individuals—including my name and the names of my husband and sons—and the names of most cities in Mainland China are pseudonyms. On rare occasions, inconsequential details, identifying characteristics, or product names have been changed.

Most of the conversations took place in Cantonese or Mandarin. The translations are mine.

FOREWORD

There are books that we *should* read, and books that we *want to* read. This book is a rare blend of both. Grace Jacob has written an important book about her 29 years as a career missionary in China with her husband and family. It is important, and one that we all should read, for three reasons:

> *Perspective on the state of Christian missions in China.* China is important to the rest of the world at a lot of levels. With the continued growth of the faith in this country, we need the relationship-by-relationship vignettes, as well as the statistical overviews we receive on a higher demographic level. When I read *Dragon Ride,* I could visualize the people that Jacob interacted with, from random meetings to strategic discussion groups she created with Chinese college students.

> *Illumination on the grace of God.* The book is a rich collection of story after story of how the conversations with seekers went, and how God reached out with Christ's saving grace and touched individuals with whom Jacob engaged. I was encouraged to see God's work through the circumstances, and the miraculous results.

> *Challenge on personal evangelism.* If you have any background on the cross-cultural aspects of missions, you will quickly see how flexible and agile Jacob had to be, often on the spur of the moment, to address a particular question or obstacle of one of her friends or students. For example, we in the Western world often make the assumption that people want to seek after truth. Jacob soon discovered that for many of the Chinese people truth is whatever they want it to be, so she quickly adapted her approach to help her students see that

everyone believes in truth in their practical everyday lives. Only after that did she move on to God and the Bible. And in another conversation, Jacob is faced with the question of whether God is just an impersonal force or if he can have relationship with us. After some trial and error she figured out how to show that God is personal.

To make things more complex, during her years in China, Jacob and her family walked a tightrope of staying under the radar, away from the anti-Christian police and Chinese FBI forces, who continued to sniff around her and her friends to find evidence to stop and deport her and her husband. This tension challenged me in how I need to address the felt needs of people I want to share Christ with, in my own sphere of influence.

There is much more to this book, and the stories are riveting. And that is the *want to* part of *Dragon Ride*. It is literally a compulsive page-turner. Jacob's writing style is clear, descriptive and emotionally accessible, and I could hardly put it down. For example, when is the last time someone told you that they were so disappointed and angry with God because of some circumstance, that they needed to yell out their anger, but since it might be recorded by the authorities, they went outside to their porch to have their protest with him?

Ultimately, *Dragon Ride* paints a clear picture of how we are to engage in obeying the Great Commission to "make disciples of all nations" (Matthew 28:19-20). Enjoy it and grow from it.

John Townsend, Ph.D.
New York Times bestselling author,
co-author of the bestselling book *Boundaries*,
psychologist and founder of
the Townsend Institute for Leadership and Counseling,
Newport Beach, California
2017

INTRODUCTION

My family and I spent 29 years living, working, and playing with the Chinese people in Hong Kong and Mainland China. When we first went to Hong Kong, my goal was to become Chinese in every way. The stress that put on me broke me physically, emotionally, and spiritually. What resurrected out of those ashes was a less idealistic but more effective missionary, who became part Chinese by the osmosis of friendship—speaking their languages, relishing their food, laughing at their jokes, and finally even learning to *tell* Chinese jokes. A spiritual resurrection also resulted, where I came to know God more intimately.

After several years of living in close quarters with the Chinese, I had difficulty speaking English—I was no longer naturally using the letters "r" and "n" in my speech. In their place were "l's." I was also using Cantonese grammar in my English. In fact, Cantonese was becoming the language of my heart.

The transformation that occurs from learning to think in another language and taking on the values of another culture is slow and painful, but it ultimately enriches and broadens the soul. It is a beautiful experience to think in another culture. But in the process, I had to decide which Chinese values I did not want to embrace because every single culture has both good and bad qualities.

In Hong Kong I became familiar with vibrant, traditional Chinese culture. But when we moved to the Mainland, it felt like I had been dropped into the West because the Communist Party had attempted to strip society of its Chinese culture. Gradually, I began to understand the hidden Chinese soul in the Mainland, but the culture was different than Hong Kong, and so were the thinking patterns. In the Mainland it was easier to develop deep, personal friendships because the people weren't naturally closed like the Hong Kongers. The Mainlanders didn't trust each other, though. They told me they felt safe confiding in me, a Westerner—because who would I betray them to?

In the Mainland, I dealt with security issues, persecution, forced abortions and many dangerous situations. I learned to trust the Lord while living in the Mainland.

I also learned how to share the gospel. When we moved to Hong Kong I had a message but no effective method of sharing it. Over the decades I learned how to depend on the Holy Spirit, how to pray, and how to challenge the atheist and Buddhist thinking. Most of the people I led to the Lord were apathetic to God and the gospel when I first met them. Learning how to share, in such an inhospitable environment, was a work of God.

Except for the exhilaration of raising kids, there is no experience I know of that rivals leading Buddhists, idol-worshippers, and atheists to Christ, especially when using their own heart language. I would watch them grapple with their belief systems until they finally realized that Jesus is the truth and he could satisfy their deepest longings. Then I would see joy rip through their lives as they embraced Jesus.

My husband and I had a code of ministry that we would put as much into one person as we would a thousand, and we would invest in someone who was struggling just as much as one who was emotionally balanced and charismatic. In some ways this made our ministries smaller, but more than once the Lord turned it around and these unlikely people reached thousands that we could never have reached.

As we submit to the Lord, growing in him, seeking to fulfill his purpose for our individual lives, we each will make small but eternally significant changes in the world. Only a few will make a big splash. I am content with doing my Lord's will.

The greatness of the smallness.

LIST OF STORIES

BLACK TRENCH COATS

1972, USA

Ambling the half mile home from school, books in hand, I was thinking eleventh grade girl thoughts—how to get past my mom so she wouldn't comment on my hippie hair or discover I had a boyfriend. I cracked open the front door of our home and peeked in, ready to sneak up to my room before Mom spotted me.

Instead, I saw two strange men in their thirties, sitting under the window across from Mom, talking to her. They were extremely clean cut and were average in every way, except they both wore black trench coats.

Mom looked both pleased and apprehensive to see me. "Grace, why don't you put your books upstairs and come back down. These men want to talk with you."

My heart fluttered as I climbed the stairs to my room. They want to see me! My mind was racing. A business proposition! They must have a business proposition for me. It turns out it was far more incredible than a business proposition.

I hurried down and sat on the edge of the black leather piano bench facing the two men.

My mother spoke first. "These men are from the FBI. They have been talking to me for two hours, waiting for you to come home." What have I done now?

Mom told me later she had not been allowed to leave the room, so she couldn't warn me not to come home!

After greeting me, one of the men opened his briefcase and pulled out a photocopy of a letter I had written to President Nixon. The president was leaving in a few months for a trip to China, where he would meet with

Chairman Mao to discuss rapprochement.

The man held the paper out to me. "Did you write this letter?"

"Yes." I couldn't figure out how that letter was getting me in trouble. This is what it said:

> *Dear President Nixon:*
>
> *When you go to China, please plead for the plight of the Christians in China. I have heard that you can be killed for owning a Bible in China.*
>
> *Thank you.*
>
> *Sincerely,*
>
> *Grace Gurney*

The men grilled me. The most startling question was, "If President Nixon were to bring a Bible into China, would he be killed for it?"

I couldn't believe my ears. "Of course not!" How stupid were these men? They looked average in every way, but evidently they were below average!

They pressed on. "Where did you get your information?"

"There's a newsletter published by Brother Andrew.[1] It suggested that we write the president."

"Do you have a copy you could show us?" I raced upstairs to find it.

After I handed it to them, they asked, "Do you have any publications from China?"

"Well, yes." I was feeling a little afraid and uncomfortable. I didn't know what they would do with my answer. "My brother subscribes to the *Peking Review*,[2] and I read it."

"That's what your mother said." So they were testing if our stories were the same. But why did it matter? I dug up a copy of the *Peking Review* for them.

After an hour of questioning, it finally wound down. "We need to take your picture." After I posed for them, they asked me for a sample from my typewriter. I made sure I remembered which typewriter I gave the sample from. You never know! They didn't take my fingerprints.

Both men relaxed and addressed my mother. "If we had known her age,

---

1. Brother Andrew was the founder of Open Doors, which published a newsletter about the persecuted church around the world.

2. The *Peking Review* was the international propaganda publication of China.

and if we had had any say in the matter, we would not have come to interview her. Sometimes people write the president a warning they're not able to spell out clearly, so they give a hint hoping we'll pick up on it. President Nixon's trip to China is very sensitive. We've been assigned to investigate every letter written to the president at this time that uses a violent word. Grace might have been trying to warn the president that he would be in danger in China."

That's how I got an FBI file at age 16. At the time I had no idea I would end up as a missionary in China.

USA

Until 1986

My parents were Canadian,

and I am a dual Canadian/American.

My father was a pastor,

and from the time I was born to the time I left home

he pastored one church.

I grew up on Long Island, NY,

the youngest of seven siblings.

I had a hard time becoming a Christian,

and an even harder time my first two years of college

when I doubted my faith and then became an atheist.

RUGGED ROAD

1960-1973, USA

A man well over two times my height, four times my size and six times my age looked into my five-year-old, upturned face, "Do you want to believe in Jesus?" We were standing on the cement steps of the church where my father was the pastor in the suburbs of New York City.

That was exactly what I wanted! I knew my parents were good people because they were always helping others. Homeless men often showed up in our living room to ask my father for money, and he would try to wrangle some of our food money away from my mother's tight fist to help the men. I was sure they were good because they were Christians.

I also knew I wasn't so good. My sister always told me that.

Every Saturday I got up at six in the morning before anyone else was up. I crept out of the house, and stayed away for the whole day so my sister couldn't catch me and make me help clean our room. Maybe believing in Jesus would fix everything.

"Yes, I want that! How do I do it?"

"Kneel down here and pray this prayer…"

Immediately I plopped to my knees, golden curls flying, and I prayed.

It didn't take. I could tell because in the weeks and months that followed I was still the same naughty little girl I had always been. I knew there was no Jesus inside me.

Time and again someone many times older than me asked if I wanted to believe in Jesus. Each time I knelt right down and "prayed the prayer," but it didn't work for me and I didn't know why. Gradually, I stopped hoping or caring. At least being naughty was a lot of fun!

By third grade I was cutting up so much in children's church, the head teacher kicked me out and exiled me to the adult worship service. She told me to never ever come back to children's church again! Children's church went until sixth grade. Three years of exile.

When I entered seventh grade, becoming a Christian didn't matter to me anymore. Having fun and outsmarting authorities were the driving forces of my life.

I loved lighting fires in the science lab.

And it was so much fun putting my French teacher, Mr. Whitebread (that really was his name!) on trial. Whenever Mr. Whitebread yelled at a student during class, I immediately convened court in the classroom and appointed a prosecuting attorney, a defense attorney, and a jury. Of course, I appointed myself the judge. We would try Mr. Whitebread to determine whether he had the right to yell at the student.

I made a plan that I'd be bad until one day I would decide to put it all behind me, completely change, and become boring good. It wasn't that I wanted to become a Christian anymore, I just didn't want to become a bad person. If in the future I could become a good person, then that would mean I wasn't really bad. The plan gave me hope and a sense of control over my life, without jeopardizing all the fun I was having. I would decide when to change; the time simply hadn't come yet.

The school started calling home, telling my mother about my bad behavior. My mother sat me down in the living room. "Grace, you're hanging around with the wrong kids!" I stared at her, dumbfounded. I couldn't believe she was that naïve. I was the ringleader.

Then, in the ninth grade, two unexpected things happened. First, my older brother, Steve, became a Christian.

Steve thought I was a Christian also because at church and at home I was pretending to be. He asked me to spend whole evenings in prayer with him. We prayed for everything in the world, even for China in the throes of the Cultural Revolution, and for Chairman Mao to become a Christian. Why I subjected myself to this when I didn't know the Lord, I don't know. But it served a purpose in my life. I was an anarchist at school during the day and a "praying Christian" in the evenings. The hypocrisy started to grate on me.

Then my best friend, Jeanette, became a Christian. Jeanette was a very artistic, petite, Chinese girl, and we spent all of our free time together. I had invited her to church with me not because I wanted her to become a Christian, but so we could have even more time together. She was the one person who knew I was a hypocrite because she saw how badly I behaved at school and how much I pretended to be a Christian at church. And now she was one of them!

6

About a month after Jeanette came to know the Lord, I decided the time had come—I needed to activate my plan to turn my life around and become a good person. So I tried to be well-behaved, kind, respectful, and quieter, but I couldn't! The problem was that all day long at school I spotted opportunities to orchestrate chaos, and I took every opportunity. As hard as I tried, I couldn't stop misbehaving. I felt helpless and scared because I realized I was already a bad person and I didn't know how to become good.

At the end of ninth grade, during the summer, I lay prostrate on the floor of my bedroom, crying, begging Jesus to change me. I didn't know where else to turn.

It took! In the summer before school started, I knew I had become a Christian because I was so different—I began treating others with respect.

When tenth grade started in the fall, everyone at school could see I was a new person. Three days into the new school year, Mr. Whitebread asked me, "What on earth happened to you? You're a completely different person!"

That was the early 1970s, the time of hippies and the Jesus movement, and many students at the neighboring high schools and colleges were becoming Christians. Steve asked me to lead a weekly Bible study for the young women who had come to know the Lord. All through high school I spent 10 hours a week studying the Bible in order to prepare, so I grew a lot spiritually. I was being challenged by what I learned from the Bible, I was learning how to teach the Bible, and I was loving getting to know the Lord.

CRASH AND REBOOT

1973-1975, USA

(Note: This story is somewhat philosophical. It traces my descent into atheism during college and how I came back to faith in God. The rest of the book is not so philosophical.)

Soon after I entered college in upstate New York, I picked up a copy of *The Communist Manifesto*. That book shook me to the core because Marx and Engels had such different presuppositions in life than I did. Were my presuppositions valid? I wondered if my beliefs had just been passed down to me from my parents. What did I believe?

Then I faced a further challenge to my faith. I was studying for a bachelor's in biology. The evolution debate wasn't an issue for me; instead, I was troubled by deep philosophical issues that came from my studies. The only way I knew about the world around me was through my senses. But what if my nerve impulses had no relationship to the world? Was there even a real world out there? I came to the conclusion that I couldn't know if the physical world existed. And since I couldn't know if the physical world existed, I certainly couldn't know if God existed.

Since the Bible makes clear that the Christian God is knowable to a certain extent, I figured that if there was no way of knowing whether or not he existed, then he didn't. As far as the Christian God was concerned, I had become an atheist.

I wrote home, "Mom, I don't believe in God anymore."

The thing is, I was a reluctant atheist. I wanted the Christian God to exist because my parents' faith was so beautiful. But I wasn't willing to pretend he existed.

8

If God didn't exist, I didn't think there was any meaning in life—at least any meaning that was worth much, because all we would have is the here and now. Some atheists talk about being brave and facing life without hope or meaning. I couldn't do it. Hopelessness and meaninglessness made me so depressed, all I wanted to do was end my life.

My all-consuming search began. I didn't have a clue how I could ever come to believe in the physical world, much less God. I decided to ask other students, "Do you know if the physical world exists?" But whenever I opened my mouth with my burning questions about the existence of the physical world, everyone was dumbfounded. They had no idea what I was talking about.

I was studying at a Christian college, and since most of the people around me believed in the Christian God, I figured they must have reasons. Maybe they could believe in the physical world without proof, but they certainly would have thought through why they believed in God!

I was so desperate for answers that whenever a friend introduced me to someone, the first question out of my mouth was, "Do you believe in God?" If the new acquaintance answered, "No," I fired at them, "Why?" If they said, "Yes," with hope and desperation in my voice I asked, "Why?" If they couldn't give me a good answer, I walked away disappointed and disgusted. That person wasn't worth knowing because they hadn't thought through the most basic things in life. And they certainly couldn't help me with my pressing issue.

My friends knew I was suicidal, and they worried about me. One of them encouraged me to make an appointment with the chaplain.

During the small talk part of the appointment, I told the chaplain that I was very concerned about the lack of fresh water on the planet. (I don't know why I was concerned about lack of water when I wasn't even sure the world existed. There was a disconnect in my thinking.)

He laughed delightedly. "That's what I love about you young people. You're so passionate about all these causes that don't matter!"

I closed up like a clam. He had just laughed at me, looked down on me, and treated me as inconsequential. I never told him my pressing issue.

I wasn't getting anywhere in my search. I read everything I could get my hands on about any related subject. Mostly I read Christian philosophers, because they were the ones who had a lot of explaining to do, but no one addressed the question, "How can I know if anything exists?" I was giving up hope because neither books, nor face-to-face conversations were at all helpful, and I couldn't figure out the answers myself.

Then one day, as I was sitting in the cafeteria eating dinner, a question popped into my head. I didn't realize it was the Holy Spirit. "Do you need to eat in order to live?" Such a simple question, but as strange as it may seem, I pondered it for a month. I had thought I couldn't know anything, but I actually did know something. I knew I would die if I didn't eat. I knew I had to earn money to be able to buy food. I knew all sorts of things; I just didn't know how I knew them. I realized then that on a practical level I knew the physical world existed, I just didn't know how I knew.

Now I could press on to the question of God.

I had become a little cynical about God in the process of all this questioning. At one point, I shook my fist toward heaven and said, "Even if I can know that the physical world exists, I certainly cannot know if a spiritual world exists!"

A month or so later the Holy Spirit asked me another question (although I still didn't know it was him), "How can you be sure you can't know if a spiritual world exists?"

I realized that was presumptuous of me. Finally I conceded, "O.K. I don't know if a spiritual world exists, but I can't be sure that I can't know." I was no longer an atheist. I just didn't know if God existed.

But even if God existed, that didn't mean the Christian God was the true God, so I read every scripture from every religion I could get my hands on—the *Qur'an*, the *Bhagavad-Gita*, the *Kama Sutra*, the *Upanishads*, the *Tibetan Book of the Dead*, the *Teachings of the Compassionate Buddha*, the *Analects of Confucius*, the *Doctrine of the Mean*, the *Book of Mormon* ... These scriptures had some wisdom, but they all seemed shallow, as if they were just written by men. Then I read the Bible with my doubter/seeker mind, and I was impressed. The Bible was richer, true to life, with mystery to draw you in to deeper truths. Although that wasn't enough to convince me, it was at least appealing, and it gave direction to my search.

Summer came and I worked at Sag Harbor, Long Island (near the Hamptons) cleaning house for a very cranky, old woman three hours every morning. Her huge house had trap doors and secret passageways from rum-running days and it was right on the beach. Except for her being cranky, it was an idyllic place to spend the summer, with afternoons of swimming, water skiing, lying on the sand in the sun; and, of course, rich boys combed the beach. But I had little interest in those attractions because I had brought a shelf full of Christian apologetics books to see if I could find some reason to believe, some reason to live.

My mother had handled the situation well. She didn't look shocked, hurt, or sad, nor did she sit down with me and try to prove God. She waited for me to talk with her, which I didn't, because I was afraid the Christian faith was my parents' faith, not mine. But she did give me an old book, *Who Moved the Stone?* by Frank Morison.

Frank Morison was a lawyer who thought the resurrection of Jesus was ridiculous, and he set out to prove it never happened. How he planned to do that was by using his courtroom experience to put the authors of the gospels on the witness stand to ferret out the fabrications in their accounts.

Right at the beginning of the book I was amazed by his truth test. As a biology major, I was used to scientific proof. But Frank Morison introduced me to a totally different kind of proof—historical proof.

He talked about the ring of truth and how you can often tell when witnesses are lying or telling the truth. For example, when the disciples wrote that women were the first witnesses to the resurrection, it had a ring of truth—a fictitious account would have put men first at the tomb since women were considered unreliable in that day. When Jesus appeared after his death, the account says that some doubted. An author who was unconcerned with truth would have said that everyone was absolutely sure Jesus rose from the dead, since to say that some doubted could make the evidence seem less convincing. And Peter's denial of Christ is such a humiliating story that is so obviously true, and clearly written by someone who is truthful. I began to realize that the authors of the gospels were writing what they believed actually happened.

By the time Morison had finished writing the book, he had become a Christian, and after reading the book, I was also teetering on the edge of faith. If the Christian God existed, I had no problem with miracles, and the most logical explanation of the facts was that Jesus rose from the dead. There were still holes in Morison's arguments, though, so I continued to research Jesus' resurrection. The more I researched, the more likely it seemed that Jesus really had risen from the dead.

But I still wasn't satisfied. Suspecting Jesus rose from the dead because of historical evidence didn't get rid of the nagging philosophical implausibility of God. I couldn't see God, so he just seemed like the product of people's imagination.

Also, I had atheist friends at college that I talked and read philosophy with. I would have been humiliated to tell them, "I believe in Jesus now because I believe he rose from the dead." I thought that sounded really dumb; it would have stopped my friends dead in their tracks and the jokes would have started. I needed philosophical respectability. Frankly, I was embarrassed by the idea of God.

In the summer, shortly before I started my junior year, my brother, Larry, called from the Chicago area where he was attending seminary at Trinity

International University. He knew the questions I was struggling with. Larry was taking a cram summer course in apologetics from Dr. Norman Geisler, and he wondered if I would like to live at his apartment and sit in on the course.

I quit my job that day, and the next day boarded the 18-hour train from New York City to Chicago. During the trip, I thought about Jeremiah 29:13—that if someone seeks God with their whole heart they will find him. I told the Christian God that I didn't believe in, "You promised in the Bible that if I search for you with all my heart I will find you. You cannot fault me on this. I have searched for you for two years with every ounce of my being, but I haven't found you. If I don't find you during this apologetics course, then I'll know you do not exist. This is your last chance."

Since I didn't see any point in living if God didn't exist, I brought extra money, so if I didn't find God, after the course I would go somewhere, anywhere, have a fling and then kill myself. I was done with a life without meaning and hope, and I was done with pretense and hypocrisy. I didn't tell anyone what I planned to do.

I sat in on the last two weeks of the three-week master's level course. I was too young to be enrolled in the class, even as an audit, and I hadn't paid tuition. Since there were only about 25 students in the class, I'm sure Dr. Geisler noticed me and knew I wasn't supposed to be sitting in on the class, but he was so gracious he said nothing. If he had commented to me on any of these improprieties, I would have followed my final exit plan.

Dr. Geisler took us through various cosmological arguments for the existence of God. Amazingly, I had never heard those arguments before; no one had ever pointed me in that direction.

I poured over the textbook every waking hour when I wasn't in class. I scribbled notes on every inconsistency I found in the logic. After class I sometimes went to the front and argued with Dr. Geisler.

In the end, I came to the conclusion that although what Dr. Geisler presented was not proof,[1] it was a reasonable philosophical defense for the existence of God and that was what I needed. I came to believe in Jesus because the resurrection is the only coherent explanation for the events following Jesus' death, but I came to be willing to confess faith in God and call myself a Christian because Christianity is philosophically reasonable and respectable.

At the end of the course, sprawled on my brother's couch, it suddenly hit

---

1. I've come to realize that even so-called scientific proof is not proof either—it's just the conclusions drawn from multiple controlled experiments.

me that I had come back to believing in the Christian God, but I had a decision to make—would I follow God or go my own way? I had wanted God all along, so the decision was easy. I returned to God and I have never regretted it. Getting to know him is such an amazing experience.

My life has not followed the "traditional" Christian path. I became a Christian and then I stopped believing in God. It's almost as if I had two conversions—one of the heart and one of the mind. I can't explain what happened.

Although I was unwilling to believe because of my parents' faith, it was the beauty of my parents' faith that made me want God so badly.

But I almost didn't survive my search for truth and God.

I realized that it is much easier to ask questions than to develop thought-through answers. Those who question feel so intelligent because they think their questions are brilliant. I know I did. But asking questions is simple, and doesn't require much intelligence. It's finding answers and defending them that's awesome. Just like, it's so easy to destroy, but difficult to build. It's so easy to kill, but so hard to raise a child. It's easy to mock, but hard to defend.

I'm now more sympathetic to people who believe in God for reasons I find insufficient. Everyone's truth test is different. What convinces one person is not what will convince another.

Finally, I ended up as a missionary in China. What could have been better preparation than my difficult conversion and my time of doubting? Atheism can be said to be the national religion of Mainland China. I understand atheism. I was able to start with the atheist mindset, gently leading the Chinese atheist to Christ. I had researched other religions and had some understanding of Buddhism, which helped me bring Buddhists to Christ. If someone had tried to become a Christian, but Christianity didn't seem to work for them, I've been there, too. I would explore with them what the missing piece was in their attempt to come to faith. By God's grace, he helped me to be successful with that, too.

These were some of the most difficult times of my life, but God, in his providence, was uniquely preparing me for the work he called me to.

BOOMERANG

1975-82, USA

After returning from Dr. Geisler's class at Trinity International University in Chicago, my journey of getting to know God began again. A few weeks later I started attending a university near my home on Long Island as a transfer student. I became the president of the university's InterVarsity Christian Fellowship (IV), which wasn't saying much; the group had been decimated by a cult before I arrived, and I was the only member.

I knew I would have to be creative to get the fellowship going. A few weeks into the semester I plastered advertisements all over campus for a free barbecue run by the InterVarsity Christian Fellowship, as if there was a group. The IV staff worker put a grill outside on the patio of the room allotted to us. Twenty-five students came out of a student body of 12,000. What would I have done if all 12,000 had come? I hadn't even thought about it. The next week only 12 returned, but we had a group! I put my heart into leading Bible studies, discipling, and running an evangelistic book table.

Combatting cults was high on my agenda as the IV president. One day I took a lunch break from the evangelistic book table and left a friend in charge. Somehow, without her realizing it, a cult member came along and replaced all of the Christian literature with their material—so before I discovered it, we were effectively witnessing for a cult!

A girl named Patti started attending our Bible studies. I didn't see anything unusual about her, but one day one of our group members said to me, "Have you noticed Patti? She cozies up to someone each week and leaves with them. That person never returns. Patti's a member of a cult." She was using our IV group to recruit converts. I couldn't believe these people! Once again the group was being destroyed. I thought long and hard about how to protect it from Patti's false teaching and how to flush her out.

I knew that the cult Patti belonged to didn't believe that Jesus is God, so I led a Bible study on Mark 2:1-11, where Jesus forgave the sins of the paralyzed man who was let down through the roof by his friends. I emphasized the deity of Christ. Patti flushed herself out. Toward the end of the study, she stood up indignantly. Walking around to each participant, she pointed a finger at them and demanded to know if they believed that Jesus is God. They all said yes. Patti stalked out of the meeting and never returned. We were safe again.

After I graduated, I set my sights on returning to Trinity International University to study for my master's degree at the seminary. I wanted more biblical training to help me be a better Bible study leader. I was also considering going overseas as a missionary.

For two years I worked as a legal secretary to earn money for school. But I had grown up poor, and this was the first time I had ever had money to buy anything, so I spent almost everything I earned rather than saving it. Finally, I packed off to seminary with only enough money for one quarter, and no car. I wouldn't be able to afford insurance payments, so I sold my old clunker for $25, and caught a ride to Chicago.

A few days before classes started, I met Justin in the backseat of one of the student's cars. A number of us were crammed into the car to go to Poppin' Fresh for pie. I was looking forward to a really good time of making friends with all these strangers who would be my classmates for three years.

Justin was brown-bearded and balding, his straight hair just a little long. His beard was cool—full and well-trimmed. We were all looking for common points of interest to talk about, and Justin and I hit upon Chinese characters as something we were both interested in. I had always been curious about China, so in college I had audited a Mandarin course. And several years before Justin attended seminary, he had hired a Mandarin language tutor because he wanted to prepare to be a missionary to China. I couldn't believe that we had both studied the Chinese language, although neither of us could speak much of it.

Justin's missionary call had come shortly after he became a Christian during his freshman year at a state college: he had such a passion to pray for China at the prayer meetings he attended on campus that he realized he was called to China as a missionary.

Justin was a very southern boy. He had grown up in a small town in North Carolina that wasn't international in any sense. In fact, the Mandarin tutor he hired was the first Chinese person he ever knew—he was called to be a missionary to China before he knew a single Chinese person! After graduating, he worked as a chemical research engineer for four years until he had saved enough money for three years of seminary, then he quit his job and went to Trinity to get the training he needed for China.

My background couldn't have been more different. I grew up in cosmopolitan New York and I had always loved Chinese people—starting in grade school, they were always my closest friends and neighbors. Because of my curiosity about China, I not only audited the Mandarin class in college, I took courses in Chinese literature and Far East history. I didn't realize, though, that these were indicators that the Lord was calling me to be a missionary to China.

Talking about Chinese characters with Justin should have been a good start to a friendship, but instead we argued! I told him what my Chinese teacher had taught me, that Chinese characters were derived from pictograms that were pregnant with meaning. Justin thought everything I said was rubbish! I was so mad at him. There was no talking to him; he just cut down everything I said. We boomeranged away from each other, and by the time we arrived at Poppin' Fresh I didn't want anything more to do with him. What should have been common interest and experience had been ruined. After school started, when I would walk into the cafeteria, I would comb the place to see where Justin was sitting so I wouldn't accidentally sit at his table.

About six months later, I heard about a Chinese church that met a few miles from campus. I kept searching for the church but I couldn't find it, and I didn't have a car to get there, anyway.

Finally, I asked a Chinese friend where the church met. She told me I should contact Justin and get a ride from him, that he led the youth group at the church. I groaned. It took me a couple of weeks to swallow my pride and ask him for a ride.

Not long after I started attending the Chinese church, the pastor asked me to become the girls' counselor for the youth group. I was excited about the job, but now I was going to have to work alongside Justin. Crud!

Between starting a typing business at Trinity, cleaning houses, teaching English to a Taiwanese woman, and landing a well-paying summer job as a Teamster at Lockheed Shipbuilding in Seattle, I made it through the second quarter of the second year of my master's studies before running out of money. I decided to quit school and go back to my job at Lockheed to earn money to finish my degree.

At lunch one day I overheard two students talking about how they had received an amazing answer to prayer. I had always made plans that made sense to me, but I hadn't even thought about praying concerning the decision to leave school. I spent the next day fasting and praying. "Lord, if you want me to stay at seminary, please provide what I need."

The very next day, my Chinese pastor, Eric, cornered me. "What are you doing next quarter?"

"I'll probably go to Seattle." I was embarrassed and didn't want to tell him I was broke.

"Why are you doing that?"

Well, he was dragging it out of me. "I don't have the money to continue studying." I was so down to the wire I was returning textbooks to the bookstore; I cut someone's hair for two dollars even though I didn't know how to cut hair; I was considering selling my blood, but it didn't come to that. I had also counted the exact number of dollars I needed to travel to Seattle so I wouldn't be stranded.

Eric asked, "If you had free room and board, would you stay?"

I thought for a minute. How could this be—the Lord was answering my prayer! If the Lord would provide my living expenses, I could probably earn enough for tuition. "Yeah, I would stay."

"Live with my family. You can eat with us, and I'll arrange transportation for you to school."

Not only did this keep me in seminary, it was the beginning of my learning to pray and see God answer. Living with Eric's family was an amazing opportunity to learn the Chinese culture, eat Chinese food, and learn to use chopsticks. I also learned a few words of Cantonese, like *m hou gaau!* (Don't touch!)

In the Chinese church, as I counseled the girls in the youth group, and shared the gospel with them, I noticed how good Justin was with the teenagers—gentle yet firm and funny—and I saw how much he loved them. My heart melted and I wanted to be around him.

I had recently broken up with my boyfriend, and there was a square dance I wanted to go to. I knew no one would ask me because they thought I was still hooked up. I tried to ask two guys out, but I didn't get very far. At supper on the night of the dance, I sat with a group of friends and was telling them about my attempts to get a date for the square dance. We were all laughing hysterically. Toward the end of my story, Justin sat down at our table. "Do you want to go with me?" his quiet voice spoke up.

In time, just as a boomerang returns, I ended up marrying Justin.

He had one condition for our marriage—he wouldn't marry me unless I would go with him as a missionary to China.

HONG KONG

1986-1995

Justin and I were married in our Chinese church in 1982,

then we joined a mission agency.

First we planted a church for Cambodian refugees

near Seattle, WA.

While in Seattle I gave birth to two sons,

Nigel and Adam.

Our mission agency then sent us to Hong Kong

as church planters.

Nigel was three and Adam, one,

when we embarked on this adventure.

In Hong Kong

we studied Cantonese full time for the first two years

and part time the third.

After that we planted two Cantonese churches.

Justin was finally fulfilling the dream

the Lord had placed in his heart.

I was passionate about evangelism.

HONG KONG KINDNESS

1986, Hong Kong

A week after arriving in Hong Kong, Justin and I made the mistake of sitting on the upper deck of a double-decker bus, with our three-year-old son, Nigel, and our one-year-old son, Adam. I carried a red, cloth diaper bag that was so big it could fit several babies in it, and a long, red and white umbrella with a hook on the end. The choice was between standing body-to-body on the crowded lower deck or taking the stairs to the upper deck. We took the stairs.

Before we could reach the top, the bus lurched forward with a loud, throaty acceleration. Every couple of seconds it swerved, throwing us to one side of the staircase. Justin was holding Adam while I steadied Nigel. We held tightly to the railings, trying to take a step between lurches.

After 30 minutes of rest on the upper deck, we approached our stop. We waited for a break in the jostling, then we headed back down. I went first, holding the diaper bag and umbrella. Justin followed, holding Adam, and Nigel fended for himself between us.

Three steps down, the bus swerved. The umbrella tumbled down the railings, lodging itself across the bottom of the narrow stairway at waist height. As I was also being hurled down the stairs, I grabbed the railings on each side, stopping my fall—barely. My head, shoulders, and torso lurched forward, and my arms and feet stretched out behind me, my hands still gripping the railings. Nigel was thrown against the back of my legs, so my already stretched arms bore his weight as well as mine. The diaper bag threatened to pull my right hand off the railing.

I felt my hands slipping, so I tightened my grip. If I couldn't hold on, Nigel and I would both be hurled down the stairs! Even if I could hold on, the

19

umbrella was wedged across the stairway near the bottom, blocking our way. I had no free hand to unwedge it.

Suddenly, an old man on the lower deck noticed my predicament. He stood, hobbled over, and pulled the umbrella out, and waited at the bottom of the stairs, holding it for me.

Pushing back on Nigel to allow my feet to move forward—a few seconds here and there to take a step when the bus didn't lurch—we made it down the stairs.

I couldn't have succeeded without the kindness of the old Chinese man who was willing to help a foreigner.

§§§

Three days later, I brought Nigel, Adam, and the red diaper bag to my Cantonese tutor's home for a lesson. When we boarded the bus for the return trip, I also carried a plastic bag filled with longan fruit I had bought at the market. Longans (dragon eye fruit) are one-inch diameter balls with a hard, wine-colored skin that encases juicy, white flesh inside.

I saw only six inches of empty bench near the center walkway. I didn't dare go upstairs since Justin wasn't with me.

I sat one bun on the six inches, Nigel on my left knee, which was extended into the walkway, and Adam perched on my right knee. I set the diaper and fruit bags on the floor at my feet.

About five minutes into the 45 minute ride, the bus lurched, throwing Nigel's head banging into Adam's head. Both boys started screaming and crying. I had no hand free to comfort them or separate them.

A Chinese woman in her 30s, who was sitting under the window on the far side of the bench across the aisle, signaled to me, pointing from Nigel to the vacant snippet of bench between her and the older woman next to her. Since I was out of options, I gestured that she could take Nigel.

Nigel and Adam both calmed down.

Just then, a man ahead of me handed me a longan; a woman two benches back handed me another longan; a woman ahead of the man passed a handful of longans to me, and on it went. What was going on? Was this the Hong Kong way of showing solidarity to someone in need?

Suddenly, I felt little round things bumping into my sandals. I looked down. Dozens of longans were rolling toward the front of the bus past my feet. The bus screeched to a stop and dozens of longans rolled in the opposite direction, toward the back of the bus. My bag of longans was lying empty next to the red diaper bag. All of the rolling longans on the bus floor were mine! The ones that had been handed to me, I put back in the bag.

My bus stop was approaching, so I signaled to the woman who was now playing with Nigel that she should return him. Instead, she stood up and, holding Nigel's hand, she headed for the bus door! I quickly gathered up Adam, the red diaper bag, and the almost empty longan bag. I raced after the woman and got off the bus.

The woman accompanied me, holding Nigel's hand along the bustling Kowloon City street. After walking 10 minutes, she pointed to a bus stop sign we were passing. She was showing me I had gotten off too early, that I should have gotten off at this bus stop. That meant that, in order to help me, she had gotten off at the wrong bus stop, too!

This Hong Kong woman had gone out of her way to help me, a woman who wasn't her race, wasn't from her land, and didn't speak her language!

§§§

Shortly after arriving in Hong Kong, my left eye became itchy and red, with a little pus. My contact lenses were holding the grit and pollution of Hong Kong against my eyes. That was the last time I ever wore contacts. They were a health hazard in Asia, as were so many things—breathing, eating, drinking the water, crossing the street …

With the help of a missionary, I made an appointment with an optometrist. Now to get there.

Justin took care of the kids, so I was alone. Somehow I found Prince Edward Road, the road the optometrist's office was on. But walking up and down this busy street didn't get me any closer to the address I was looking for. I hoped I could find someone who spoke English.

I walked into a shop, which was about 15 feet long by eight feet wide. Behind the waist-high glass display, sitting on a shelf, was a cream-colored phone. I had a phone number and decided I would try to call the doctor's office for directions.

"Could I use your phone?"

"We don't have a phone."

"But look, right there—there's a phone!"

"Oh, that." Annoyed, she turned around and stared where I was pointing. "That doesn't work."

The phone rang.

"See, it does work!"

"No, it doesn't work," she said, as she answered it.

I was flabbergasted. That was when I first learned that if a Chinese person gives you an answer that doesn't make any sense, then the answer is "no." There's no fighting it. You might as well give up and move on.

So I walked out to the street, confused and frustrated, with no idea how to find the optometrist.

I walked into another store, same small size, but this was a jewelry store. A middle-aged man stood behind the glass display case at the far end of the store. There was a black phone sitting on the glass.

"Could I use your phone? I have an appointment with an optometrist, but I can't find his office. He's on this road, Prince Edward Road."

"What's the address?"

I handed him the card.

"Hm. Let me call him. I don't know where this office is, either."

I heard the sing-song clipped sound of Cantonese as the jeweler conferred with the optometrist's office.

When he hung up, he said, "Getting there is complicated. I'll take you."

I stood there amazed as I watched him lock the jewelry cabinet, make another call, then walk outside with me. He rolled down the metal gate across the storefront and locked it. Then he said, "Come with me!"

We walked together down Prince Edward Road, under the busy overpass, across the road, into a building, and up a flight of stairs to the optometrist's office.

I felt a sense of awe. What kind of place had we moved to, that a shopkeeper would close his shop and take me, a stranger, right to the door of my doctor's office?

I knew Hong Kong would be a difficult place to live—with the heat, humidity, overcrowding, pollution, and difficult language, but I wanted to be here! The old Chinese man from our double-decker bus ride, the woman on my return bus ride home from my Cantonese language class, and now this man in the jewelry store, they all left profound first impressions, and bent my heart toward loving my adopted land. I wanted to get to know the Hong Kong people!

PIRATE

1988, Hong Kong

"Mom, I'm so lonely. There's no one to play with." Five-year-old Nigel looked up at me with sad blue eyes.

We had recently moved from our first apartment in Hong Kong, which was in an area where many foreigners lived, to a 555-square-foot, first-floor apartment in a Chinese village, because we wanted to live around Chinese people.

"Nigel, let's pray that Jesus will give you a friend." Holding hands, we knelt down on the white tile floor and prayed.

Five minutes later, a little Chinese boy, about Nigel's age, banged on the door, panting and out of breath. "Can the boys who live here play with me?" he said in Cantonese.

Loh Sei Hoi lived five minutes away. He was named after a pirate, Sei Hoi, which meant "Four Seas." He was a little out of control, but he was the friend the Lord provided. The boys played with him almost every day.

Loh Sei Hoi (Ah-Hoi) taught Nigel to curse fluently in Cantonese.

One morning, when Ah-Hoi thought no one was looking, he dropped one of our sons' toys, a Transformer, out of their bedroom window. His friend was hiding under the window in order to catch the toy and run.

But a Chinese friend of mine was visiting, and she saw the whole theft and told me.

When Ah-Hoi realized he had been discovered, he ran out the door. I was furious and yelled at his retreating figure, "You can't play with Nigel and Adam anymore!"

That afternoon, Nigel noticed a note folded in the bars of our living room window. In a child's scrawl of Chinese characters, it read, "I'm sorry. Please let me play with Nigel and Adam again."

I sent the boys to Ah-Hoi's home to get him. When they came in, Ah-Hoi just stared at the floor he was so sad. The four of us sat around the dining room table.

"Ah-Hoi, stealing the toy was bad."

"Yes, I know. It was wrong. I've done a lot of wrong things I wish I hadn't done."

I told him about God and that Jesus died to forgive his sins. "Do you want God to forgive you?"

"Yes, I want that." He confessed his sins and decided to live for Jesus. He even started going to church with our family.

Years later I saw Ah-Hoi again, long after we had moved away from that village. Smiling, he told me, "I still follow Jesus and I go to church every Sunday with my grandma!"

NOT BY POWER, BUT BY MY SPIRIT

1988-1995, Hong Kong

Most people think that when missionaries go overseas, they're experts at sharing the gospel. I sure wasn't, and it became obvious when I tried to share my faith with the women in my basic level English class.

Two years after we moved to Hong Kong, I started an English class for Chinese mothers who were struggling to help their kids with English homework. In addition to teaching them English, I hoped to share Christ with them. The women and I became friends. Their English level was so low we always spoke Cantonese outside of the class.

I took them out for dim sum[1] one at a time so we could talk about Jesus. Telling them about God wasn't easy because the women were idol worshippers, like most Hong Kong people. Not only did they find it hard to believe in a creator God, but they found it hard to put aside their idols because worshipping idols comes with a lot of fear and obligation. The women were required to perform rites, like burning incense and offering sacrifices of fruit, so their families would prosper and their idols wouldn't be offended. If they didn't perform these rites, they were afraid their gods would hurt them.

One of them voiced the fears of the group when she told me, "If I believe in Jesus, the gods I worship are going to retaliate. They'll hurt me really bad. Is Jesus powerful enough to protect me from them? Whose power is greater? If Jesus isn't stronger than my gods, then I don't want to become a Christian because I won't be safe."

I should have had some brilliant answer to her questions, but I couldn't think of anything to say, so I was silent. How do you convince someone that Jesus is stronger than their idols? Unless, of course, you have a power demo

---

1. Dim sum is a Cantonese breakfast of small pastries, dumplings, and delicacies.

like Elijah did on Mt. Carmel.

They also had another heartfelt objection: "Jesus is not Chinese, so I won't believe in him." I countered with what I thought was a convincing answer. "Jesus was born in the Middle East. He was born between the East and the West, so he's for all of us."

They persisted: "But he's not Chinese."

It was then that I began fervently praying for the gift of evangelism.

What finally interested some of them in the Lord was when I invited them to an evangelistic meeting at the Cantonese church my husband and I were planting. I don't know what the Chinese evangelist said that was so convincing because my Cantonese wasn't good enough yet to understand him, but his preaching was effective. After that meeting, two of the six women came to faith and started attending our church.

But my heart longed for one particular student, Mary, to become a Christian. She lived in the worst conditions I have ever witnessed, in what was the most densely populated place on earth—the Kowloon Walled City, where 33,000 people slept, ate, and raised their families in a space the size of a city block. It was a cesspool of drug dens and brothels, controlled by the Triads (the Chinese Mafia), and it was lawless. The Hong Kong police rarely patrolled the area.

One day Mary invited me to her home in the Kowloon Walled City for lunch. I followed her along a narrow walkway several stories up, tripping on the uneven cement as it veered between "buildings." Originally, the residents had built many small rooms on top of each other forming one-room-wide buildings, which topped out at 14 stories—the max allowed because of the airport. These buildings were constructed right next to each other, so the residents finally built a labyrinth of hallways connecting them. Because of poor construction, the walls jutted and the floors dipped where the buildings joined.

Many years ago, the residents had strung electric wires along the pathways. The cords now sagged between hooks, almost touching our heads. It was hard to distinguish the black electric wires from the decades of gray cobwebs that embraced them. A dark, greasy shine covered everything. I didn't want to touch anything.

We turned left to enter her 15-by-15-foot home. An eight-dish dinner was waiting for me on her short square table. I breathed in deeply. The smell of pork stir-fried with garlic and soy sauce whetted my appetite. Bowls and chopsticks were laid out.

This was where Mary and her husband were raising their three daughters. I couldn't understand how she was able to raise her kids in this criminal,

26

drug-infested environment. Mary had a sweetness that attracted me to her. I wondered how she could be so kind and considerate when I would have been frayed beyond recognition living here. I could see the strain on her face and the premature thinning of her hair.

But Mary had far more stress from living in that environment than I could have imagined. The vice of the Kowloon Walled City had entered their home; her husband had become addicted to heroin.

I found this out in a backward kind of way. Connie, Mary's sister, who was also a student in my English class, asked me to get "a friend's husband" into Christian rehab. The government detox program had a three-month wait list, but this "friend's husband" wanted to get off drugs now. "You're a Christian. You might have connections with a Christian rehab so he could start right away." I got him in.

Three months later I went out for dim sum with Mary. Partway through the meal, her face clouded over and she said: "Grace, I want to tell you something very personal that I don't tell many people. My husband is a heroin addict. He's now in Christian rehab."

My heart ached to hear about her husband, and I sympathized with her. Then I asked, "Has he been in rehab for three months, by any chance?"

"Yes, he has."

So Connie's "friend's husband" was actually Mary's husband! I knew that in the Christian rehab program they would be sharing the gospel with him, so I was hopeful this would be the turning point for Mary. That day, after she confided in me, I told her about Jesus in more detail and encouraged her to become a Christian.

"I won't become a Christian unless my husband does first."

Smokescreen. The Chinese often put up a smokescreen to avoid answering with a direct "no." I didn't know how to break through her barriers.

A few months later, after Mary's husband, Louis, got out of rehab, I invited them to my home. It was my first time to meet him. All the way from the bus stop to my apartment Louis talked about the Lord!

When we sat down in my living room, I turned to Mary, "Has Louis become a Christian?"

"Oh no, he would never do that!"

I was pretty sure from the way Louis was talking that he had come to know the Lord, so I turned to him, "Have you become a Christian?"

"Yes, I have!" Louis was beaming.

Mary stared at him in shock.

"But, Louis," I said, "you never told your wife!"

"I was afraid to." I could see why.

I turned to Mary. "You said that if Louis became a Christian, you would, too. So are you ready to become a Christian then?"

"No. I won't become a Christian!"

I sighed. I had no idea what to say.

Mary and I eventually lost contact. Several years later, a week before we moved away from Hong Kong, in that city of six million people, I bumped into her in the MTR (subway). We were excited to see each other. Waving her arms expansively, she told me all the news of her family. In every sentence she praised the Lord for what he had done for them! Had she finally become a Christian?

I had almost no time to spare, since we were about to move halfway around the world, but I invited her and Louis out for Chinese fast food. When they arrived, I asked Louis, "Is your wife a Christian?"

He looked sad. "No. She never became a Christian."

"Louis, how would you know if she had become a Christian?"

Louis said that if she believed Jesus is the creator God, that he died for her sins and rose again, and if she repented and wanted to follow Jesus, then she would be a Christian.

After each point he made, I turned to Mary and asked, "Do you believe this?" "Have you asked Jesus to forgive you?" "Have you decided to follow Jesus?"

Every time Mary responded with an enthusiastic, "Yes!"

Finally, I turned back to Louis, "Your wife already is a Christian!"

"She is?"

Then I looked at Mary, "You already are a Christian!"

"Really? I'm a Christian?"

Three of the six students from the class had become Christians, and so had one of their husbands! What had I done in all these conversions? Not much. I had diligently shared the gospel, but without effect. Part of the problem was that I didn't know how to think like they think in order to make the gospel appealing.

But the beautiful thing is that the Lord worked in these women's hearts anyway, drawing them to himself! And he used what little I had to offer him. If I had never taught that English class, I wouldn't have been able to invite the women to an evangelistic meeting where they would hear the gospel. And with Mary and Louis, the Lord gave me the strangest role. I got Louis into Christian rehab without knowing it was him. I let the wife know her husband had become a Christian. I let the husband know his wife had become a Christian. And I let the wife know that she herself had become a Christian! It wasn't much, but it was significant.

It was not by my power, but by the Spirit of God.

BROKEN

Starting 1989, Hong Kong

We had only been in Hong Kong two and a half years when the breaking began. When I went to Hong Kong I had a lot of misconceptions about the Lord, about serving him, and about my significance and insignificance as a person. My misconceptions caught up with me in Hong Kong and began to destroy me. I finally broke, and the Lord used it to make me the person I am, the Christian I am, and the missionary I became.

§§§

Every night I slept on a barely padded board that the Chinese called a mattress, in our bedroom that was hardly larger than the bed, with an air conditioner blowing cold air directly on my muscles all night. Hong Kong was so hot and humid we couldn't sleep without air conditioning. Every morning after I woke up, I winced as I tried to shift my stiff body into a sitting position and reach my feet down to the cold, white, tiled floor.

We had finished our two-year intensive Cantonese language program and I could now speak like a two-year-old. For this third year I was studying half time with a tutor. Finally I had time to make friends and share the gospel.

I was so excited to be able to serve the Lord, I didn't care about the pain. Everything I could find to do for the Lord I jumped into. And I juggled it all while raising our five- and three-year-old sons and continuing my language study.

Justin was also under a lot of pressure because he was pastoring the church plant, which meant preaching in Cantonese, doing the administrative work, and a lot of late-night meetings.

The Hong Kong culture placed stringent requirements on social behavior. And for some reason, the Hong Kong people considered me to be one of them, so the extensive workaholism and courtesies, which came natural to them, were imposed on me. They censured me whenever I didn't conform or even know what to do. I kept trying to prove myself, but I felt unaccepted and unacceptable.

Eventually the stress, coupled with the poor sleeping conditions, caught up with me. My back muscles froze up in disabling pain.

My life came to a halt. All I could do was lie flat on my back. Even simple everyday responsibilities, like shopping for food, cooking, cleaning house, playing with the boys, were impossible because I could barely hold my head up. Month after month this was my pathetic life.

Doctors in Hong Kong gave me very bad advice and an even worse prescription.

"Sleep on a board at night. Your bed's too soft." My back stiffened even more.

"Don't do anything that hurts." So I did nothing, which further stiffened my back. Doing *anything* was agonizingly painful.

"Here's a prescription for Xanax®," one doctor said.

"Doctor, is it addictive?"

"No, of course not."

I got addicted. All the while, he continued to write scripts, for a full year, and my back seized up worse every eight hours if I didn't pop another pill.

If serving the Lord had made me worthwhile, I was now worthless. I couldn't even take care of myself or my family. I had no value.

"God, I gave you everything I had to offer, but you rejected it," I told the Lord. "Why? Why don't you want my service?"

I fell into deep, suicidal depression.

After I had suffered for six months, Justin invited our co-pastor, a young, godly man, Mr. Chan, to come pray for my healing. I sat stiffly on our sofa. Justin and Mr. Chan scooted easy chairs over to huddle near me to pray.

Mr. Chan prayed in Cantonese. While he prayed, I concentrated on how badly I needed the Lord's touch, how much pain I had suffered, how much I would love to be healed, and what it would be like to function again, pain-free. Oh, how I wanted that!

After 20 minutes, Mr. Chan closed the prayer and looked up at me. My face must have shown all the pain and longing, because his face filled with consternation. "Grace, don't think about your back or the pain or how much you want to be healed. Put your mind on the Lord!"

Closing my eyes, I tried to bow my stiff neck as he again led in prayer.

And then, all of a sudden, I saw the Lord! He took my breath away.

He was seated on a large throne of unfinished blond wood. I had always thought his throne was gold and embedded with precious stones. That had never made me feel close to him. But I could relate to the King sitting on a throne of unvarnished wood.

I was completely mesmerized by his eyes, which were intently focused on mine. They were filled with love, compassion, concern—beyond anything I had ever seen before.

He was leaning forward on his throne, with his left arm reaching toward me. I knew that nothing mattered to him but the pain I was suffering.

He said nothing, but his eyes and body language said everything. My pain hurt him deeply, yet I knew he wasn't going to heal me physically.

But that was the beginning of the greatest healing I have ever experienced as a believer.

Over the next three years, I spent a lot of time flat on my back with the Counselor, the Holy Spirit, ministering to me, and the Lord tore down my previous false beliefs: *If I'm strong I have value, but if I'm weak, I'm worthless. God is only interested in what I do for him. My worth comes from how productive I am. I don't need anyone's help. If I'm emotional, it means I'm a weak person. I'm inferior because I'm a woman.*

Then he built into me a whole new value system based on his perspective.

My value didn't come from what I do for the Lord, but from who I am and who I am to the Lord. The Lord wasn't so interested in my service for him; actually he could do everything himself if he wanted to. Instead, he delighted in the fact that I am and that I am his. That was enough. It didn't matter if I was unable to be productive or strong, I still had the same worth.

Before I was broken, I was so busy finding ministry to do for God. After being broken, I realized that I must follow his leading, and not run ahead of him. Any work I do for the Lord is actually him working through me.

I came to realize my inestimable value as a woman. I always used to want to be a man so I would have value, but I began to celebrate my womanhood.

I had always been told, with a sneer, that men are intellectual and women are emotional, so I had suppressed the embarrassing emotional side of myself. But I discovered that I am a very emotional being, and I began to celebrate my emotional side. I found that emotions are a reflection of what a person really believes. If I wanted to know what was going wrong in my thinking, my emotions were the clue to where my mind and beliefs had gone astray. If I ignored my emotions, I was less able to straighten out my thinking.

I found that when part of my true self was suppressed, I couldn't have as deep a friendship with God. Now that I was giving fuller expression to my whole being, my relationship with the Lord became so much richer and deeper.

I became less judgmental and more compassionate toward others as I accepted myself and my weaknesses. Before, I could never ask for help, but I became comfortable with needing other people.

And I was no longer ashamed of myself.

When I had been sharing the gospel like a workaholic, hardly anyone came to faith. At the beginning of my breaking, when all I could do was pray, the women I had witnessed to came to believe in Jesus! This really opened my eyes. I realized that although it's vitally important to share the gospel, it is even more important to pray, because the power is from God.

The changes I experienced are almost too many to tell. In those few years of excruciating physical pain, my spirit came to health. It was almost like a new birth.

ILLITERATE

1990, Hong Kong

Illiterate
adj. unable to read or write
(The New Oxford American Dictionary)[1]

I became illiterate when I was 34.

It happened nine months after my back muscles froze up. I was lying in bed, reading a book in Chinese, trying to do something worthwhile, when my eye muscles seized up in pain. I couldn't focus on anything near my face, much less read.

It took nine months and returning to the States before I got a diagnosis—adult strabismus. My left eye turned in slightly, my right eye turned up a little, and my eyes couldn't track together.

The brochure in the doctor's office informed me that these problems are all perfectly curable—that is, if you're six years old or under!

I couldn't believe what happened to me. I have my master's degree and I'm an avid reader. Being unable to read made me feel like my mind was atrophying.

So I began to learn braille. I listened to books and magazines on vinyl records sent by the U.S. government Services for the Blind, and I listened to the Bible on tape. It was hard to remember what I heard, though, because I'm a visual learner. That always makes my husband chuckle—a visual learner who can't read.

The doctor started me on a vision therapy regiment that I still do each

---

1. *New Oxford American Dictionary.* Edited by Elizabeth J. Jewell and Frank Abate. New York: Oxford University Press, 2001.

day. After nine months of vision therapy I started to be able to read a little, but it took 15 years of exercises and pain before I could comfortably read for 10 minutes at a time.

But the Lord was amazing—he used my inability to read! Many of the women my age in Hong Kong were illiterate. When they became Christians it was difficult for them to cope with the level of literacy we assume in our churches. But now I understood what they were up against.

When I taught the women's Sunday school class, I prepared by listening to a tape of the Bible passage over and over again at home. I thought up questions to ask them, but I had to remember the questions since I couldn't write them down.

In class we first listened to a tape of the Scripture passage and then we discussed it from memory. I had noticed that the literate teachers gave the women lengthy passages of Scripture to memorize, which the women were unable to learn. So I picked out a short key memory phrase from the passage, like, "*Bat yiu pa, ji yiu seun.*" ("Don't be afraid; just believe.") Months later the women told me, "We learned so much from what you taught us in Sunday school. And the memory verses are still helping us because we can remember them!" I had been specially gifted to teach them because at that time I was illiterate, too.

There is a big difference between literary and colloquial Cantonese (like the difference between Shakespearean English and modern speech). Any Hong Kong person who is educated can speak literary Cantonese, and that is the language that is used for prayer in Hong Kong. Since I could no longer read Chinese, I learned colloquial street Cantonese from my friends. And God used my simple Cantonese to convince my illiterate friends that they could pray!

I often sat with these friends in church. At the end of the service, we always broke up into small groups for prayer. In our prayer circle, the women told me, "We can't pray because we don't know all those fancy words everyone uses to pray." I tried to explain to them that God just wants to hear from our hearts. But their response was, "You wouldn't approach a king the way we speak, so how can we approach God? We can't pray." So I said, "O.K., then I'll pray." We bowed our heads, and in my simple Cantonese I talked to God. When I finished, they all looked up at me surprised, and said, "We could do that! We'll pray, too." They each prayed in the circle. Simplicity was what they needed, and that simplicity came from my inability to read.

CURSE

1991-92, Hong Kong

We had an uneasy relationship with the villagers after we moved into Hang Hau Village. Some of the women embraced me—they loved to talk with me and we went for walks together. Mrs. Ho, the matriarch of the village, enjoyed sitting with me under the one tree in the center of the cement landscape of the village, telling me stories in Cantonese of the Japanese occupation of Hong Kong during World War II.

But our kids didn't make a good entrance into village life. Right after we moved in, Adam took off his shirt and asked me to paint black circles all over his skin. After he went outside, I stood on the porch and watched him sneak up on our new neighbors, raise his arms and growl at them.

At ages eight and six, Nigel and Adam were energetic and active, which Hong Kong people considered naughty. In fact, the Cantonese word *wuht put* (active) actually implies naughty. But I was determined not to restrict the boys from being normal, active American kids, even though it meant we wouldn't fit in. It was very difficult to be the mother of the naughtiest children, and always berated, but I decided that if the people of Hong Kong yelled at my kids for innocent, lively play, I would bear the brunt of it.

Nigel and Adam liked to play on the hillside behind the village because it wasn't cemented over; there were trees and dirt. Whenever a group of old Chinese women passed by, they would always show concern for our kids in the Chinese way—they warned them of dangers.

"Siu pehngyauh, yauh seh a!" ("Little children, there are snakes there!")

A Chinese child would have heeded the warning and come down off the slope.

My children, being American, looked around, didn't see any snakes, and called back, *"Poh po, mouh seh a!"* ("Grandmas, there are no snakes!")

This frustrated the grandmas, who were being loving to our kids and were worried about their safety. The grandmas argued back and forth with the boys.

"There are snakes!"

"No, there aren't any snakes!"

"Yes there are!"

"No, there aren't!"

And on it went, until finally, the grandmas marched off in a huff. Nigel and Adam were so disobedient! They wouldn't even listen to their elders.

One spring afternoon, the boys were biking around the village. I kept hearing Mrs. Ho yelling and yelling in Cantonese.

Finally the boys burst into the apartment. "Mrs. Ho keeps yelling at us all the time!"

"What's she yelling at you for?"

"She says we're going to hit the propane tanks in the alleys and they'll explode. But we aren't even near the propane tanks when we bike between the buildings. We're careful. She won't stop bugging us. And we can hardly play!"

"O.K., I'll go down and sit outside."

I grabbed a pile of unread mail and sat under the tree to read. The boys resumed their play while I drew all of Mrs. Ho's ire.

She was screaming now. "Your kids are going to run into the propane tanks!"

I didn't say much to her. I thought she was being totally unreasonable; the boys had often biked between the buildings and there had never been a problem. That day, when I didn't get alarmed or stop the boys, she tried to rally support against me. Turning to residents as they returned to the village, she pointed at me and shrieked, "Her kids are going to hit the propane tanks, and she doesn't even care! She won't stop them!"

I had never seen Mrs. Ho melt down like this. I sat out there for more than an hour being yelled at and criticized while the kids played.

The next day Mrs. Ho died! Maybe she hadn't been feeling well and that was why she was screaming. But it seems the villagers understood it differently. No grandma ever yelled at our kids again after she died. The boys were shocked at the change. Some villages have witches and warlocks who put hexes on people who cross them. I think the village people thought I had supernatural power to kill them. If you yell at Nigel and Adam, Grace will put a curse on you and you will die!

LITTLE BOY DYING

1992, Hong Kong

I stood on the roof of our apartment in Hang Hau Village one afternoon hanging up laundry. For several weeks I had planned to call Maggie Ng, a single mom who attended the Chinese church we were planting. I kept putting it off because I didn't like calling people who weren't my close friends.

I had just put a clothespin on the shoulder of a shirt, clipping it to the line, when I was startled by a supernatural presence right above me, and an urgency that I needed to call Maggie now! I left the shirt hanging by one clothespin and ran down the stairs. I didn't know why I was supposed to call her and I had no idea how important this simple phone call would be.

"Maggie, how are you doing?" I asked in Cantonese.

Her voice was trembling. "Not well. I don't know what to do. My son, Jeff, is real sick. I took him to the doctor, but the doctor didn't think there was much wrong with him so he sent him home. But he's real sick! I guess I just have to take care of him at home."

"What's wrong with him?"

"He has a fever of 39 degrees (C) and his tongue and lips are very swollen. He also has a rash on a lot of his body."

Hearing this made me anxious; 39 degrees Celcius was 102 degrees Fahrenheit. It sounded like an allergic reaction. "Is he taking any medicine?"

"Yes, he started on antibiotics."

"You need to get him to the hospital right away! I don't care what the doctor said. Take him to the hospital!" I shouted into the phone in a panic.

"But the doctor didn't think it was very serious, so how can I take him to the hospital?" Chinese people tend to believe everything a doctor says implicitly because he's the authority.

"Listen, he may be having an allergic reaction to the antibiotics. My sister had an allergic reaction to eggs once and almost died! I heard it was like that, with her tongue swelling up. You need to get Jeff to the hospital right away! Do you want me to come with you?" I wanted to make sure she actually took him.

"No, I'll take him myself." I could hear the fear in her voice.

Maggie didn't call me for several days. When she did, she sounded exhausted. "Grace, you won't believe this. You may have saved Jeff's life by calling when you did and convincing me to take him to the hospital! That night, 11 doctors gathered around his bed trying to figure out what disease he has. Every hole in his body had turned black, his arteries were inflamed, and he had a fever. They had never seen anything like it. They finally figured out it was Kawasaki disease. It's a strange disease kids can get. He's only the third child ever in Hong Kong to get it, and the other two kids died!"

I shuddered. "How is he doing now?"

"They got him on the medicine just in time and he's getting better. He's still quite sick, though."

I sighed in relief.

Jeff was ill for several months but he completely recovered.

God is so great—he had saved this little boy's life through my phone call. But what if I hadn't dropped everything and called Maggie the moment God told me to—would Jeff have lived?

IDOL STORE OWNERS, MY FRIENDS

Starting 1992, Hong Kong

An acquaintance from our village ran up to me. "Grace, Mr. Dow was hacked to death!" he said in Cantonese.

"What?" I gasped. "No! That can't be! We went out with them for dinner just a few weeks ago."

"Two weeks ago Mr. Dow went into the market at five in the morning to set up his idol store. Five men followed him in. They had cleavers and they chopped him!"

I closed my eyes and tried to make sense of his murder. The Dows were our friends. He was only in his early 30s and they had two toddlers. Why would anyone kill him—and in such a horrible way? Who could hate him that much?

The story had been in the newspapers two weeks earlier, but I had missed it because we had our own trauma at home. I hadn't been out much or seen Mrs. Dow for two weeks. Apparently she hadn't wanted to tell me about her husband. Hong Kong people are astoundingly private. Even though I was her close friend, I knew less than anyone else about the tragedy. I hadn't been invited to the funeral because in the Buddhist ceremony they had worshiped Mr. Dow, and since I'm a Christian they assumed I'd feel uncomfortable.

Our neighbors told me Mr. Dow was killed by the Triads, the Chinese version of the Mafia. "Chopping" was the Triads' signature execution method. The Dows once told me that the Triads charged protection money from all the vendors in the market, but Mr. and Mrs. Dow had refused to pay. Such a small thing. Did he die just for that?

The Dows owned two newspaper stands—one open-air stand, and another in front of their stall in the market where they sold idol worship paraphernalia. I first met Mrs. Dow at the open-air stand. She was so friendly and fun, we couldn't stop laughing and joking with each other. Cantonese is a great language for telling jokes. Being monosyllabic with seven tones, there's no end of puns. In English, the pun is the lowest form of humor. In Cantonese it's the highest.

We fast became friends. Eventually we felt comfortable talking about marriage, kid issues, and finally Jesus. She was excited when I offered to read Bible stories to her. But then she shocked me by setting up a chair in her idol store for me to sit and read! There I sat in the center of her idol store for all to see, reading and discussing Bible stories with her. Didn't she feel the contradiction? I felt like I was bringing Christ to Satan's throne.

One day, a few months after I started reading Bible stories to her, Mrs. Dow stopped me on the street. "Do you know what happened to old Mrs. Boe? She was shopping in the market and fell down right in front of my stall. She was in a lot of pain. It turns out she had broken her hip. I asked the young men in the market to help me put her on a merchandise cart to get her to the hospital." Mrs. Dow looked angry. "But you know the old Buddhist superstition that if you touch someone and afterward they die, then someone in your family will also die? Well, the men turned their backs on me and refused to help! And they all know Mrs. Boe! It was really hard, but I rolled her onto our cart and brought her to the hospital."

Mrs. Boe was my dear friend and walking partner. Two weeks later she died.

And Mr. Dow was murdered just four weeks after that. I expect the curse was demonic. Had it come true?

I'm a curious person, and I wanted to know all the details of his death. But when praying for Mrs. Dow, the Lord impressed on me that the best way to show love was to have no curiosity at all, particularly since Hong Kong people are so private.

I waited a month after her husband's death to ask Mrs. Dow out to dim sum. We talked about everything but Mr. Dow's murder. We were both somber, though—no jokes. Finally Mrs. Dow said, "Everyone—relatives, friends, acquaintances, and then some—have been constantly calling and knocking on my door, wanting to find out how and why my husband was murdered. But you, you're different. You didn't take me out to eat because you're curious about his murder. You're my true friend. You haven't tried to find out anything at all!"

After her husband's death, Mrs. Dow was even more interested in talking about the Lord. She finally told me, "I want to become a Christian, but if I do, it's going to cause a lot of problems in my husband's family. As the daughter-in-law, I'm still responsible to worship my husband's ancestors and maintain the god shelf, even though my husband passed away. If I don't do that because I've become a Christian, there'll be no end of trouble."

The last week I lived in Hong Kong Mrs. Dow took me out for a farewell dim sum. Out of the blue, she said, "While I was in the shower this morning, I was thinking about the things you said. I think I'll become a Christian!"

I was so excited. "Are you ready now?"

"Not quite yet."

§§§

Every time I return to Hong Kong, I call Mrs. Dow. When she hears my voice on the phone she screams, she's so excited. She takes the day off work and we bum around Hong Kong together, and sharpen our puns. I love seeing her.

On my first visit back, she and her kids went with me to the church Justin and I planted. She had never been to church before. Both she and her children loved it, so she decided to get connected with a church.

She started taking her kids to a tiny church in Hang Hau Village for tutoring. But the second time I visited, she looked at me sadly, "That pastor at that Hang Hau church told me, 'You shouldn't keep coming here to get our help. You don't have any interest in becoming a Christian, so why should we help you?'"

He only helps people who will come to faith in Christ? I thought we were supposed to help all people, and without a price tag. And how come that pastor hadn't talked with Mrs. Dow to find out that she actually was thinking about becoming a Christian?

Mrs. Dow continued, with a little anger rising in her voice. "It's so hard for me as a widow and single mom. I was really hurt when he said that. I stopped taking my kids over there for tutoring. In fact, I'm not interested in Jesus anymore because of that pastor."

Whenever I see her now and I bring up Jesus, she changes the subject.

My years of witnessing were all undone by one Christian's unwillingness to help this needy family—whether they became Christians or not.

MAINLAND CHINA

1996-2015

We loved Hong Kong,
but the churches there were already
strong, vibrant, and reproducing.
They didn't need our help planting churches.
The Hong Kong Christians begged us to stay,
but Justin set his sights on
Mainland China.

The only suitable international school
Justin found for the boys in the Mainland was in Wuran,
so that was the city we hoped to move to.

To live in the Mainland, we needed student or work visas.
That meant that in addition to being employed by the
mission agency,
we would also need to be students,
or at least one of us had to have a job outside the ministry.

First, we studied Mandarin for three years;
and after that, Justin worked a variety of jobs:
engineer, manager, program coordinator,
and English teacher.
I also taught English.

For his main ministry, Justin taught Bible school level
courses to house church leaders,
and I was learning from the Lord
how to effectively share the gospel.

China was not such a tame place when we moved there.

SECURITY—SPY GAME

1996, USA

I woke up panting and sweating. It was a small thing, really, but it cut at the heart of our privacy.

We had left Hong Kong, were spending a year in the U.S., and were considering moving to Mainland China. After much prayer, we asked the boys how they felt. At ages 13 and 11, they were old enough to give input into the decision. Adam piped up, "China is closer to Hong Kong than America is. We should move to China! We want to be near Hong Kong." So the decision was made.

But that night, I woke up flooded with anxiety. Our China home might be bugged! If Justin and I had a fight, the government would hear. When Justin and I made love, it could be public record. If I yelled at the kids, China could know the details of every misbehavior. And if I cried, one of the greatest countries in the world could delve into my deepest personal feelings. Could I live with that?

Early the next morning I raced down to the living room to talk with the boys. "Our home in China could be bugged! Do you still want to move to China?"

The boys squealed with excitement. This was better than anything they could have imagined—their lives were about to turn into a spy game! First they huddled together, then Nigel ran over to the phone, lifted the receiver and gave secret coded messages to his spy counterpart.

If we moved to China, the security issues were going to make our lives full of anxiety, but the boys put a light-hearted turn on it, and made the security issues into a fun game. Because of that, we were able to joke about security for our first few years in the Mainland until we learned to trust the Lord.

We decided to take an exploratory trip to Wuran, China, to see if we could live there.

DANTE'S INFERNO

1996, Wuran

My face was almost touching the taxi window, my eyes fastened on the scenes flashing by. Justin and I had come to Wuran for a five-day exploratory trip to see if we could arrange everything we needed in order to live here. We were seeing the city for the first time, and we hoped it would be our home for many years to come.

Since it was a city of nine million, I had expected a trim expanse of sky-scrapers joined by freeways. There were a few high-rises, but almost all the buildings topped out at seven stories. They were boxy, concrete structures with no character—like you see in pictures of third world countries, where the government was desperate to build somewhere for the population to live. The buildings, the roads, the cars—everything looked grimy.

As we traveled toward our destination, I was shocked by what passed for traffic in this metropolis—horse-drawn carts full of lumber or bricks, and adult-sized tricycles attached to flat-beds, with merchandise stacked several times higher than the cyclists' heads. Masses of slow-moving bicycles were creeping along both sides of the street. Yellow van-taxis spewed out black exhaust, with fumes so pungent they stung my eyes and throat, and so oppressive they made my head feel like it had been stuffed into a tailpipe.

I didn't see any traffic lights; in fact, there seemed not to be any traffic laws at all. Cars sped toward us, *in our lane*, swerving to avoid head-on collisions.

The sound of horns was so constant I could barely hear anything else, as drivers seemed to honk for every reason—*I'm passing. I'm turning. I'm behind you.* It wasn't the frantic bearing down on the horn like Americans do, out of fear or anger; it almost sounded friendly—*beep, beep, beep*—except that every car was beeping all the time!

We slowed down as we neared our destination. I gasped when we turned off the main road onto a dirt and gravel road. I've camped off of roads that were better maintained than this. You could almost fit a basketball in some of the potholes! Garbage and bricks cluttered the sides of the road, and the manhole cover sunk into the ground at a 45-degree-angle. Everything looked shoddy. How could I live in a place like this?

The driver turned right, drove past an old brick wall, and stopped. In front of a sooty, rectangular housing unit stood several tattered men, warming themselves around a three-foot-high barrel with flames skittering out the top. The place looked like Dante's Inferno.

The ground was bare, with no grass cover and almost no trees. I was trying to be brave. Justin was excited and I didn't want him to know I was about to cry.

The driver motioned for us to get out. We didn't think we were at the right place because Allen, a friend of a friend, who invited us to stay at his apartment, had described his housing complex, and this wasn't it. We used hand signals to try to communicate with the driver that this was the wrong place, but he was surly and impatient. He waved his hand from us to the door. He didn't care if it was the right place or not. He wouldn't take us any farther.

We hauled our two suitcases and backpacks out of the trunk and set them on the ground. We stared silently at our dismal surroundings. We were lost in a city of nine million people, in a foreign country where we didn't speak the language. We had Allen's phone number, but no phone. In fact, there were almost no phones of any sort in Wuran in the year 1996.

As we tried to figure out what to do, a man walked up to us. He looked a lot better than the ragged men clustered around the fire. In clear English he asked, "Can I help you?"

Hope! Had the Lord seen our predicament?

"We need to call someone."

"I have a phone in my apartment on the third floor. You can use it." He pointed at the apartment building behind the men warming themselves. He had one of the few phones in Wuran!

I watched the luggage while Justin accompanied the man up to his apartment to make the call. I stood with my back to the building and the flaming barrel.

One man, then two, then a few more, until finally a dozen men came and stood in front of me, all whispering to each other and staring at me. I stiffened. They were very interested in something, so I followed their gaze down to my shirt. Not just one, but two buttons had popped open! Not only could they see me, they could see our whole stash of cash, which was stuffed into my bra—200 flame-red bills! All were 100 RMB (Renminbi) notes. Twenty thousand RMB was the equivalent of 2400 USD—four years' salary for a laborer in China. We had thought that was the safest place to carry the money, but staring back at the men, I wasn't so sure.

There was nothing I could do but turn around and button myself up. The men lost interest and dispersed. I was shaken up. This was my introduction to the men of Wuran; and worse, it was their introduction to me! I couldn't wait until Justin came back.

When Justin returned, he told me, "Grace, I got ahold of Allen, but I couldn't tell him where we are because I don't know. He told me that's no problem. He would find us somehow." Justin chuckled.

We waited in that bleak place. It seemed impossible that Allen could locate us.

As I looked around again, I hoped we would find a place to live that looked nothing like this.

About 10 minutes later a taxi drove up and a tall, smiling American jumped out.

"How on earth did you find us?"

"I went to a driver I know and asked him, 'If a taxi driver thought he had driven my friends to my home, but the place he drove them to wasn't my home, where would he have taken them?' He brought me right here! Apparently the names are similar."

I held out until Justin and I were alone in the loft of Allen's apartment, getting ready for bed. I didn't mean to ruin Justin's excitement about his calling and dream, but I couldn't help it. I broke down, and sobbed and sobbed.

"What's wrong, Grace?"

I told him about the men who surrounded me, and then I said, "I hate it here! I don't want to move here. I hate Wuran. And there are no trees!"

Justin held me close and tried to give me hope, "Let's see if things improve tomorrow."

We had come to Wuran to arrange several things. We needed an affordable international school for our boys, and we had to rent an apartment. We also had to find a university for Justin and me to study Mandarin that would offer dependent visas for the boys and allow us to live off campus. Both the dependent visas and permission to live off campus were impossibilities. At that time China didn't offer dependent visas for kids if the parents came on student visas, and in Wuran, foreign students weren't allowed to live off campus. The police wanted to keep tight tabs on foreign students to make sure they weren't sharing the gospel or teaching the Bible, so they required them to live in the dorm. But Nigel was 13 and Adam 11, and we were not going to raise them in a dorm.

We had only five days to arrange the five things we needed. If the Lord wanted us to come to China, he would have to open the ground before us.

The next morning I was willing to try again. Right after breakfast, we flagged down a taxi and flashed a card in the driver's face—"Foreign Language Institute." Off we sped into the exhaust fumes and honking.

The campus of the local university wasn't pretty, but it was prettier than anything I had seen in Wuran. A brick wall surrounded a myriad of buildings that had at least a little style to them. And there were a few old, gnarly trees in beds of grass, an oasis in this barren city.

We found the admissions office and talked with the admissions officer.

"Yes, we offer a Mandarin language program." "Oh, you want to live off campus? I'm sorry, there's no provision for that." "You have children and want dependent visas for them? We don't offer dependent visas. Don't bring your children with you—leave them in America!"

Leave them in America? We weren't about to do that. We didn't know any other universities with a Mandarin language program, but maybe we'd get a breakthrough somewhere, so we soldiered on.

Justin called the international school to make an appointment with the principal. This school in Wuran was the cheapest international school that we could find in all of China that was large enough to be suitable for the boys. But tuition for our two sons would still be one and a half times our annual salary!

However, we didn't even get to discuss tuition. "I'm sorry, the principal can't meet with you. He's away for the next five days."

By the end of the fourth of our five days in Wuran we had succeeded at nothing. I knelt at the edge of the mattress on the floor of the loft of Allen's apartment, "Lord, we want to move to Wuran, but there is not one door open. If you want us to live in China, you have to arrange the five things we need to be able to live here. We only have one more day. If you don't give us all these things tomorrow, we're going to leave the next day and we're not coming back. It's up to you."

We got a call. "A board member of the international school can meet with you at nine o'clock tomorrow morning." I couldn't stop grinning.

The next day we met with the board member. We never told him directly that we were missionaries because the place was probably bugged, but it was obvious to him. Why else would a couple in their 40s with a teenager and a pre-teen move to Wuran to learn Mandarin? "People in your situation get a 75 percent discount on tuition." We couldn't believe our ears! It was only 9:30 a.m. and God had already answered one of our needs.

Doug, someone we had met at the International Fellowship, told us he could help us find a university. He told us to meet him at 10 a.m. at the gate of the Institute of Technology.

The Institute of Technology was all asphalt and imposing Soviet-style cement buildings. Almost no trees. Doug led us around the buildings and into the Foreign Student Affairs Office.

Everything in the office was in tattered disarray. About five worn-out desks cluttered the center. Directly ahead sat a frayed, olive-green couch.

A beautiful advertisement for the university hung from the door. It showed the school nestled in a lush, verdant forest. I turned to an office worker and asked, "Where is the forest? I haven't seen it yet." He shrugged. As I studied the pictures, I recognized the forest; it was the rainforest on the Olympic Peninsula just west of Seattle!

I turned away, disappointed, and we sat down on the couch. Doug explained our situation in Mandarin to Mr. Wang, the admissions officer.

Mr. Wang turned to us and in passable English said, "We have a Mandarin language program."

Justin said, "It's only four months until school starts. Is there enough time to get our transcripts to the school so we can be accepted?"

"You already are accepted. Just bring your tuition in U.S. dollars."

What kind of school was this? He didn't even know our names!

"We have two sons. We need visas for them."

"No problem. Just bring the tuition in U.S. dollars."

"And we need to live off campus because of the ages of our sons."

"That can be arranged. But remember, U.S. dollars!"

We almost danced out of the Student Affairs Office.

Doug turned to us, "We just rented an apartment. We are told that the police will allow three foreign families to live in our apartment complex. We and another American family are moving in. You could be the third. Do you want me to take you over there?"

We taxied to a garbage and brick-strewn, pot-holed road. At the end was a run-down, sooty, U-shaped building. The chipped and scuffed bare cement of the stairwell led up to a fifth-floor apartment.

We entered the cement shell of the apartment—a large, dreary, windowless living/dining area with two bedrooms shunted off. I headed straight to one of the bedrooms to look out the window to see if there were any trees. The view was depressing. All I could see were blackened cement buildings that had no soul. There were almost no trees in sight. I tried to see the street, but where the street must have been, all I could see was garbage. I stared in shock—pigs were rooting through the garbage! And what was that smell?

Rotten shrimp? It smelled like it was coming from the garbage on the street.

And outside I could hear the constant pecking on car horns—*beep, beep, beep.*

Four months later, shortly after we moved in, I explored the apartment complex. On the road I found potholes so big you could almost fit a basketball in them. A manhole cover was sunk in at a 45-degree-angle. Rounding an old brick wall I saw a three-foot high barrel, now cold. We had moved into Dante's Inferno! That's what the Lord provided.

But we were happy; the Lord had paved the way for us to live and minister in Mainland China. And we knew it was his will for us to be here because on the last day of the exploratory trip he had given us all five needs that I prayed for.

HOME VISIT FROM THE POLICE

1996, Wuran

Shortly after we moved to Wuran, the Foreign Affairs Officer from our language school called our home. "The police will come to your apartment today for a home visit."

Justin and I raced down the two flights of stairs to Doug's apartment. Doug was the missionary who helped us find the language school and apartment.

"Doug, did the police ever check out your home or the home of any foreigners you know?"

"No, I've never heard of it."

Justin and I looked at each other apprehensively. Justin had only been in China three and a half weeks, and the boys and I had come a week and a half ago. We had already had a serious problem with the police that had almost ended with us moving back to the U.S. Were we going to have to move back to America after all?

§§§

Half a week before, Justin and I were headed over to the police station to register. This was required of all foreigners within a month of arrival. It should have been routine.

I got out of the taxi and stared at the imposing, concrete police station. The massive-looking, three-story edifice was clearly influenced by Soviet architecture—lacking in artistic value, but dictating power and the ability to crush the masses. I knew a little about the police brutality and murders that went on in Chinese police stations. I shuddered, wondering if the violence happened in the basement. Would anything happen to us when we stepped through the doors? The building held its secrets. All the windows were carefully shuttered.

We climbed the stairs into the bowels of the police station, past a wooden bench on our right, then handed our passports through the window on the left. We were directed to an office down the left hallway. In that office, behind the desk sat our personal policeman—he was in charge of our family. Justin handed him our documents and the address of our home.

"This is where you're living?" he snorted. "You can't live there."

"But the Institute of Technology, where we will be studying, told us we could live there," Justin objected.

"Well you can't."

"But I've already renovated the apartment."

"You can't live there. It's for your safety!"

"It's for your safety" is the Chinese police euphemism for "No," while they pretend to care about your welfare.

"But other foreigners are living there."

"Are they students like you?"

"No. They're businessmen."

"Well, there you go. You're not in their classification. Foreign students can't live there. Foreign businessmen can."

"But ..." We tried to object.

"Don't come back here again!"

We were flabbergasted. We had thought registering was just a formality and that when the Chinese government granted our visas, it meant we could live in China. We didn't understand that if the local police didn't approve our stay in China, our visas meant nothing. It had never crossed our minds that he would refuse to register us. If we couldn't register at the police station, in less than a week, Justin would be in China illegally! Two weeks after that, the boys and I would also be here illegally.

"But ..."

"Don't come back here, I said!"

Well, that was final. Should we quickly pack our bags, and again move halfway around the world and cut our losses?

But we were sure the Lord had called us to Wuran because of how he provided everything we needed on the last day of our exploratory trip. If it hadn't happened almost miraculously we wouldn't have been so sure.

In a daze we found our way to the bench near the entrance. We sank onto the bench and tried to pull ourselves together. At first we were silent.

Then Justin spoke. "The Institute of Technology told us we could live in our apartment. We need to go to the school and talk to them. Maybe they'll straighten it out for us. And, you know, we haven't paid our tuition yet. If they don't resolve this, they don't get our U.S. dollars!" Justin gave me a wry smile.

We flagged down a taxi and showed the driver the Institute of Technology business card.

At the institute, we wound our way through the maze of buildings into the Foreign Affairs Office. We glared at the Foreign Affairs Officer, Mr. Wang. Justin spoke first. "You said we could live in the apartment we rented. We just visited the police station and the police said we can't live there!"

"The police are right. You can't live there."

"What! How can you say that? You told us it was O.K., so we signed a year's lease on the apartment, paid almost 2,000 U.S. dollars for the deposit and three months' rent, as well as 5,000 dollars to renovate it!"

"The police are right. We have some very nice suites on campus you could rent."

Justin countered, "No, Mr. Wang. This is our bottom line! We would not have moved to China if our family had to live in a dorm. We have two sons—a teenager and a pre-teen. When we talked to you a few months ago, before we moved to China, you assured us that we could live off campus. We would not have planned to attend this university if you had told us we had to live in the dorm."

Maybe that was the point. Mr. Wang had merely told us what we wanted to hear, a common malady of the Chinese. If he had told us the truth, we would not have planned to attend the university and they would have lost all those U.S. dollars. So we had moved 6,000 miles on the basis of false information designed to lure us in.

"These suites on campus are very nice," Mr. Wang said. "You need to move!"

Justin spoke firmly. "If we move, Mr. Wang, we will be moving back to America!" I jarred up. Justin was giving the Foreign Affairs Officer an ultimatum and threatening to leave China! I was more shocked hearing Justin say this than anything the police or Mr. Wang had said so far. I knew how badly Justin wanted to be in China and how much he felt called. But I was gratified he was putting our family first.

We suspected being deprived of our U.S. dollars would hurt Mr. Wang personally. From what we had seen of his lifestyle, we were pretty sure he got a cut of the tuition.

I held my breath, waiting to see what would happen.

"I'll see what I can do."

Mr. Wang called the police right then. After he hung up, he turned to us and smiled. "You can live in your apartment. You don't need to move."

54

I could feel all the tension in my shoulders relaxing. We could stay!

§§§

Now, a few days later we heard Mr. Wang telling us on the phone that the police were coming for a home visit!

How could this be? We had thought we were done with the police unless they caught us doing our mission work.

The policeman who arrived for the home visit, Officer Li, wasn't our personal policeman whom we had seen at the station. Mr. Wang accompanied him to act as a translator. We have learned since then that when a policeman in China acts like he doesn't understand English, he may be fluent in English, just waiting to hear what you say to each other that you don't think he understands.

When Officer Li entered our home, the first thing he did was race over to the closed door of the storage room off the living room. He paused in front of it dramatically, then swung the door wide open and peered in. He acted like we were keeping illegal immigrants or contraband Christian literature in there. All he saw were a chessboard, Monopoly, and other games we played with the boys. I couldn't believe his theatrics. I think he must have watched too much TV.

After the two men sat down on our gray cloth sofa, the four of us pulled up wooden chairs facing them. I had told the boys (13 and 11) not to say a word.

Officer Li asked friendly questions about the neighborhood, our adjustment to China, and so forth. We relaxed. It was going to be a friendly visit.

Then, without warning, Officer Li leaned forward and began firing questions at us. Eyes narrowed, he spit out at Justin, "Are you a Christian?"

"Yes."

Addressing me, "Are you a Christian?"

"Yes, I am."

Turning to Justin, "Are you a devout Christian?"

"Yes."

To me, "Are you a devout Christian?"

"Yes, I am."

I was so nervous I jumped up to get more water for the teapot, giving me a moment to compose myself. When I returned he fired at us, "Do you attend the foreigners' Christian fellowship?"

"Yes, we do," Justin answered.

Officer Li looked disgusted.

"Do you have an organization?"

Now I was scared. His meaning was a missionary agency.

"Yes," Justin said.

"Is there anyone else in this city with your organization?"

"No." We were pioneering for our mission in Wuran. The Chinese police are very regional, so we have learned, and only care about their own backyard. He liked this answer because it meant our organization didn't have a nest of missionaries in Wuran. He became less interested in us.

As quickly as Officer Li had turned the visit into an interrogation, he switched back to being sweet. Apparently it was the good cop/bad cop routine. This was a budget interrogation, though, with only one cop playing both roles!

"Let me write down the phone numbers of the fire department and police station. You are new to our country and we want your stay to be pleasant. If there is any way I can help you, do not hesitate to call!" Did he really think we would call on him to help us after he interrogated us?

After about an hour, he and Mr. Wang left. We could stay in China!

We should have been elated, but we were too exhausted. We just leaned against each other, then I looked at Justin in amazement. "He as much as said that he knew we're missionaries. Why didn't he kick us out of China?"

"I think he was saying that as long as we're not a problem for him, then we can stay."

"Then this is the key to doing ministry in China. I'd never understood why the missionaries don't all get booted out. The police know what we're doing, but if we keep our ministries small and quiet, they'll probably turn a blind eye."

"Yeah, we need to look incompetent and ineffective as missionaries."

The police visit that was intended to intimidate us, actually emboldened us, and taught us how to avoid being discovered!

AGAINST ALL ODDS

1996, Wuran

"*Ni hao*," our middle-aged Chinese teacher greeted us with a big smile when Justin and I arrived for our first day of Mandarin study. We had been in Wuran for a few weeks, and I couldn't wait to learn this language. It would be the gateway to forming friendships, sharing the gospel, and just overall functioning in China. We planned to study Mandarin for three years.

I liked the pleasant attitude of our professor. But she didn't speak a word of English; her only qualifications were that she was a native speaker and she cared.

Our fellow students—all at least half our age—filed in: eight South Koreans, a Brit philosophy graduate, an American college graduate, and a young woman from Israel. The South Koreans trudged in as a clump with the enthusiasm of a hangover. We later learned their parents had forced them to come to China to learn Mandarin. Every one of them stopped attending class after a few weeks.

The Brit philosophy graduate and the American came in together, laughing and talking, and took seats next to each other. The American was very loud. From the first day, we always knew exactly what he was thinking.

The young woman from Israel entered quietly and sat down. We came to the conclusion that she was a spy, but not a very good one—she always mixed up her stories about herself, especially the location of any trips she had just taken.

Teacher Yang assumed her students could already read Chinese characters! She was primarily teaching us oral Mandarin, using Chinese characters. This was OK for the South Koreans, who had learned to read Chinese in high school. Justin and I could read Chinese from studying Cantonese in

Hong Kong. All Chinese dialects use the Mandarin written form; but each dialect has a different pronunciation and in the case of Cantonese, a different grammar, too. But the Brit-American-Israeli trio didn't have a clue how to read Chinese.

We were afraid we wouldn't be able to get anything out of the class, so we asked a Chinese friend to teach us three sentences. "What does that mean?" (*You shen me yi si?*) "Say it again!" (*Zai shuo yi bian!*), and "I don't understand." (*Wo bu dong.*) We taught the trio these sentences, too.

A typical class went like this: the teacher said a sentence that none of us understood. One of us would raise our hand and ask in faulty Mandarin, "What does that mean?" To explain, the teacher wrote what she said in Chinese characters on the board. An exclamation of understanding came from the Koreans. A collective groan of dismay and frustration rose up from the trio because they had no idea what she had said *nor* what she had written.

Justin and I would then turn around to the trio and explain the meanings of the teacher's written words and grammatical points. We couldn't understand her spoken words either. And even though we understood the meaning of what she'd written, we could only read it with the Cantonese pronunciation.

Every day we were almost beyond our limit after three hours of this. One time in class I was so frustrated and discouraged, I ran out sobbing.

We *had* to learn Mandarin. Our ability to perform everyday tasks in China and our effectiveness as missionaries depended on it.

Learning the language was especially difficult for me. Six years earlier, in Hong Kong, my eyes had gone into painful spasms one afternoon while reading Chinese characters. I was unable to focus up close, so I couldn't read English or Chinese.

After nine months of vision therapy, I could still barely read and I had frequent setbacks that would last up to a year. During these times, I couldn't read at all and my eyes hurt a lot.

When I started studying Mandarin, I was able to read Chinese off the blackboard because it was distant, but I struggled to read the textbook because it was close. Humanly speaking, I wouldn't be able to learn Mandarin. But we were sure God was sending us to China, so we waited on him to enable me to master the language.

I managed for the first four days of class. But the grit in the air in Wuran was so severe that by the fifth day, the non-reflective coating on my glasses was so scratched, I couldn't read through the bifocal part. I needed the bifocals because they reduced the stress on my eyes when I read.

That wasn't a problem because I had packed an extra pair. But when I put them on, the prescription was too strong and they hurt my eyes. I had brought the wrong glasses!

How could God have let this happen? I was trusting him. Couldn't he have prevented my glasses from getting scratched? Couldn't he have prodded me to bring the right backup pair?

I asked the foreign community for advice. "Don't go to a Chinese optical shop," they told me. "They often fill prescriptions incorrectly." But out of desperation, I went to an optical shop anyway. When I handed my glasses to the optician, she pointed at the bifocal part and chuckled. Then she passed the glasses around for everyone to see. They had never seen bifocals before!

An American friend suggested I try an optical shop in South Korea. The South Korean shop I contacted said they would be happy to make glasses for me, but first I needed to mail my current pair to them so they would know the prescription. (Asia uses different glasses prescriptions than America does.)

My vision was 20/700. For three weeks, while I waited for my new glasses, I couldn't even go to school or leave home. It wasn't safe for me to walk down the street. My situation was getting worse, and I was getting farther and farther behind in my studies.

When the glasses finally arrived from Korea, I was shocked. Korean opticians didn't know how to make bifocals either! They had pasted something on the glasses where the bifocals should have been, and I couldn't read through them at all! I not only cried, I was getting angry at God.

At least I could see through the main part of the new glasses, so I ventured outside and attended class again, but I still couldn't attempt to read the textbook.

Finally, I asked a friend in Seattle to go to LensCrafters®, where my original glasses had been made, and ask them to make another pair (without the non-reflective coating). About two weeks later, the glasses arrived in Chinese customs, but they wouldn't release them to me! They wouldn't tell me why or what I had to do to get them. I was too new in China to realize they wanted a bribe, but couldn't say it outright.

After 19 days of waiting for my glasses to clear customs, I began to feel severe pain in the back of my eyes, most likely because the Korean glasses had been made poorly. It could be months before my eyes would stop hurting. I lost hope. Any possibility of studying Mandarin was gone.

I fell apart. I had sacrificed everything to serve the Lord in China, but he hadn't noticed. Couldn't God do simple things like make my glasses not get scratched, or show the Chinese or Korean optical shops how to make bifocals, or make customs release my glasses? Isn't the heart of the king in the hand of the Lord? Are opticians and customs officials exceptions?

But what cut me to the heart most was that I thought the Lord had forgotten me. He didn't care about me.

I went out into our enclosed porch in case our home was bugged. I didn't want the Chinese government to hear a missionary do what I was about to do. On the porch I screamed and railed at God.

The next day, on the twentieth day that my glasses had been held up by customs, a foreign-run company found a way to get my glasses out of customs. As soon as I put the glasses on, my eyes stopped hurting and I could read! That had never happened before. I started studying. It had taken two months to get a usable pair of glasses, and it was as if I had never missed those months. I could speak and read what the rest of the class had learned in the time I had been gone! I cannot explain how that happened. The Lord had not forgotten me; he purposely delayed helping me because he was teaching me to trust him.

I went on to develop a good facility in Mandarin: able to teach the Bible at a Bible school level, develop close, intimate friendships, and lead people to Christ even when it required scientific or philosophical discussions. I can only attribute this to God's grace.

I've often looked back at what happened with my glasses, when God was so silent, letting my situation get worse and worse. Even in writing this, I am in the middle of two serious situations where God is silent. I can't see what God is doing or what he'll bring about in the end—but I've learned to trust the Lord with these problems as a result of that scratched pair of glasses that took two months to replace.

QUALITY OUT OF CONTROL

1996-2002, Wuran

When we moved to Wuran, it was a backwater town of nine million people.

The new apartment building we lived in was rigged to deliver a maximum of 60 amps of electrical current to the 12 apartments in our stairwell—only five amps per apartment! We constantly counted how many light bulbs were burning. To heat water for a shower required seven amps, which was over the limit, so we unplugged the fridge, turned off the lights, and hoped our neighbors hadn't maxed out their usage.

The fuse for the apartments in our stairwell was just a piece of solder wire, and it frequently melted through. One of my first memories living in the apartment of the housing complex that we called Dante's Inferno, was of all the men in the stairwell gathered on the ground floor around the melted solder fuse.

"I have two children—three dependents including my wife, so I should not replace the solder," one of the men said.

Another man pointed a finger at a third man. "You have only one child. You should be the one to replace the solder!"

"No! I have to support my ill mother, so with my wife and child I have three dependents!"

The men were counting dependents to decide whose life was most expendable, and that man should change the solder! The problem was that since nothing in China was well-made—in fact, nothing seemed to work at all—no one was sure if the main switch to turn off the electricity really worked. Since China's electricity is 220 volts, if the main switch didn't work, the man changing the solder would be electrocuted!

Finally, two weeks after we moved there, the men were fed up with risking their lives. No one was willing to change the solder anymore. We were on blackout until the apartment manager installed a circuit breaker that could supply 100 amps to the 12 apartments. It wasn't much improvement, but it made a big difference. We still counted light bulbs and held our breath when the fridge turned on, but the power outages were fewer and not life-threatening. We just flipped the switch.

Everything in our apartment was brand-new since Justin had just renovated it and bought all new appliances. The quality of everything was so poor that Justin spent eight hours a week repairing the new appliances, pipes, and hoses as they burst, exploded, and leaked.

The Lord was vigilant in protecting us through these almost daily disasters. When the hose to the hot water heater split open, I was standing only a foot from the heater. Boiling water shot straight out, missing my face by only an inch!

Exploding light bulbs was a common occurrence. Each time, amazingly, we were across the room as slivers of glass shot out in every direction. But one time I was right next to a light bulb when it burst. I stood completely still, afraid to move, expecting the shards of glass to embed themselves in my face and eyes. Instead, I watched in amazement as the fragments of glass shot straight down as if Someone had placed a two-inch invisible funnel under the light bulb restraining the shards. Not one piece even scratched me!

We returned from a weekend away once, only to find that our kitchen hot water heater had fallen off the wall and water had flooded the two apartments below us. We were glad no one had been standing under it when it fell. Although we were already living simply, we came to understand something after that incident. Less is more. If we had fewer appliances, there was less that could break, which meant we had more time, peace, and safety. We never replaced the kitchen hot water heater, so it couldn't fall off the wall again. I went into the bathroom after that to fetch hot water for washing dishes.

It wasn't just the poor quality of appliances in our apartment that made our lives difficult. A year after we moved to Wuran, a Chinese company came up with a scheme to make some easy money. They put a powder mixture in a bag and labeled it laundry detergent. Praval, being a foreign product, was the expensive laundry detergent, so they labeled the mixture "Praval" in order to make the most money.

I had chosen to use Praval instead of the local "Fast Dog" laundry detergent because the clothes came out fresher and cleaner. Then one day, the clothes I pulled out of the washer were streaked with a white, sticky goop.

It stuck to the clothes, which still smelled like damp body odor. The laundry detergent was fake! So I scrubbed. And I scrubbed. After 20 minutes of scrubbing the goop off one piece of clothing, I realized that the company had added one real ingredient to the detergent—bleach! Where the goop had been, the cloth was bleached white. The whole load of clothes was ruined! We had bought all our clothes in America and hauled them over to China to cover our American-sized bodies. Chinese clothes didn't fit us. We couldn't afford to lose too many of these clothes.

I studied every itsy-bitsy mark on the Praval packages to try to differentiate which bags contained real Praval and which ones were fake. That didn't help because the real Praval's packaging was not completely standardized.

So I bought a package of Praval, noticed what shelf it was on in the store, and tested it by washing a rag. When I found a package that did not leave sticky goop on the rag, I bought all the Praval on that shelf, assuming it was from the same factory. That was no help either because the real Praval was on the same shelf with the fake Praval!

I switched to the cheaper, inferior Fast Dog detergent. That worked until the other consumers had also discovered that much of the Praval was fake and switched to Fast Dog, like me. Then the company also had to switch from making imitation Praval to imitation Fast Dog, with a cut in profits, of course.

For several years we had to schlep laundry detergent from America to China!

The laundry detergent was a small problem because it wasn't something we ingested. In 2008 it was discovered that much of the milk for sale was laced with an industrial chemical called melamine, which makes the milk creamier, but damages the kidneys. It was horrible because babies were dying around the country. My husband now has stage three kidney failure. We'll never know if melamine was the cause, but we always wondered why his low fat milk was much creamier than the whole milk I drank.

SECURITY—LEARNING TO TRUST

Starting 1996, Wuran

If we were too afraid of getting caught, we wouldn't do ministry. If we weren't careful enough, China might kick us out and, more important, people's liberty and lives could be in danger. It was a difficult dance.

When we moved to a new city, we would ask the foreigners about police action against missionaries so we would know what to expect and how careful we should be. Every location was different. In some cities the police were serious about investigating Christian activities, especially on college campuses. But even in those cities, it was like the swing of the pendulum—for a while the police cared, then for a while they didn't. We watched the pendulum closely, noticing the persecution of local Christians or missionaries. If there wasn't any persecution, we increased our ministries; if there was, we pulled back.

Shortly after we moved to Mainland China, some 50 missionaries in our city were kicked out of the country when the police discovered their ministry. It was shocking, especially since we were friends with one of the families.

Our first few years in Mainland China, we assumed our apartment was bugged, so when we wanted to discuss ministry we would take a walk. Even then, we kept our eyes and ears open in case a passerby understood English. We had friends who were certain their apartment was bugged because their government employer knew information they had only shared in the privacy of their home. But we noticed that many foreigners were cautiously doing ministry in their homes. So after the first year, although we preferred not to study the Bible with locals in our apartment, sometimes that was the only place available. When there were no repercussions, we eventually concluded that our apartment wasn't bugged.

For talking on the phone and writing emails, we used code words. We were glad we did when we heard of a foreigner who was kicked out of China after the government hacker read his Instant Messages.

We avoided house churches altogether as we didn't want to endanger them or draw attention to ourselves. When Justin trained house church leaders in other cities, he kept a low profile. Sometimes his Chinese co-workers even brought him to the training center in a van with darkened windows. When they arrived at the apartment where the training would take place, a Chinese friend first ran up the stairs to make sure no one was in the stairwell. Only then did Justin race up to the apartment, where he hid for the duration of the training, with shades covering the windows, and soundproofing lining the walls and floors. He didn't see the sun for a week or two while he trained the leaders.

Despite all of our vigilance, we had a few close calls. Justin and I were discussing ways to dispose of sensitive documents once at a restaurant. We used a special code during our conversation—every other word was English, and every other word Cantonese. Any eavesdroppers would have to be fluent in both English and Cantonese. Not many people knew English, and we had almost never met a Cantonese speaker in our city, so we felt safe. About ten minutes into the conversation, a Chinese man at the next table turned around and said in perfect English, "I couldn't help but overhear what you were saying. I'm fluent in English, Cantonese, Mandarin, and Swedish!" I gulped. We tried to carry on a casual conversation with him. We never used that code again in public.

Another time, our Mandarin professor, who had recently become a Christian, dropped over for a visit. As soon as she walked in the door, she yelled at us: "You need to be more careful! Your upstairs neighbor just asked me who you guys really are—she saw you passing out Christian books to a number of Chinese people in your living room!" Justin was preparing to teach a Bible school level course, and we had taken the precaution of inviting the students over one by one. The students were sitting on our couch near the living room window of our first-floor apartment when he handed them the texts. Our window was high off the ground, so no one passing by could see in. After our professor left we checked, and sure enough, if we craned our necks, the part of our couch that was next to the window was visible from the porch one floor up! Our neighbor had been watching our apartment that closely, and even knew the textbooks were for studying the Bible!

One evening we got off a train at the main train station in our city of nine million people, where thousands of foreigners lived. We flagged down a taxi. We had never seen this taxi driver before, and as we started to tell him our address, he waved at us to stop. "I know, I know." And he proceeded to tell us our address! It was creepy.

On another occasion, a taxi driver Justin had never met before was waiting outside our apartment building. The drivers outside our building were always the same because that was their turf, so it was odd to see a new driver. As soon as Justin got in this new taxicab, the driver said, "I want to study the Bible. Could you teach me?" You didn't have to be living in China long to realize that situations like this were not opportunities! In this case, it was probably a trap—it happened too fast! Justin replied, "You should go to the government church to learn the Bible." Everywhere Justin went that day, that same cab was waiting outside to give him a ride and he kept asking Justin to teach him the Bible. After that day, Justin never saw that driver again! We have no doubt he was sent by the police to spy on Justin's whereabouts and to trap him into offering to teach him the Bible.

The security issues made living in China very stressful, especially during our early years, until we finally learned to commit them to the Lord as a result of a serious security violation. A few years after we arrived in China, our mission leader, who lived in another country, emailed us a multipage document, "Our Mission's Plan for Reaching China with the Gospel." When we saw the email, we were stunned. This email wasn't encrypted, so it was open for the Chinese government hackers to read.

Because the boys had turned the security issues into a spy game, we had been able to joke about it while still taking precautions. But this time our sense of humor failed us—we were scared and wondered if we would be kicked out of China for something that was totally out of our control.

That's when we started to trust the Lord with the security issues. We realized that this mess-up was in his hands, and that he truly is sovereign. I prayed, "Lord, please make China's email monitoring device malfunction so they can't read this email. Or else, please let it be that the Internet policeman assigned to read our emails was in the bathroom when this one came through. But, Lord, if you want us out of China, this is your chance. We wait on you." Peace came over us, and after that, we didn't fret so much about getting caught. In God's sovereignty, the police never did contact us about that email.

Coming to trust the Lord through the many difficult and frightening situations we faced was one of the greatest lessons I learned in Mainland China.

THE PRICE OF FAITH

1996, Wuran

This was my first encounter with persecution in China. It was different than I had imagined.

Nineteen-year-old Peter was our first Chinese friend in Mainland China. We loved him. He had come to believe in Jesus less than a year before we met him. When Justin first arrived in Wuran, Peter helped him renovate the apartment, and before we could communicate in Mandarin, he translated for us and tutored us. He spoke fluent but simple English.

We spent every Saturday together. Peter had a unique way of looking at everything and such an amazing sense of humor that we laughed our way through each Saturday.

He took the boys on adventures—exploring, paintballing, getting massages with flaming alcohol, eating strange foods like donkey or snake, riding dirt bikes, and "dating missions" (which were practice rounds to get up the courage to ask a girl on a date). Most of the adventures were "secret missions" that I've never been told about to this day.

Peter was just starting to go bald, which was very unusual for a Chinese man, so he was afraid no woman would want to marry him. Every few weeks he asked me to examine the top of his head to see if more scalp showed. We discussed hair growth creams and hair transplants.

The only thing we couldn't figure out was why he always had free time. No school. No job. He was afraid to tell anyone because the police had ordered him not to, so it took half a year before he was willing to tell us.

One December afternoon he asked us to sit down in our living room because he had something important to tell us. I thought he was probably pulling another stunt to tease us, but when I looked at his face I saw that he was tense and sad. I had never seen him like this before.

He began. "It was hard for me to get into college because I had a learning disability when I was young. All my teachers thought I was stupid. But I worked real hard and made it in."

At that time the Chinese government only allowed three percent of Chinese high school students to go to college, so that was an impressive achievement.

"Last year was my first year of college. I had looked into Buddhism because my grandpa is Buddhist, but Buddhism is stupid. Then an American English teacher of mine, Max, told me about Jesus. When I heard about him, I knew it was true. I told my friends about Jesus and they believed, too.

"Max studied the Bible with me, and I taught my friends what he taught me. Max lives in the foreign teachers' dorm, and that's where he was studying with me. I had to sign in every time I went to see him."

Justin and I were both tense, and silent, wondering where this was leading.

Peter shifted in his chair. "Another American teacher, who also lived in the foreign teachers' dorm, lent a Bible to one of her students. When the police discovered what she had done, they kicked her out of China. I didn't know this teacher."

I asked, "But what did that have to do with you?"

His face looked pained. "The police wanted to find out what students she had shared the gospel with, so they checked the dorm sign-in list and found my name on it. I had gone in a lot of times, but I wasn't visiting her since I didn't even know her. But when I signed in, it didn't ask who I was visiting, so they didn't know I wasn't visiting her."

My heart sank. I wish Max and Peter had been more careful and had found a safer place to study the Bible.

Justin asked, "So did the police investigate you?"

"Yeah, first they questioned me, then they investigated me."

"What happened? Did they discover anything?"

"When they investigated everybody I knew, they found my friends who had become Christians, then they discovered that I was teaching them the Bible. I didn't even know this would be a problem! No one ever told me!" Most non-Christian Chinese don't know the government wants to stop the spread of Christianity, and new Christians have to be told so they can be careful while they serve the Lord.

I groaned.

"I thought it was okay until I took my final exams. Believe me, I did well on my finals. But when they posted the grades, I had flunked every exam!"

"What? What happened?"

"I knew there had to be a mistake, so I went to the teacher and said I needed to see the exam papers. He wouldn't let me see them! I kept pushing—I knew the grades were wrong and I needed to get it straightened out.

"Finally the police called me in and told me that because I'm a Christian and telling my friends about Jesus, they were kicking me out of college! The police said I'm not allowed to tell anyone the real reason I was kicked out of college. I can only say that I flunked out." Peter couldn't look at us anymore. He looked so sad and humiliated, and I could see it had been hard for him to tell us, even though we were his close friends.

The police have enormous power in China. They control the education system, especially the colleges. Peter was now blacklisted and could not attend any college in China. Not only had the police taken away his college education and made it hard for him to get a good job, but they had made sure Peter would be humiliated the rest of his life—having to say he flunked out of college. In this "face" oriented society, that humiliation was hard to bear.

I cried quietly.

Peter looked up, surprised at my reaction. "When I told Max what happened, he was happy! He told me I should rejoice because I'm being persecuted for the Lord."

"Eventually you may feel that way, Peter, but it's really sad you've been kicked out of college. How could Max be happy this happened to you? You've lost everything!"

"When Max said that he was happy I was kicked out of college, it really hurt. I haven't been able to be happy. I feel so much better because you're sad with me."

"Do you still see your old college buddies who became Christians?"

"Yeah, all the time. I still study the Bible with them."

I was surprised. "But what if the police find out?"

"Well, I love the Lord, and I'm going to serve him no matter what the police do. They already took college away from me, they can't take it away again!"

RIGHT UNDER THEIR EYES
First English Camp

1997, Outside Wuran

After six months of praying and making arrangements with a high school principal, our whole family was finally in the van with a team of three Westerners on our way to English camp. I could hardly sleep the night before, I was so excited. This was to be our first English camp in Mainland China. But I was also apprehensive. Not only was the camp illegal, but the government especially wanted to prevent children under 18 from hearing about Jesus. And it would be so easy for the authorities to discover that we were sharing the gospel.

This was an English immersion camp. We would use English songs, games, skits, and stories to introduce 50 atheist high school campers to American culture and to Jesus. In the stories and discussions, we would talk about a lot of topics: family, food, sports, making introductions, and solving problems. We would intersperse those topics with pre-evangelism stories about love, trust, sin, forgiveness, the limits of science, and the meaning of life. We would also teach Bible stories and the gospel.

This camp was an unprecedented opportunity for these high school students to learn English, as we were not charging for our services. From previous experience in Hong Kong, we knew that in the three weeks of camp we could take most of the students from a low English level to a level of being conversant in English.

During the hour-long ride to camp, Nigel, 14, and Adam, 12, joked and laughed with the three Westerners. Finally, we turned left through the iron gate of the remote, 50-acre site for the camp. It was the campus of a vocational school that was not in session.

A brick wall, taller than a man, enclosed the whole area, keeping it safe from prying eyes, or so we thought when we saw it.

Wide cement walkways crisscrossed the campus, connecting large brick academic buildings, dorms, and a cafeteria. Grass grew sparsely in the sandy soil, but a few trees had been planted to beautify the area.

I craned my neck trying to catch sight of the students. I couldn't wait to get to know them and tell them about the Lord! Probably none of them had ever heard about him before.

We spotted the students standing on the road, and after unpacking in the teachers' dorm I went out and started making friends with them.

The next day the heat was oppressive, with the temperature in the high 90s and stifling humidity. The camp began with a lively time of large group activities. Then we broke up into small groups with a Westerner teaching the story and leading discussion with each group.

On the second day of camp, though, the students were lethargic during the large group activities. When we broke up into small groups, many couldn't even hold their heads up at the tables. We asked them what was wrong, and they told us, "The camp isn't giving us any water to drink!" You can't drink from the tap in China, so the camp was supposed to supply water. When Justin investigated, he was told that the principal had probably siphoned off some of the students' fees into his own pocket so there was no money for the camp to provide water. If we couldn't get water for the students, not only could we not run the camp, but dehydration became a real possibility. All the Western teachers complained to the staff about the camp until watery carrot soup made from boiled tap water was provided. Camp could go on.

We soon learned that the high walls surrounding the campus were not able to keep our sharing the gospel secret because the high school had sent its own English teachers to the camp to spy on us.

The head English teacher, Cassius, was their master spy. He didn't care about the camp or how much English the kids learned. It became obvious that he had two goals. First, he wanted to impress the American teachers with his English ability. But Cassius had learned English from books, not real people. Every evening he commented on the "SW wind" that was blowing. We told him that we say "southwest wind," not "SW wind." He didn't believe us. He had read "SW wind" in books, and, of course, we didn't know as much as books.

His second goal was to please his handler, the school principal, by making sure we didn't teach about God. Every day he hunted around the meeting room for printed lessons we'd accidentally left behind. Because we were afraid this would happen, the printed copies of the stories we taught from were "sanitized"—no mention of God, Jesus, or the Bible. When we taught a parable of Jesus, we simply told the students that it came from the Bible and that Jesus told the parable. That way there wouldn't be any concrete evidence of our sharing about the Lord.

The journals were our biggest security risk, and Cassius figured that out quickly. Every day we asked the students to journal their responses to what we'd taught, including the Bible lessons. One day we accidentally left the journals stacked in the meeting room. Cassius walked in and furtively looked around. I was in a corner and he didn't see me. I watched as he sniffed around the room for evidence that we might be teaching the kids about Jesus. When he saw the journals he rushed over to grab them. I ran up to him and snatched the stack of journals right out from in front of him. We were more careful after that not to leave them lying around.

Another day, after class, a student asked me about the Lord, so I took her outside to talk. I didn't want any of the local teachers overhearing our conversation, so I chose a secluded walkway, which was bordered by a thick hedge and dead-ended at a wall for us to talk. Cassius came biking down the sidewalk, staring hard at us, craning his neck to hear our conversation. He was so intent on what we were saying, he nearly ran into the wall!

Cassius was difficult, but, even worse, we soon discovered the school had assigned an English teacher to spy on each small group! They sat right in on our teaching times to make sure we wouldn't teach about the Lord.

The first few days having a spy in my small group wasn't too bad because I was just doing the early stages of pre-evangelism, talking about love, forgiveness, and the purpose of life. My spy probably didn't even realize that I was preparing the students to hear about God.

But the first time I taught a miracle story from Jesus' life—the feeding of the five thousand—I was nervous. Not only was this going to be a hard sell for the atheist students, but the spy would know exactly what I was doing.

As my eight students crowded around our rectangular, folding table that day, I gasped as not just one, but two spy teachers joined my group!

"Lord, blind the eyes and ears of the spies, and please help me explain a miracle to these atheists I'm growing to love!" God did beyond what I asked or thought.

After we read the story together, I asked a few questions. Silence. They hadn't understood a thing. Since miracles don't make any sense to an atheist, they couldn't figure out what I was talking about. It sounded like nonsense.

To help them understand, I sketched on the whiteboard: two fish + five loaves = food for 5,000 people + 12 baskets of food left over.

The students just stared at the board. I was so frustrated I was about to end the class session, and I was already rehearsing in my mind my report at the teachers' meeting about what a failure this lesson had been.

I stood there, feeling sorry for myself, when one of my students, looking confused, broke the silence. "There's something missing in this story."

I looked at her hopefully. She was starting to understand.

The eyes of one of the spy teachers widened. "It's God!" she said with wonder in her voice. "God is missing in this story!"

Then she leaned back, and a look of shock and dismay crossed her face. I think she remembered that her assignment was to make sure the students didn't come to that very conclusion. Clearing her throat, she spoke in a loud, authoritative voice, "Students, this story teaches us that we should help the poor."

Anger welled up in me, but I kept my voice calm. "Yes, it does show us that we should care for the poor. But it also makes us question who Jesus is."

Again, the spy teacher forgot her role. In a moment of epiphany, she gasped, "Maybe Jesus is God!"

"Maybe he is." I said and quickly ended the lesson before she could realize and "correct" what she had just said.

The spy had been teaching the lesson for me!

Nigel and Adam had only agreed to go to camp for one week, so shortly after that, I left camp with the boys.

Two weeks later, the boys and I returned for the last day of camp, to attend the farewell party and to say goodbye.

That day, when the students journaled their final entries, one of the girls, Shar, wrote that she wanted to become a Christian!

I bumped into her outside and shared the gospel with her. She responded, "This is great! Yes, I want to become a Christian. My roommates and I have been talking all about it. We've got to go to my dorm room and tell my roommates how to become Christians, too."

We went up to her room, which was long and narrow with four beds against the walls, two on each side, and a window at the far end. Basic—no rugs or décor. We sat on the beds facing each other. She prayed and committed her life to Christ. I felt such a sense of awe.

One of her three roommates, Ann, returned to the room. Shar said, "Ann, I became a Christian! Do you want to become a Christian, too?"

"Yes!" Ann sat down, and I again explained the gospel very simply, and helped her pray to give her life to Jesus.

As soon as Ann lifted her head, another roommate, Colleen, entered. Shar and Ann shouted at her, "Colleen, we became Christians! Do you want to become a Christian, too?"

"Yes!"

As soon as Colleen finished praying, the last roommate, Lily, returned. The girls shouted at her, too, with the same results. When Lily prayed to become a Christian, she first stood up and walked over to the little window at the end of the room. She craned her neck to look up at the sky and only then began to speak to God. Lily thought God was in the sky and he couldn't hear her if she wasn't close to the window!

I got the impression that if there were enough time, the whole dorm would believe in Christ!

Then one of their friends, Pat, popped her head in the door. The four told her, "Come on in! We became Christians. Do you want to become a Christian, too?"

"Yes, I'd like to!"

In explaining the gospel, I asked her, "Pat, have you ever done anything wrong?" (The American teachers had talked about sin in the small groups.)

"No, I've never done anything wrong." She was adamant.

Her four friends were shocked. "You must have done something wrong!" "You're not perfect. We know you!" "You've never ever lied?" No matter what they said to her, she insisted she was perfect and sinless.

When teaching about sin and forgiveness, the American teachers had taught the students a phrase. The four, in unison, chanted the English phrase several times at Pat, "You can't be forgiven unless you say you're sorry! You can't be forgiven unless you say you're sorry!"

Pat was unrelenting.

"I'm sorry," I told her. "I can't help you become a Christian until you know you've done wrong things."

Then we heard the call to load up the buses. Camp was over.

For over half a year I met with these four young women in our home to study the Bible. They were a delight! Two of them began reading the Bible on their own, and the father of one of the girls even started reading his daughter's Bible as a result of her witness to him. I then connected them with a local believer who discipled them.

Many others in the camp came to believe in God and the resurrection of Jesus.

How was it possible to lead students to Christ and help them come to believe in God, right under the eyes of the spies? We were careful, but we were also courageous. And the Lord was with us, blinding some and making others see.

WE NEED A MIRACLE TO BELIEVE
Second English Camp

1998, Outside Wuran

Our whole family was riding in the van with a short-term team of Americans, again on our way to the same location for English camp. Justin and I were nervous. We were being blackmailed and didn't even know if there would be any students at the camp!

Roman, a friend of ours, had enlisted Lance (both Chinese) to recruit high school students for the camp. Instead, Lance recruited adults because he could charge adults extra and pocket the money. When Roman told him we would only teach kids, Lance threatened that if we didn't teach the adults he recruited, he would make sure the camp was ruined and that no kids showed up.

We found this out when the American short-term team was already over the Pacific on their way to China, so we couldn't tell them not to come!

Roman agreed to talk to another principal and see if any kids could be rounded up to attend camp. He had only a few days to find some, or camp would be closed.

Justin and I prayed together, begging God to thwart Lance, and help Roman find students, but we didn't know what the Lord would decide.

That night in bed Justin held me close. "Grace, it will be so humiliating if I'm responsible for a short-term team coming over from America and there's no camp for them to teach at."

When we picked the team up from the airport, Justin sighed and told them, "Someone threatened us yesterday that if we don't meet his demands he'll make sure there'll be no students at camp. We can't meet his demands, so we have no idea if there will be any students. Yesterday and today our

Chinese friend has been trying to find students. You have traveled all this way, but there may be no camp." Justin looked down.

One of the women spoke up. "If there's no camp, that's O.K. We'll take it as from the Lord. We can have fun sight-seeing in China." Those were some of the kindest words I had ever heard in my life. This team was enthusiastic about teaching at camp, and it would be awkward for them to report to their supporters, who had paid for the trip, that there had been no camp, but they wanted us to feel better, so they put it in a positive light.

A few days later, on the way to camp, the team was excited and jovial in spite of the uncertain situation. As we drove through the gate of the camp, I was getting more and more tense. Would there be students or not?

When we pulled up to the teachers' dorm, we counted 38 secondary school students standing at attention along the sides of the road to greet us! Camp was on! There were tears in my eyes. Even though we'd hoped for more, these were 38 students we would grow to love, and who would hear the gospel, probably for the first time.

The next day we played games, sang songs, and discussed a story with the students. They were lively; the camp provided water; and we had no spies.

Our sons (15 and 13) had loved camp so much the previous year they agreed to come for the full two weeks this time. I hardly saw them they were having so much fun with the campers.

Everything went well for three and a half days. Then, the unexpected happened.

Thursday afternoon one of the campers asked me, "Have you seen Adam?"

"Not recently."

"You need to see his head."

I ran over to where Adam was having dinner in the dining hall, laughing and joking with the campers. When he looked up at me I gasped. A lump about two inches by one inch was bulging almost an inch out of his forehead!

He grinned. "Hi, Mom."

"Adam, how did this happen?"

"What?"

"Your head!"

"Oh that. I was running toward the pool, and there was a metal bar in my way just above eye level. I ran into it. I didn't see it." He smiled and shrugged.

If it were as serious as it looked, Adam should be in more pain. But then, that was the problem with Adam—he never complained. He had a high pain tolerance and, on top of that, he had taught himself Asian focusing techniques to further anaesthetize himself to pain. He never told me he was sick when it was minor enough that a simple doctor's visit could solve it. By the time Adam ever acted ill, he needed to be hospitalized.

We were an hour's drive away from poor quality medical care, and at least four hours from international standard medical care, which didn't always reach international standards. To take him to the doctor was a huge endeavor.

And I didn't want to leave camp because my small group was starting to talk about spiritual things. Why would God pull me out of this ministry?

I called an American nurse I knew in Wuran. I needed help deciding how serious this was.

"Could his skull be fractured?"

"It's possible."

"If it is and I don't seek medical attention, what are the possible consequences?"

"It could be bad."

Within an hour I rented a car and driver to take us to Wuran and a taxi to take us on to the International Clinic in Huangdi. We left a little after 6 p.m. The trip to Huangdi took over six hours. In the back seat, I looked over at Adam. His right eye was dripping pus. I was concerned, but how bad could an eye infection be? Any eye infections we had ever had were always easily cured.

We arrived at the clinic after midnight. It was already closed, but I had called ahead and requested that a doctor and x-ray technician come in to meet us.

The technician took an x-ray of the side of Adam's head. The doctor looked exhausted. When he examined the x-ray, he inadvertently turned it 90 degrees, so Adam's face was at the bottom. Pointing at the image of the back of Adam's head, he smiled. "See his forehead. There's no fracture!"

I shuddered. He was pointing at the back of Adam's head instead of his forehead! I didn't want the doctor to lose face, but I needed to know if his skull was fractured. "Uh, aren't these his teeth?" I pointed, trying to politely orient the doctor to the location of Adam's forehead.

The doctor stifled a gasp and straightened the x-ray. He barely glanced at the image of Adam's forehead and quietly said, "There's no problem. What really concerns me is his eye." He gave me a topical antibiotic for his eye infection.

Relieved, I hired a taxi to drive us back home, with plans to return to camp as soon as Adam's eye improved.

But his eye didn't improve. It deteriorated, rapidly. The next day, every hour, I had to clean matter out of his eye. And he didn't want to get out of bed anymore.

Sunday morning, at the International Fellowship, I stood up and asked for prayer for Adam.

I didn't think Adam was well enough to make the trip to the Huangdi clinic again, and I didn't trust them anyway with how the doctor had handled the x-ray.

In Wuran, where we lived, there was only one international clinic, but we were not allowed to be seen there. An international company had set up the clinic for their employees only. That afternoon I called the Wuran clinic doctor and begged him to see Adam. After a while he agreed, against company rules, but we had to wait until the next day.

That evening one of the young women from the fellowship showed up at our apartment. "I could tell you were worried, Grace. I came over because I want to be here for you."

I was glad to see her; I had felt so alone and scared, and there was no way to get ahold of Justin, who was still at camp. I took her over to Adam's bed. Adam was past being willing to talk. "How about we lay hands on Adam and pray over him for healing?" I suggested. We prayed, but I saw no improvement.

The next morning I took Adam to the clinic. The stoic German doctor examined him, then crossed the room to wash his hands. "I'm afraid for your son," he said without looking at me.

I was already scared, but now I was really scared! "What are you afraid of?"

"I'm afraid the infection will go into his brain." The doctor spoke evenly, without emotion. Only his words communicated what he was feeling.

I shut my eyes, trying to take this in. "How do you know it hasn't already gone into his brain?" I like to know what we're dealing with.

"Because he would have more symptoms."

He gave me oral antibiotics for Adam. I helped Adam stand, and supported him as we left the clinic and waved down a taxi to head home.

As foreigners living in China we felt like we had no medical safety net. Local medical doctors are only required to get a bachelor's degree, the first year of which is devoted solely to studying Communist political theory! Sanitation in the local hospitals is often non-existent. In fact, when I was ill and a nurse was taking my blood, she refused to change her gloves which were covered in blood! That's probably why the German doctor didn't hospitalize Adam. His chances were better at home.

That evening, 24 hours after we prayed over him, Adam finally spoke, "Mom, did you know I was seeing double last night?"

A chill ran down my spine—was this the "more symptoms" the doctor had talked about? "Are you seeing double now?"

"No."

"When did you stop seeing double?"

Adam lowered his eyebrows as he replayed the last 24 hours in his mind. His eyes widened as he looked up at me. "It was right after you and your friend prayed over me!"

Two days later I took Adam back to the German doctor. "The night before I brought Adam in last time, he was seeing double. What does that mean?"

The doctor looked over from the sink. "It means the infection was already on his optic nerve, which is part of the brain!"

I cringed. "He's not seeing double now. What does that mean?"

"It's no longer on his optic nerve."

I let my breath out slowly. "When an infection is on the optic nerve, is there anything a doctor can do?"

"No, there's nothing doctors can do once the infection is in his brain like that. It's over." He spoke with surprising bluntness.

I blinked back the tears as I looked at Adam. The Lord had saved his life! Thank you, Lord.

When we prayed over Adam, it seems the Lord pushed the infection out of his brain, but God hadn't healed his eye. It was improving, but was still obviously infected.

After two more days, he was well enough to return to camp, just 24 hours before the camp was over. We had been gone a week. It seemed so pointless to show up just for the final party.

After we arrived at camp, I told the other English teachers what the Lord had done for Adam. They were amazed. One of the teachers said, "We told the campers about miracles in the Bible, and they asked if we had ever seen a miracle. They told us they would believe in God only if we have seen him do a miracle. But we have never seen God do a miracle, so we didn't know what to tell them. We've just had a miracle! And it was for Adam—everybody loved Adam! We want you to tell this to the campers."

I spent the rest of the day telling Adam's story to small groups of campers. Their response: "So God does exist after all!"

Because of the camp, and especially because of the healing, many students threw over the atheism they had been taught all their lives at home and in school, and embraced belief in God. Quite a number even came to believe that Jesus rose from the dead. Many said they would start reading the Bible to find out if Christianity is true. One girl came to faith in Christ.

When I was despairing about Adam's condition, how could I have known that not only was the Lord going to save Adam's life, but he planned to use

Adam's sickness for his glory, to bring many atheists to believe in his existence?

MENTAL WARD OPTION

1998, Wuran

After I spent the night taking Adam to the clinic in Huangdi, the next day, I heard a gentle knock at the door. When I opened the door, Peter, our friend who had been kicked out of college for his faith, was standing there, slumped over and looking haggard.

"Peter, how did you know we would be here? We told you we would be at English camp."

"Yes, I knew you weren't supposed to be home, but God told me to come here." His voice was flat and depressed.

I let him in. "What's wrong? You look terrible!"

"I need to tell you something. but we have to find a place that's not bugged." We carried folding chairs out to our porch.

"What happened?" I asked anxiously.

"The police, they went to my mother. They asked her if I'm mentally ill!"

"What? I can't believe they did that! What did your mother say?"

"She thought my Christian faith had gotten me in trouble with the police again. She figured she had two choices. If she said I was normal, then they'd say I'm responsible for all my actions and they'd put me in jail. She thought the better answer was to say I'm mentally ill. She hoped if she said that, they would think I couldn't be held responsible and they'd leave me alone. My own mother! I can't believe my own mother said that I'm mentally ill!"

"Oh, this is terrible! Why did the police come to your mother? And why now? It's been two years since they bothered you."

"Nate and I were helping a group of Americans who were visiting China on a group visa. Their visa required that they stay together, but the group split up, some going sightseeing in a different province. When the police discovered they weren't together, they checked to find out who was helping them. My name came up and I guess they looked at my old police file. Now they're after me again."

It made me mad. Couldn't these American visitors just obey the laws in China? It was a simple law. And they disobeyed it just so they could go sight-seeing. The consequences to the locals can be devastating!

"Oh, and I forgot to tell you. The police also went to my high school teachers and asked them if I'm mentally ill!"

I cringed and closed my eyes. I read the international news which Peter, as a local Chinese, had no access to, so I knew that Chinese police some-times put dissidents and Christians in mental institutions and gave them drugs to destroy their minds. "You know what this means, Peter? They're trying to find evidence to put you in an insane asylum!"

Peter just stared at me as if he was having trouble taking in what I said.

I couldn't believe that this was to be the fate of this funny, intensely loyal, gentle, loving young man who felt like part of our family.

I was so afraid he would "disappear" and we wouldn't be able to find out what the police had done to him. "If we can't find you, how will we know what happened to you?"

"They're sure to tell my family, and then my sister would know. I'll give you my sister's phone number and I'll tell her you might call." Peter still looked bewildered.

"Peter, I can't call her from here because they're sure to be tapping your family's phones. I'll have to call from a pay phone."

We set up code words for me to communicate with his sister so she could tell me what happened to Peter. My heart was breaking. I was actually mak-ing preparations in case I never saw him again. This might be our last con-versation so everything had to be said.

My mind was racing, trying to devise a plan to stop the police from put-ting him in a mental institution. "Peter, there are some U.S. senators I could contact who are interested in religious persecution in China. They might take your case. If you're committed to a mental institution, do you want me to try to get the U.S. government to pressure China for your release?" I was sure he would say yes. Everything in me wanted him to say yes.

He replied defiantly. "If the U.S. tries to help me, then China will know that an American friend living in Wuran is behind it. They will clamp down on all the Americans here and make it even harder for you to share the gos-pel. I do not want that to happen! If leaving me in the mental institution will further the gospel, then leave me in the mental institution! Do not contact the U.S. government!" I looked down, not wanting him to see my tears.

82

"But, Peter, they will pump you full of drugs that will destroy your mind! That is their goal!" I was begging him.

"If leaving me in the mental institution will further the gospel, then leave me there!"

ESCAPE

1998, Started at Wuran

"We're going to take you on a dangerous vacation." The boys whooped and cheered. Justin had no idea how true his announcement would turn out to be.

Before Adam's eye infection, Adam (13), Nigel (15), and Peter had been planning a rafting trip down the Li River, the beautiful river that traverses the magnificent, jagged mountain peaks of Guilin. But Adam still had tiny lesions on his eye, so the doctor wouldn't allow him to get in dirty water. The cool rafting trip was off. The dangerous vacation was a consolation prize.

We were merely planning to take the boys to the Lake of Heaven, a volcanic crater lake on the China/North Korea border. The "danger" was seeing North Korea from across the border.

We decided to take Peter along because he was running from the police. They had already kicked him out of college because of his faith; now they were preparing to incarcerate him in a mental institution. But the police in China often get tired of chasing Christians who aren't really criminals. We hoped "out of sight, out of mind" would work for Peter like it had for one of our other Chinese friends. The police had hunted for that friend, but couldn't find him because he was in the hospital; by the time he was released from the hospital the police had forgotten about him.

The plan was for the five of us to take a train to a little town in Jilin Province called Baihe, and from there, to hire a car and driver to take us to the Lake of Heaven.

Our train tickets were for hard sleepers—the beds were just boards covered by thin mats. Hard sleeper compartments had triple bunks on either side of a narrow walkway. Since we didn't buy the sixth ticket, a stranger slept in the compartment with us. Across from the entrance, an 18-inch window opened about nine inches, providing the only ventilation on that sticky August night. The compartment had no door so there was no privacy. All night I tossed and turned, listening to the commotion in the main walkway and the train screeching to a halt as it entered the different stations.

We only had tickets to Shenyang, where we had to change trains. We couldn't buy tickets right through to Baihe, because the rule in China was that you had to buy tickets along the way.

We arrived in Shenyang early the next morning. Justin and Peter stayed with the boys, while I, eyes half open, found my way to the station's ticket hall. No one formed lines in China, so I shoved and elbowed my way through hundreds of other passengers to the wicket. By the time I got there, the only tickets available were *wu zuo* (no seat tickets). Great! We would have to stand for nine hours on the next train!

We settled ourselves and our luggage as best we could on the enclosed, sloping metal platform between cars. The boys kept goofing with Peter, so they were having fun, but Justin and I, half asleep, kept an eye on the luggage.

Shortly before we pulled into the Baihe station, a creepy man, young but hunched over in an ill-fitting Western-cut suit, shuffled through the train. He leered at us with beady eyes, like we were his prey. "Hotel, hotel, you want a hotel?" He said in Mandarin and thrust an advertisement in our faces. Repulsed, we pushed it back. He slunk back and forth across our platform, repeatedly targeting us. Each time he passed us, he shoved his face in ours, "Hotel, hotel, you want a hotel?"

After about 20 minutes of this encroachment, the train finally pulled into Baihe. We raced down the steps to escape the man, only to be surrounded by a swarm of young men shouting in our faces, "Hotel, hotel, you want a hotel?" These young men grabbed our arms and pulled at our luggage, each one trying to drag us to a different hotel. We struggled to hold on to our bags and stay together. We could only slowly move forward by pushing back at the men. We stared straight ahead, not replying to anyone so we wouldn't encourage them. But we couldn't shake them.

Suddenly, into the throng stepped a calm, pleasant-looking woman, like an angel. "Do you want to get away from them? I'll help you." She gently took my arm and led us into a restaurant she owned. We went willingly, relieved. No one followed us into the restaurant.

We sat at a large round table. The woman, Mrs. Jin, cooked a delicious dinner for us, including a dish of wild mountain mushrooms. After dinner she sat at our table and chatted with us.

"What brings you to Baihe?" she asked us in Mandarin.

"We want to go to the Lake of Heaven tomorrow," Justin said. "Could you refer us to a trustworthy driver to take us?"

"What a coincidence! My husband will be returning tonight with the van. He can take you."

We smiled. Everything was working out.

"What about a hotel? Could you refer us to one?"

"My friend owns a hotel up the street. I'll take you there."

The accommodations were bare, but adequate—linoleum floors, very hard beds, and a "squatty potty," which is a ceramic hole in the floor. We asked Peter to call Mrs. Jin to make the arrangements for us to go to the Lake of Heaven, so there would be no misunderstanding due to language. At seven the next morning, her husband would pick us up for the all-day excursion. We would have the whole van to ourselves, which was good because we wanted to bring our luggage and find a hotel close to the lake. Also, we could take our time touring, lingering at each spot as long as we wanted to. The Chinese liked to run from one place to another, taking pictures as they went. The price was 600 RMB (about 75 USD) for the whole van for the day. That was a lot of money in China at that time.

The next morning we were all excited. Finally, we were getting to the "danger" we had promised the boys. We checked out of the hotel and Mrs. Jin led us to the van. There were other passengers sitting inside!

I was dismayed. "We were supposed to have the van all to ourselves."

"It doesn't matter. They're also going to the Lake of Heaven."

"But that was not the agreement. We need the whole van."

"If you want the whole van, it will be 800 RMB!"

"No, the agreement was that we would have the whole van with no other passengers for the day for 600 RMB." We couldn't give in on this, or she might keep changing the agreement in any way that suited her.

"You misunderstood the agreement." That's what Chinese people say when they want to change an arrangement.

"O.K., then we won't go to the Lake of Heaven with you," I told her. Turning to the family, "Go back up to the room, everybody!"

Mrs. Jin followed us up the stairs and into the hotel room, arguing all the way! The Mandarin language becomes shrill and staccato when a woman is angry. She sat down on a chair in our room, her piercing, sharp voice mounting argument after argument why we should go with her husband to the Lake of Heaven. The boys and Peter stayed silent, watching the drama unfold. At first Justin and I tried to reason with her, but it was pointless. The more she screamed at us, the more confused and frustrated we were. We stopped talking and just listened to her scream. How do we get her to leave our room? How do we get to the Lake of Heaven? And how did such a simple transaction turn into such an intractable problem?

Finally, she threatened. "I'll take you to the police!"

Baihe was a very small town. It had only two roads that formed a T. For sure everyone knew each other and probably most of the people were Mrs. Jin's relatives. She was the one breaking the agreement, yet she wanted to take us to the police. If the police were her relatives, according to Chinese Confucian culture, they would automatically side with her. Or, she might not be planning to take us to the police at all, but to, say, a warehouse where her friends would beat us up or rob us.

"We will not go to the police," I countered. "We have no problem with you because we're willing to forget the agreement and not go to the Lake of Heaven. If you have a problem with us, then bring the police here." I figured we were safer in the hotel than some place she might take us. She never mentioned the police again.

The situation was spiraling out of control. Mrs. Jin wouldn't leave or stop railing against us, and we no longer trusted her enough to take the trip with her husband. We were afraid of where this was leading and we wanted to get out of town as fast as possible. I was most afraid for Peter. If, because of Mrs. Jin, the five of us were arrested in Baihe, the police from our city wouldn't need any more excuse to lock Peter up in a mental institution. We had to get Peter away.

We decided to split up. Justin would stay in the hotel room with the luggage so Mrs. Jin wouldn't steal it. Nigel, Adam, Peter, and I would walk to the train station to buy tickets out of town.

On the way to the station I told Peter that if we could only get one ticket, no matter what the destination, I really wanted him to get on that train. "If there aren't any trains, what do you think about you walking the tracks to get out of here? I would give you enough money so we could meet up somewhere." He never got a chance to answer.

In front of us, as we neared the train station, was Mrs. Jin! She hadn't stayed at the hotel. She was here, in the town square, her arms waving above her head and her shrill voice inciting a mob against us! We could feel the rage building in the horde of villagers.

Her back was to us. We quickly passed on the other side of the square and tried to sneak into the one-room station.

A short row of attached, yellow plastic chairs sat with their backs to the entrance of the station. I was so hopeful we could get a train away from this place, but as we sat, my heart sank. I could see from the train schedule posted on the wall in front of us that Baihe was the end of the line. Only two trains a day left the station. One train had just gone, and the next wouldn't depart until ten o'clock that night. Fifteen hours is a long time to wait when a mob of villagers are mad at you.

We heard the commotion before we saw it. Mrs. Jin, chin held high, arms sweeping wildly in front of her, was leading about 20 villagers into the station. She was still yelling. They surrounded us—pointing, accusing, threatening. A security guard passed by and, seeing the mob, even hearing all the threats, he ignored the rabble. It was just the townspeople terrorizing some foreigners. No need to interfere.

Nigel and Adam huddled closer to Peter and me. I wasn't just concerned about Peter now. I was afraid for all of us, afraid we wouldn't make it out of the station alive.

Adam looked up at me with trust in his eyes, but Nigel's face was set like flint, as if he were willing a wall to separate himself from the danger.

An older woman slipped through the crowd. Her shoulders sagging, she drew close to me and in a hushed voice said, "I'm sorry for what my daughter is doing to you." So there was a break in the ranks! Hope surged in me, but quickly died as I looked at the mother's downtrodden face. She wouldn't be of any help.

In the midst of all the shouting, Peter leaned over and whispered to me, "Mrs. Jin has come back to the original agreement, but I told her that we would never get in the van with her husband."

Then a short, thickset man shook his fist in Peter's face. With his chest puffed out, he loomed over Peter and growled, "I'm going to beat you up!"

I whispered to Peter, "All I want to do right now is get out of this train station alive! We'll figure out how to get out of town later. Peter, I've only been in China two years, so I don't know how to deal with a situation like this in your culture. But there are two things I know to be true for any culture. If someone threatens to beat you up, you can't just cave in and agree with them. It makes you too weak. The second is that since Mrs. Jin came back to the original agreement, if this goes to the police, we are in the wrong. Peter, this is your culture. Please come up with a plan to get us out of this train station. You have all our money at your disposal. We can go with Mr. Jin to the Lake of Heaven or not go. We'll do whatever you decide. Just get us out of this station! I'll be praying."

Peter came up with a brilliant solution. Shoulders back, he looked Mrs. Jin straight in the eyes. "We'll go to the Lake of Heaven with your husband if we have a written agreement." That made it possible for us to agree to go, even though Peter had been threatened and had said we would never go with her, as if lack of a written agreement had caused the impasse. It was laughable, though, because written agreements didn't mean much in China.

Mrs. Jin looked around at the crowd. "He wants a written agreement. He wants a written agreement," she taunted. But then she agreed.

Peter wrote up a contract. He leaned over to me, "I'm not putting my name on that!"

"I'll sign it," I told him.

I pocketed the agreement after it was signed. The crowd broke and let us pass! We raced back to the hotel.

In the hotel room I told Justin that we had signed an agreement with Mrs. Jin to go to the Lake of Heaven.

"You what?" Justin cried out.

I didn't have time to tell him the full story.

All we had accomplished was getting out of the train station. Now we had to survive the trip with Mr. Jin to a remote area. We didn't know if he would rob us or harm us, or maybe worse. We exchanged passport and ID card numbers and made sure each of us had the phone number to the American Embassy.

I said, "That way if one of us gets away, he can report what happened." What was I thinking? If one of us gets away? We had a 13-year-old and a 15-year-old with us! But we saw no other solution—at least our chances were better than they were in the hands of 20 angry villagers.

I continued, "And I don't want to sit in the front seat with Mr. Jin. I really think I might punch him if I'm too close to him. Could someone else sit in the front seat?"

Mrs. Jin arrived at the hotel, and we went downstairs to the lobby to meet her. "There are a couple of other passengers going in the van with you."

"Back up to the room, family!"

Mrs. Jin had overbooked, and the other passengers she had promised to take were unwilling to forgo their trip. If other passengers were going with us, that broke the agreement, so we didn't need to go with Mr. Jin after all!

But we still had to get out of town fast because the villagers might soon come after us. In the room Justin stared at the floor, trying to figure out if there was any other way out of town. "I've got it! I've seen long distance buses pass through here. They don't come very often, maybe once an hour."

Peter had noticed the bus routes. "This is not the terminal station for them, so the drivers won't be from this town, and they won't be Mrs. Jin's relatives. We'll be safer."

"It's our only hope."

Adam looked calm, but every few seconds Nigel jumped up to look out the window. He was keeping an eye on Mrs. Jin's van. I hadn't even thought to watch the van. "The van's leaving!" he called.

"We only have about two minutes, guys, before the whole town will be here. Go to the road," I said. "Hurry!"

We picked up our backpacks and ran down the stairs. As soon as we were outside, Nigel looked down the road to see if the Jins were returning. A moment later he cried out, "Look, they're coming back!" Nigel ran away from the road, panicked.

The Jin's black van pulled up next to Peter. Mr. Jin rolled down the window. "I'm going to kill you!" he threatened and drove off.

The moment the van was out of sight, a long distance bus drove up! If it had come a moment earlier, Mr. Jin would have seen it. If it had come a few minutes later, the townspeople might have already arrived! We believe the Lord sent it right at that moment to save us. We waved it down. We didn't even think to look at the destination until later; we didn't care where we were going, only that we were leaving. The bus was traveling four hours in the wrong direction, farther away from home.

Nigel was studying the oncoming traffic on the two-lane road. About five minutes into the trip, he whispered urgently, "The Jin's van! I see it! And the silver car that was following their van is right behind it! They're coming back for us!" I could almost taste the fear in his voice. I had never noticed the silver car following the van, but Nigel noticed everything.

"Duck! Duck down!" I called out.

The Jin's van and the silver car passed.

About 10 minutes after that, the bus came to a roadblock! The roadblock looked hastily constructed. We were sitting in the back of the bus, clustered, but not all together.

Again I called out quietly, "Duck, everybody! Quick, duck!" I felt panic rise into my throat. Somehow I was sure the roadblock was for us.

The man at the roadblock spoke to our driver, who then turned around and examined the passengers. We were all crouched down, not visible. The driver spoke to the roadblock man. He let us pass.

Once we were far enough away from Baihe, peace came over me. I had never felt so safe in all my life. The Lord had protected us. I kept thinking how I could now identify with the apostle Paul—fleeing, but with no destination.

We rode the bus along lush fields. The fresh farm smells of soil and cut crops wafted through the windows. Chinese fields are a patchwork of small garden plots. Even though the roads were crowded with motor vehicles, and China was modern in many ways, there was never any large machinery plowing and harvesting. Everything was done by manual labor. So the fields were much more beautiful than the monotonous single-crop megafarms in the U.S.

After four hours we arrived in the city of Dunhua. We asked a taxi driver to bring us to a hotel that fit our budget. We had to check out five rooms before we found one that was not moldy, and the faucets, shower and toilet worked! We showed our passports to the clerk, because in China a foreigner must be registered with the police anywhere he stays overnight, and we paid for the room.

All I wanted to do was sleep after we had run for our lives that morning. But the men were hungry, so we went to the market first to eat. After lunch, Peter and the boys stayed to explore the market, and Justin and I headed off to the hotel to sleep.

As soon as we entered the lobby, the clerk at the front desk informed us, "You can't stay in this hotel."

"But we already paid for our room!" Justin objected.

"We'll reimburse you, but the police said you can't stay."

"Why did the police say we can't stay?" Justin wanted to know.

"Because this hotel is too dangerous for foreigners."

"Wait a minute. What you're saying is that this hotel is not rated to allow foreigners to stay here?"

"Yes, that's right."

"But didn't you know that when we walked in? You must have known foreigners weren't allowed to stay here. We spent all that time finding a suitable room."

"Well, we were confused. There was a big trade conference in Dunhua, with many foreigners attending. There weren't enough hotels rated for foreigners, so the police temporarily changed the rating of our hotel to allow foreigners to stay only during the conference. The conference ended two days ago. Now we are again not allowed to let foreigners stay here."

"So, what you're telling us is that two days ago this hotel was safe for foreigners, but it has suddenly become unsafe."

"Yes. That is correct."

There was no point discussing it with her. She was just doing what the police said. Justin and a clerk headed upstairs to get our luggage. I went out and sat on the semicircular front steps of the hotel, feeling sorry for myself.

It was hardly a minute before an old, wrinkled man hobbled over to stand in front of me. He was holding a three-legged, foldable stool. He canted his head from side to side, silently studying me, then he unfolded his stool and sat down directly in front of me. Apparently, he found me interesting.

"We fought them in Nanjing. We fought them in Wuhan, but we couldn't defeat them. We fought real hard and took some bad hits …"

It dawned on me—he had fought in the Nationalist Army against the Communists in the 1940s. He was describing how they were defeated by the Communist army. This was a taboo subject in Communist China. Just to mention the Nationalists was taboo.

"Do you want to see the bullet holes I have? I was hit three times."

"Sure."

He rolled up his pant leg to his thigh. "This is where it went in, and it came out here." He pointed at the scars. Lifting his shirt, he revealed another scar on his belly. "A bullet is still lodged in here." Then he touched his head. "Another one grazed me here."

Suddenly his eyes narrowed and he focused in on me. "Why are you sitting on the steps of the hotel? Did something happen?"

"They kicked us out of the hotel."

"They what? Listen, you are welcome in my home. Come and stay with my wife and me!" The Chinese are extraordinarily gracious about hosting people. In fact, the common man in China is often very kind. It was whenever money was involved that we ran into problems.

Justin came out right then with our luggage and heard the old man. He said, "In our country, America, you could stay in any hotel you want. You would be a guest in our country and we would welcome you!" Justin and I were normally very careful what we said in China. We didn't criticize China, or talk against the government or government policies, but that day we were so exhausted and fed up that we were spouting off.

The old man nodded in pleasure at the welcome we gave him to come to America. A crowd of the disadvantaged was forming around him, and was listening to our conversation and staring at Justin and me. They also smiled at us, delighted with the welcome they would receive in America.

"But why did they kick you out of the hotel?" the old man asked.

"Because they said this hotel is too dangerous for foreigners to stay in," Justin replied.

"Oh." A sigh of disapproval went up from the crowd.

"And why do they say it's too dangerous?" Justin asked the crowd.

"Why?" The crowd looked at each other, puzzled.

"Because of you!" Justin said. "You live near the hotel. They think you are going to harm us! It is you they say are dangerous!"

"No, that can't be!" someone yelled out. "We would never harm you! How could they say that? We welcome you."

Right then, the manager of the hotel stepped out, drawn by the incensed crowd. She was alarmed. "No, no! You have it all wrong! It's not because it's too dangerous that you can't stay here. It's because there's karaoke singing at night. It's too loud. We want you to be able to sleep well."

Justin's hand swept out in front of him to take in the whole crowd. "The hotel doesn't care if its karaoke keeps you awake at night. They don't care if you sleep well. They only care if foreigners sleep well."

A gasp went up through the crowd. They looked enraged.

Our boys returned right then with Peter, relaxed and happy from their explorations, only to find their parents once again surrounded by an angry crowd. This time, though, the crowd was supportive of us.

The manager slipped inside. She called two taxis, helped us put our luggage in them, and even paid for them! She wanted us out of there before the crowd got completely out of control.

The drivers took us to a hotel that was rated for foreigners, but was too expensive for us to take our full two-week vacation. Having been chased out of two places that day, being extremely exhausted, and seeing how quickly our money would run out if we stayed in police-approved, upscale hotels, I thought Justin would never be willing to continue the vacation.

But after a good night's sleep, he announced: "I've been looking at the map. There's a town north of here called Tumen, and North Korea is just across the Tumen River from it. We can see North Korea from there. And, there's an added bonus. It's also close to Russia! We'll be able to see Russia and North Korea!"

"Let's go!" the boys shouted.

We headed off. Soon after we arrived in Tumen we discovered a road that bordered the Tumen River. Walking along it, we had a good view of the North Korean town of Namyang, which was on a mountainside, sloping down to the 100-foot wide Tumen River. Namyang was a primitive farming village. People worked the fields with oxen and they traveled by ox cart or on foot. Only twice did we see a motor vehicle. We noticed that none of the farm hands seemed to want to work. They congregated in groups of three and four in places that, because of the slope, were hidden from other North Korean eyes, but were in plain view to the Chinese. They squatted on the ground and talked for hours.

At one point along our walk, Nigel burst out laughing. He pointed at a huge sign painted on a stone face on the hillside above Namyang. The sign, which said "Work Harder!" was written in bold, black Chinese characters, but both of our boys could read Chinese. Nigel looked at us. "I can't believe that North Korea is trying to convince China to work harder! Look at how backward North Korea is, and how modern China is!"

Facing the river, on the North Korean side, stood a little wooden hut, a lookout, about seven feet square, raised up on four 10-foot stilts. At the front of the lookout was a narrow porch where a stiff, armed North Korean guard in gray-green uniform stood—a chilling reminder that North Korea deployed marksmen on the mountains and the river's edge to shoot anyone who attempted to cross to the China side. I didn't expect to see anyone in the river, but on the China side, there were fishermen wading, careful not to cross the center of the river to the North Korean side. As we walked the dusty river road away from Tumen, it gradually gained elevation until we were overlooking the Tumen River from about 50 feet up.

We were strolling along that road the next afternoon. At four o'clock we passed a bluff that obscured our view of North Korea. I climbed the bluff to see it better, and when I reached the top, I gasped. A man was in the water, swimming from North Korea to China! I turned around and called to the family, who scrambled up after me. I was afraid a marksman would shoot him. Why would someone cross in broad daylight? We were all transfixed.

I had binoculars so I watched him carefully. He came up out of the water on the China shore. He was stark naked!

I breathed a sigh of relief that he was safe.

On the shore was a package, wrapped in clear plastic. The man picked up the package, tied it to his back with a rope around his neck, walked into the river again and swam back to North Korea! It was dangerous enough swimming over here, but to swim back? He was risking his life for whatever was in that package.

I studied the river. The man crossed at a spot on the outskirts of Namyang where bushes obstructed the view of the water. North Koreans wouldn't see him—and neither would the Chinese as there was a bend in the river and this bluff. The only place he could be seen from either country was the spot right where we were standing on the bluff!

The man climbed up onto the North Korean bank with the package still fastened to his back. He walked up the slope and into some short bushes where he dressed in hobo clothes. We hadn't seen any North Koreans dressed like hoboes, so the man actually stood out instead of blending in. He opened the package and laid the contents on the ground. He held up the plastic wrapping and shook the water off. Then he picked up what looked like a large portfolio, about the size of a small briefcase, and inserted it in the right side of his jacket.

Keeping his head down, the man began walking. For an hour I continued to watch him through the binoculars. Just before he passed the lookout, the guard slipped inside. We had seen that guard many times. He had always been outside, carefully watching, never inside. Had someone paid him to go inside when the man walked by?

The man ambled up to the tracks and passed a policeman, all the time hunched over with his eyes staring at the ground in front of him. Finally, he went into a gully on the hillside. Five minutes later he came out walking erectly, with confidence. It appeared that he had made a drop-off. Another man met him and they walked together, conversing and carefree.

Finally, we had seen something dangerous that didn't involve us. That night as we discussed the man, we realized he was probably a spy. We could see no other explanation. That worried Peter. "If North Korea is spying on China, then I need to inform the Chinese police. I'm a Chinese citizen, and we Chinese are very patriotic."

But Peter had no proof without me. I was the one with the binoculars, and I wasn't quite ready to become an informant.

As we talked more, we realized that the man was as likely a Chinese spying on North Korea as he was a North Korean spying on China. Peter quickly changed his mind. He said, "I keep forgetting that the police aren't here to help us. I was taught as a child that the police are good, and it's hard for me to shake that belief."

Later, an American friend told us it was good that we didn't tell anyone what we saw. He said that a Christian missionary couple on the China side of the border had recently been murdered by a North Korean hit squad because they were part of an underground railroad giving North Koreans safe haven after they escaped! Our friend suspected the Chinese government was in complicity with the hit squad because otherwise they wouldn't have been successful on Chinese soil. He was afraid that if we had told anyone what we saw, a hit squad might have murdered us too!

The next day in Tumen we got in a taxi and asked to be taken to the Russian border. The driver was surprised, but he took us to the People's Liberation Army outpost near the Chinese/Russian border. "You have to register with the PLA to go to the border. I'll park here until you get back."

We sent Peter because we thought he had the most chance of getting a "yes."

Peter came back all smiles, trailed by a PLA soldier. "The soldier says that he has to accompany us. If only I, a Chinese, were going, I could go by myself. This is a first! Americans can usually go anywhere, and we Chinese are always restricted. Now it's the Americans who have to be accompanied by the army!"

The soldier sat in the back of the taxi with Peter and the boys. We got out of the taxi on the Chinese side of the border.

The road between the countries had no fence at the border, not even a chain! Only two stone pillars, one on either side of the road, labeled with each country's name, marked the border.

In the distance I could see a guard post on the Russian side, just a wooden shack. Since I could hardly see it, I assumed the Russians could hardly see us. But I wasn't thinking clearly. Of course, the Russian guards would have binoculars and could see us clearly. Standing right at the border, I pretended to study one of the stone pillars, then I slipped my foot over the border. "Hey, guys," I whispered to Justin and the boys, "step into Russia, but don't let the soldier see you!" Both boys stepped onto Russian soil. But before Justin could put his foot over, the People's Liberation Army guard waved his hand to stop him.

The boys had another "dangerous" event under their belts.

This was our reprieve day.

Every day in Tumen the locals had tried to cheat us. When we ordered food at a restaurant, I always added up what the total bill would be. At one meal our bill should have been 49 RMB. The proprietor charged us 100 RMB. So I asked for the menu and added it up again to 49 RMB. While I was calculating it, two large Chinese men entered the restaurant from the back door, and stood with arms akimbo staring hard at us. They were thugs, there to force us to pay the 100 RMB. I asked Justin and Peter to help me put together exactly 49 RMB in small bills. Then I told all the males with me to get out of the restaurant immediately. The thugs would be less likely to beat up a middle-aged woman. When I paid them in the small bills they had to count the bills before they knew if I had paid 49 or 100 RMB. That gave me time to run out of the restaurant.

We found a store that sold North Korean stamps. I was picking out which North Korean stamps to buy when Peter came over and whispered to me, "The store owner just tried to make a deal with me to split the profits if I would help him cheat you. He thinks I'm your tour guide." I yelled at the storeowner and we stomped out without buying. Peter was shaken by me yelling at the stamp seller because, according to Chinese custom, I shouldn't have made the storeowner lose face—even though he was out to con us. That's a part of Chinese culture I will never understand. If I make him lose face, won't he think twice about ripping off the next guy?

Nigel and Adam found all the cheating a little annoying, but they were having the time of their lives goofing around with Peter. Justin and I were getting more and more tense, though. We were responsible for making the vacation happen, keeping us safe, and holding on to our money.

Part of the problem was that we insisted on not being cheated. We didn't differentiate between small or large amounts of money, and we didn't evaluate the consequences of insisting that an agreement be honored or a price not be changed midstream. We had a strong sense of justice in a country where justice was a luxury.

I was so exhausted from trying to outsmart the cheaters I couldn't take it anymore.

We had wanted to go to a hill that overlooked a section of North Korea we hadn't seen yet. We hired the drivers of two motorcycles, with flatbeds attached to the back, to take the five of us over a bridge to the base of the hill—five RMB for each motorcycle. We assumed the drivers would try to cheat us, so we drew out a map and wrote down the price. That way there would be no misunderstanding, no change of destination, and no change of price. We had thought of everything. In the middle of the bridge both motorcycles stopped. "This is as far as your five RMB will take you. If you want us to take you to the hill, it will be an extra five RMB for each motorcycle."

I completely lost it. I turned to Justin and rolled up my sleeves. "O.K. I'm ready to fight."

This is the only time in our marriage that Justin has ever ordered me. "Grace, walk!"

"But you'll just pay them the 10 RMB!"

"Grace, go!"

Reluctantly, I obeyed him. He paid them each five RMB and we walked the rest of the way to the hill.

Peter and the boys scrambled up the hill effortlessly. I was trailing Justin. With my over-reaction to the motorcycle drivers, Justin could have climbed the hill fast to get away from me. But he didn't. He climbed slowly to stay near me.

The incline was very steep and covered with small rocks. I kept slipping down the hill. At one point, I looked down at the road, and I froze. I couldn't move I was so scared.

Justin turned around and saw me. "Are you O.K.?"

"Justin, I'm scared. I'm afraid I'm going to slide right down onto the road!"

Without hesitation, Justin retraced his steps. He lay flat on his stomach on the ground, with his hands holding onto a tree and his feet stretched down to me. He said, "Grace, climb the hill holding onto me."

I crawled up the hill on my hands and knees, holding onto his body. When I reached his hands, he got up, walked a body-length up the hill and lay down again. He grabbed another tree and extended his feet down to me. I crawled up him. He did this for me again and again until I reached the top of the hill!

The next day was my birthday. And it was the first time in Tumen that we had gone through a whole day without being cheated! Then came the night. Adam got sick after our dinner of stir-fried silkworms. Justin and I had an argument, and in the midst of it all, we forgot to bolt the door. We only locked it. The next morning, my fanny pack was not on the dresser where I had left it. After searching the room, I finally found it on the floor just inside the door—with no money inside!

The fanny pack had held our passports and almost all of our cash. Justin, Peter, and I had split the money among us at the beginning of the trip so if any was stolen from one of us, the other two would still have some. During the trip, Justin and Peter had spent down their money, but I hadn't. So when the thief stole the money from my fanny pack, he took almost all we had left!

It was obviously an inside job. After the thief had browsed around our room to find the fanny pack and left to sort through its contents, he had the temerity to return the pack with the passports tucked back in! He wasn't afraid to be seen in the hallway, or to open our door a second time.

We went to the police, who had an office right in that hotel, and reported the theft. But they blamed us because we hadn't bolted the door. Later, the hotel staff told us in hushed tones that the police had recovered the money. The police never returned the money to us. We couldn't help but wonder if they were in on the theft.

Justin and Peter pooled their remaining money and it was just enough to buy train tickets home, so our adventure was over.

Justin and I returned far more exhausted than when we left, but Justin had made good on his promise to give the boys a dangerous vacation.

And not only did Peter escape from the police because he'd left town with us, they never bothered him again! That made all the stress and danger worth it!

As a family, we never went on vacation in China again, but for years we had a lot of jokes and shared stories from that vacation. Nigel loved to make us laugh by slinking around the living room, hunched over in an oversized suit jacket. "Hotel, hotel, you want a hotel?"

LAWLESS LANDLORD

1998, Wuran

Two weeks after we returned from our vacation, two of the employees of our landlord company, Xing Hui, stopped me on the street just outside our apartment. I couldn't read their expressionless faces as they stood there, motionless in their identical uniforms.

"You need to move," one of them said in Mandarin.

"Soon," the other added.

"How soon?"

"Very soon."

They gave no explanation, and it didn't really matter. What did matter was that this was going to be difficult. Almost any apartment we moved to would just be an empty, cement shell, like this one had been—no linoleum, carpet, paint on the walls, light fixtures, water heaters, or closets. And possibly no toilets, sinks, or counters. It would take at least six weeks and about 5,000 USD to fix up a new apartment.

But first we had to find one that was available. Since China had just begun its transition to capitalism, private property was a new thing and there were no realtors or "For Rent" advertisements in the newspapers. We would have to know somebody who had one. And even if we could find an apartment, the police had to approve our move.

Furthermore, we were still in our intensive language study program. Where would we find time to do all this?

Eventually, the Xing Hui employees told us our apartment building was being sold and Xing Hui was building an upscale apartment complex nearby. The word came down, "You need to move into one of the new apartments Xing Hui is building."

We asked to see the smallest and cheapest of those apartments. We didn't have much money. They showed us an extremely small unit that was more expensive than the one we were living in. The landlord would renovate it for us, so that would solve most of our moving problems. We decided to put a deposit on the tiny apartment.

Every few days we had the same conversation with the two employees of our landlord company.

"You need to move."

"Soon."

"Is our apartment renovated yet?"

"No."

"Then how can we move?"

"You really do need to move."

"Soon."

"When our apartment is renovated we'll move." We couldn't understand what was going on. Why were they pushing us when they hadn't even renovated our apartment?

To ease the tension, my husband and I made a silly bet. If the apartment was renovated by the date Justin thought it would be finished, he won, and I had to take him to play badminton. If it was renovated after that date, then I won, and he had to take me to play badminton. Neither of us won. The apartment was never renovated. We were eventually told that we would need to choose another unit.

We were exasperated! We had chosen the smallest, cheapest of their new apartments, and they had accepted our deposit for that apartment. In fact, they had two deposits from us—one for our current apartment, too. We suspected they wanted us to choose something much larger and more expensive.

Some Chinese have the assumption that Westerners have a bottomless purse and they are hankering to get a piece of that purse. But we were living on a shoestring. There was no bottomless purse they could dip their hands into.

We didn't know what to do so we agreed to look at the larger apartments. They took us to see two gigantic units. They were so big they had two-foot diameter support pillars in the living room just to hold the ceiling up! The rent was over two times what we were currently paying.

They offered to give us the first year for the same price we were paying for our current apartment. But they wouldn't guarantee that price for the second year.

"We don't know what the new landlord will charge," they said.

"What new landlord?"

"We hope to sell the apartment in a year!"

Justin and I looked at each other, shocked. This was worse than them charging us full rent the second year!

"We are not going to rent an apartment you're planning on selling in a year," Justin said. "We're not going through this again!"

The next day we heard the same clipped message from the two goons. They cornered us all the time now.

"You need to move."

"Soon."

Finally we realized the only solution was to find another apartment, one not owned by Xing Hui. We had been talking with our language professors about our landlord problem and one day one of them told us she could solve it for us. She would move out of her own apartment and rent it to us! She and her family would move to her sister's apartment. She checked with the police, and foreigners were indeed allowed to live in her apartment. There was only one glitch. Her sister couldn't vacate her unit right away because she was waiting on visa approval to move overseas. Our teacher guessed that it would take six weeks.

We kept praying together as a family that Justin and I would have wisdom in dealing with Xing Hui, that we could be kind to them, and that God would watch over us, because we didn't have a good feeling about where this was headed.

The threats began.

They called us. "The apartment you're living in has been sold. If you haven't moved out by this time tomorrow, the new landlord will turn off your water and electricity." Justin put the phone down and relayed the message from the landlord. His eyes were wide. We had only been in the country two years, so we didn't know the laws and customs that governed rental agreements. *Were* we in the apartment illegally? But they had two deposits from us, and they were still accepting our rent.

Instead of moving out, I went to the market and bought 10 large red pails. I filled them with water and lined them up against the wall in the dining area. Then I made arrangements with a downstairs neighbor who was on a different water line. She said we could buy water from her, as long as we did the hauling.

When we talked to our professors about the threat, we knew we could handle all the issues except for one. If the landlord company turned off the electricity, our kids (15 and 13) wouldn't be able to do their homework. One of the teachers said he had the key to the university and the classroom.

"If you need a place for your kids to study, just call me," he said. "I'll open the school for you."

We were bracing ourselves.

At 3 p.m. the next day our water was turned off. Right after it was shut off, Justin saw the landlord's goons exiting the room on the ground floor that housed the water valves. About 10 minutes later the phone rang. Justin answered.

"The head of Xing Hui wants you to come to the office right away."

"I'm not going to the Xing Hui office."

"This is the very top head of Xing Hui! You have to come."

"I'm not going to the Xing Hui office."

"I'm sending a taxi to bring you."

"I'm not going. If the head of Xing Hui wants to talk to us, he can come here. Goodbye." Justin hung up, then turned to me. "Well, it's obvious they turned our water off to try to force us to talk with them. But that shows no respect for us. All they needed to do was ask."

About 20 minutes later we heard the click click of high heels coming up the cement stairs. When we opened the door, a chic lady in her late 40s, dressed in a Saks Fifth Avenue suit, stood before us.

The contrast between this elegant woman and our apartment building was overwhelming. Sans graffiti and bullet holes, our apartment stairwell could have been lifted from a 1960s Brooklyn tenement housing project. Except for the iron railing, everything was plain cement, which was chipped and scuffed all the way up. A few months earlier, someone had lit the garbage chute on fire, filling the apartments with smoke and leaving soot residue throughout the stairwell.

The street our apartment looked down onto had a morning market selling fresh seafood and vegetables. At the end of morning market hours, the vendors scraped the unsold food off the makeshift tables onto the street. Often the stench of rotten shrimp wafted up the five stories into our apartment. Pigs from the nearby sewage canal rooted in the putrid food on the street. Whenever the waste on the street grew to several feet high, the government sent a bulldozer to plow the rotten food away.

The elegant woman standing in front of us looked around with the snooty air of never having stepped foot in a dump like this. She seemed to want to get the upper hand over us. We were the low-life residents of such a place. But she wasn't really that classy—she ran this pigsty. Her two goons, who had been harassing us, stood a few feet behind her.

We had opened our door, but not the outer iron gate. We didn't want them in our home, so we talked through the gate.

102

"You turned our water off," Justin said. "We're not talking until it's on." He shut the door in Her Elegance's face.

Justin had turned the tables. He wanted them to respect us before we'd talk with them.

The confusion outside the door was audible. The questions and the shuffling. Then we heard one of the goons race down the stairs.

"Quick!" I said to the boys. "Go to the bathroom! They'll be turning on the water for a short while. And fill up the tub, too! I forgot to do that. I don't know how long we'll have water."

"The water's on!" the goon yelled through the door.

We checked both water lines in our apartment, but they had only turned on the bathroom side, not the kitchen. I yelled through the door, "Only one side is on. We're not talking until both sides are on."

The goon charged back down the stairs.

When he returned, they shouted, "Both sides are on." We opened the door.

Justin took the lead. "You said the new landlord would turn off the water today. It wasn't the new landlord. It was you!"

"No, it was the new landlord!"

"Then how could you turn it back on?"

They gave an obtuse answer to cover their lies.

Justin dropped the subject. He had made his point. They knew that he knew they were the ones trying to intimidate us, and not some new landlord.

Her Elegance squared her shoulders and raised her chin. "Why haven't you moved?" she asked.

"Your employees never told you?" Justin asked. "Because the new Xing Hui apartment we chose and put a deposit on has never been renovated."

Her Elegance looked confused, then she turned toward the goons. "Is this so?" she asked them. Apparently the goons were lying to her, too. She gave them a withering look.

She turned back to face us. "Everyone has moved out of this building, but you."

"That's not true," I said. "The people who live above us are still here. Their new Xing Hui apartment renovation is not finished yet, either."

Her face registered shock and distain as she again confronted the lying goons.

"There's no point in talking," I said. "Your employees have been lying to both you and us. We're tired of all the lies." I shut the door in their faces. I regretted having spoken that way, but if everything is a lie, how is communication possible?

They didn't turn the water off again when they left. We were relieved.

That night at 9 p.m. I heard someone very slowly shuffling up the stairs. One deliberate step at a time. He stopped—on our landing! A prowler was lurking outside, waiting for us! We were the only ones still living on this landing.

Immediately, I raced to the phone. Nigel was at a friend's house and he could return any minute.

"Hello?"

"Is Nigel still there? I need to talk to him before he leaves!" I rapid fire talked into the phone.

"Nigel, don't leave your friend's house!" I said when he came to the phone.

"What's the matter, Mom?"

"There's a prowler outside our door. Don't come home for an hour. Maybe he'll have left by then. And when you come home bring some friends with you. And bring some sticks in case he tries to attack you!"

"All right. We'll do it."

"I'll be praying, Nigel."

"Thanks, Mom."

I spent the hour pacing, praying, and worrying.

At 10 o'clock I heard Nigel and his friends. I could hear the anxiety in their voices as they talked the whole way up the stairs. If the prowler was still there, what would happen? I didn't want the boys to attack the prowler, but would they?

I heard a knock; I called through the door. It was the boys. The prowler was gone.

The next evening I opened the door to go out. The prowler was on the landing! His back was to me and he was dressed in a thick, long, green Soviet coat, the coats that were popular with workmen. I quickly shut the door, my heart pounding.

Night after night the prowler returned. Slow, even footfalls, ascending the stairs. Ever so slowly.

Whenever the boys went to a friend's house at night, I told them, "Call us at the kiosk before you get to the apartment complex. We'll meet you there and bring you home." But sometimes when they called, I wasn't sure if it was safe to go out because I didn't know if the prowler was on the landing. I found a way to figure it out. Our cat, Daniel, was deathly afraid of strangers so I held him near the door. If the prowler was there, Daniel's fur stood on end and he stiffened. Then I knew it was too dangerous to go out. Only if Daniel was calm did we go. And even then, Justin and I went together to meet the boys, and I always carried a stick.

Almost every day at language school we reported a new trauma we had been put through. We were anxious to hear our professor's take on the situations because we didn't understand what was going on and we certainly had no idea how to make it stop.

"Are we in the apartment illegally?"

"No, they're still accepting your rent," we were told. "And anyway, because this is a Communist country, Chinese law favors renters over landlords."

But if we took them to court, we wouldn't likely win because Xing Hui was owned by the city of Wuran, our professors told us. They would have the judge in their pocket. Our teachers said that the new method of getting justice in China was publicizing an injustice in the newspaper. They suggested we call the newspaper and get them to publish an article on our situation. But we didn't want to do that. We were in China to share the gospel and teach the Bible—things China didn't want us doing. When you're doing something illegal, you certainly don't want your names and faces splashed all over the newspaper.

I asked the teacher, "The prowler, was he sent by our landlord?"

"Probably."

"Why would they send him?"

"To scare you into moving. I mean, who wants to live in a home that has a prowler outside the door every evening? Actually, we should move the class to your home. I'm sure the prowler knows you're both at class every weekday morning, so he might try to break in during that time."

Justin and I were the only students in the class, so from then on the teacher came to our home each morning for class.

Our professors were always kind, considerate, and extremely sympathetic to our plight. Talking with them about our landlord kept us sane.

Peter, who visited us every Saturday, was the other part of our support system. He tried to encourage us, but he was only 20, so he didn't understand all the legal and cultural implications.

We no longer knew what lengths our landlord would go to. They had already crossed what we thought were inviolable lines. Just in case the landlord or the prowler tried to break in while we were asleep, every night I wedged a mop handle between the wall and the door of the apartment, braced by the radiator. But that might not be enough! I leaned a chair at an angle against the door. If someone tried to push open the door, the chair would act as an alarm as it bounced back upright. But what if we didn't hear it? I placed a bowl, balanced precariously on the slanted chair, as a further alarm. Barricaded in, we tried to sleep at night.

We needed peace. We needed safety. We needed the goons to stop accosting us every time we went out. It was hard to find time to study our intensive language program with all the harassment, so Justin decided to hire a lawyer to put more distance between the landlord and us. If Xing Hui wanted to talk to us, we would refer them to our lawyer.

Justin asked the locals we knew for a referral to a good lawyer. Hao told him about a "very good lawyer" who had won a lawsuit for him.

His law firm was on the second floor in a downtown building. It was just a large room housing many cubicles of lawyers. But the cubicle walls were only chest-high so there was no privacy between cubicles—every consultation could be overheard. The room was disconcertingly seedy, with filthy walls and cheap linoleum flooring. Crossing the room into our lawyer's cubicle, I was astonished. His legal library consisted of only three books! I began to understand that as a country, China doesn't have many laws.

We sat down and started talking fees in Mandarin. We didn't want him to bill us for unlimited fabricated hours, so we decided to pay a flat fee—1,000 RMB (about 125 USD). That was a lot of money in China at the time.

After we explained our situation, he told us that he would solve all of our problems. We asked him to get our two deposits back from Xing Hui, too. He said no problem. We went home. Peace at last.

Two days later we heard a knock at the door. It was our lawyer, working on the problem. He said, "You need to move! Soon! I just talked with Xing Hui."

My whole body sagged. "What about our deposits?"

"Don't try to get your deposits back," he said emphatically. "You need to move. Soon."

Justin and I were aghast. Our lawyer was saying the same thing as the goons!

"The new landlord is very angry that you haven't moved. He's a hippie! He has long hair and he's dirty."

I tried not to smile. I grew up in the U.S. in the 1960s, so those things didn't mean much to me. But the Chinese thought hippies were bad people.

The lawyer continued. "He's going to come and loiter around your apartment!"

The prowler? He had just described the prowler! Justin and I were sure then that the prowler had been sent by the landlord.

"You need to move right away so he won't hurt you!"

We were being threatened, and by our own lawyer!

"Don't you want to have a peaceful Christmas?" The lawyer used that further implied threat as his clinching argument. Xing Hui had told the family upstairs the same thing while they were waiting for their new Xing Hui

106

apartment to be renovated.

"But what about our deposits?" Justin asked again.

"Don't, whatever you do, don't ask for your deposits back!"

"Why?"

"Just don't!"

We showed our lawyer out. After we shut the door, I crumpled into Justin's arms and sobbed. "Even our lawyer is telling us to move. Is it illegal to be here? But we can't move yet—our professor's apartment isn't ready."

Justin soothed his hand down my back. "Listen, our lawyer is telling us exactly what our landlord said. He's representing our landlord to us, not us to the landlord. I bet he was bought off by our landlord."

"And he was so afraid that we would try to get the deposits back," I added. "I bet they told him he could keep our deposits if he could get us out." I began to suspect it wasn't illegal for us to be here. I stood straighter.

That evening in the shower I sang hymns at the top of my lungs. I was still quite jittery, so I tried to look to God by singing hymns. I didn't realize how alluring the sound of my voice was.

The bathtub shared a common wall with the public stairwell, and the exhaust fan was positioned high above the foot of the bathtub, blowing out into the stairwell.

I gazed at the bars we had installed on the inside of the fan. Nine months earlier we had caught a burglar dismantling the fan in the middle of the night so he could break in. To prevent further break-ins we installed the bars, but I could see now that they weren't much of a deterrent. Anyone on a ladder in the stairwell landing could reach his hand through the fan to the inside of the bathroom and unscrew the bolts from the wall. I took the showerhead in hand, turned toward the fan and sprayed the bolts, willing them to rust in place. How stupid! I had come down to trying to protect us in ways that didn't make any sense.

As I turned to replace the showerhead on the wall, the louvers of the exhaust fan jiggled. I paused. There could not possibly be wind in the stairwell. Someone was watching me shower from a few feet away!

Without thinking, stark naked, I crept over to the bathroom door, in full view of the fan. "Justin, Justin," I whispered loudly. "There's someone in the stairwell watching me shower through the fan!"

Justin opened the door of the apartment, just a few feet from the exhaust fan. We heard stumbling, toppling over, and dashing down the stairs.

I got dressed and came out, totally shaken. We talked over what to do. We didn't want to call the police because we didn't want to jeopardize our Christian work, but we had reached our limit. We called 110, the emergency police line. When they heard that the complaint was a Peeping Tom watching a foreign woman shower, a dozen policemen in their early 20s showed up to investigate. The young policemen kept staring at me. As they gently asked me questions, I looked down, embarrassed, and asked Justin to tell my story.

The police found the overturned woven basket the Peeping Tom had perched on to watch me, and they traced the origin of the basket to work-men who were renovating an apartment. But they never found the Peeping Tom, and the prowler never came back.

Adam was 13 when this happened, and when the police showed up, he went into his room and shut the door, only coming out after the police left. Face drawn, he called us over, "Mom, Dad, I need to talk with you. Sit down on the couch." We sat facing him. "Mom, if China is going to treat you like this, we can't live in China anymore." My heart ached hearing him say this. Adam believed in us being in China, and he was willing to sacrifice for us to be here, but the Peeping Tom had pushed him over the edge. We told him that God had sent us to China, but it sounded a little thin.

I also lost my equilibrium after the Peeping Tom. I was unsure of our decision to stay in the apartment, and I felt extremely unsafe. I questioned whether we should move into a hotel. We found a temporary home for our cat, in case we needed it, and I put valuables at a friend's home for safe-keeping. We were preparing to move out at a moment's notice. I called my father and stepmother, and asked them to tell our family and their church to pray for us—I asked them to pray that we would know if we should move out. Within 24 hours I knew the answer. If we were physically in danger, or if we knew for sure our staying here was illegal, then we should move out, whatever the cost. If not, we could wait until our new apartment was ready.

The day after the Peeping Tom incident, someone knocked at our door. Even though we had the iron gate locked, I only opened the door a crack. I didn't know what danger was lurking on our landing. A very handsome, clean-cut Chinese man, in his early 30s, stood outside. After a simple greet-ing, he told us in Mandarin, "I'm the new landlord." My eyes widened. Some hippie! But we didn't know what to believe anymore.

"Why aren't you moving out?" he asked.

Justin shouted toward the door, "Talk to our lawyer!"

I turned to Justin. "If by some chance he is the new landlord, this could be the breakthrough we've been praying for."

Justin agreed, and I let him in.

"I'm confused why you haven't moved out yet. I'd like to work this out with you. I'm sure we can reach a solution," he smoothed.

He was so good-looking and charismatic, it was easy to believe him. We were desperate so we poured out the whole story—the harassments, the intimidations and threats, having our water shut off, and the prowler. We told him we had a place to move to but it wasn't ready yet, and that we were trying to cooperate. He was very kind and listened with deep concern. He expressed sympathy for what we had been through.

"When can you vacate the apartment? Could you give me a date?"

My suspicion of him flared again. "Are you employed by Xing Hui?" I was wondering if he wasn't just an attractive, charming goon of Xing Hui.

"No."

"Do you work for a subsidiary of Xing Hui?"

"No."

I suspected a trick. "Then show me your business card."

He fumbled around. "Oh, sorry, I forgot them." Chinese people are very proud of their business cards. This was fishy.

We willed ourselves to believe him because we needed a solution. "We could vacate by the middle of January. Our new apartment is sure to be vacant by then."

"I would want you to pay rent for the time you are in my apartment. You'd have to pay a deposit, too."

"But we still have a deposit with Xing Hui on this apartment!"

"That's with Xing Hui. I'm the new owner. These are my conditions for you to stay here. Also, this is the end of November. You have to pay full-months' rent, so you would have to pay through January 31. That would be two months' rent plus the deposit."

With no other option, we settled on exact figures for rent and deposit.

"We need a contract," Justin said. "When do we sign and when do we pay you?"

"On Monday. You can find me on the first floor."

We were still suspicious, so as soon as he left, Justin called our lawyer and explained about the visitor. "I need you to call this man and check him out. Does he actually own our apartment building? Is he the new owner or is he employed by Xing Hui? Does he have the right to rent the apartment to us? And furthermore, how does it work for us to give him a deposit when Xing Hui still has a deposit on this apartment?"

"Don't try to get the deposit back from Xing Hui!" the lawyer said. "I'll check on the other issues."

The next day the lawyer called and told us that everything checked out. The man was the owner of the building and he had authority to rent the apartment to us. He was not an employee of Xing Hui.

We could finally get this problem behind us.

On Monday Justin went to the first floor, cash in hand, ready to sign. Justin asked the man, "Could I see the contract?"

"What are you talking about?"

Justin was confused. "We talked to you about a contract to rent our apartment until the end of January."

"We never talked about any contract or you renting an apartment from me."

Justin was angry and stalked out.

He called the lawyer. "Did you talk to the man who agreed to rent the apartment to us?"

The lawyer was evasive.

"Did you talk to him?"

Justin had to ask him several times before he got the answer. "No, I never talked to him."

Justin was livid. "You're fired!" he shouted into the phone. Since we had already paid him, the only thing accomplished by firing him was getting him out of our lives. Now we would only have to fight Xing Hui, not our lawyer as well. (Later, Hao, the man who had recommended this lawyer, apologized to us. He told us he had just found out that the lawyer was corrupt and was being arraigned on charges of international malfeasance.)

It took us a while to understand why the slick man would back out of negotiations since he was about to be on the receiving end of a big pile of money. We suspect he was employed by Xing Hui and assigned to get us to vacate the apartment. He would have taken another two months' rent and a third deposit, except for one thing. Justin had insisted on a contract. The slick man couldn't provide us with a contract since it was all illegal.

We had peace for three days—and then our sons were attacked, as you will read in the story, *Attack the Foreigners*. To this day, we don't know if the attackers were sent by our landlord. Since Xing Hui was owned by the city of Wuran, they had a lot of resources and power, and little fear of justice.

Xing Hui seemed to run out of steam in December, as we waited for our new apartment. They had harassed us for four long months and we were still living there. Justin and I had agreed that neither of us would ever talk with Xing Hui alone. All of our communication with them was in Mandarin. Since we were just learning Mandarin we needed both of us together, listening and figuring out how to respond. It was our safeguard.

On Christmas Eve, Justin had to go out for a while. I was in the apartment with the boys, who were doing homework. As soon as Justin left the building, our lights went out. Apparently Xing Hui had been watching our comings and goings. When they saw Justin go out, it was their opportunity to talk to me alone. Their way of trying to get my attention was not a polite knock on the door, but cutting off our electricity.

I quietly slipped over to where the boys were and put my index finger against my lips to warn them not to make any noise.

The goons started pounding on our door. They pounded for a full half hour, shouting at me through the door. I was fairly calm—we had been through a lot worse. I could tell it was unnerving the boys a little, but they too had been through worse. We kept perfectly silent in the dark and I never opened the door.

I must have been more shaken than I realized, though, because a few days later when I heard workmen in the stairwell working on our electric box I grabbed a broom and charged out the door. I rushed at them, screaming in Mandarin, "You can't take our electric box! You can't take it!" I thought Xing Hui had sent them to dismantle our electric box so we would never have electricity again.

The workmen fell back away from me, scared of this screaming foreign woman about to attack them with a broomstick. "We're fixing the electric box of the apartment upstairs," one of them explained.

How embarrassing! After apologizing, I slunk back into our apartment.

A few days after that, our new apartment was finally ready. Chinese friends stood guard at strategic points between our apartment and the moving van to protect us and our possessions as we moved out. They were afraid Xing Hui would attack us.

Our Chinese friends later told us they respected us for standing up to Xing Hui and not giving in. It was Peter's comment that moved me the most, especially considering his own experience of having been kicked out of college and almost put in a mental institution for his faith in Jesus. Peter viewed our ordeal as our initiation rights to be accepted as Chinese.

"Everywhere you turned you hit a brick wall," he said. "There were no solutions to the problems Xing Hui caused you. That is exactly what life is like for us Chinese. We hit brick walls all the time. There are no solutions to make life work. Now, you are one of us."

ATTACK THE FOREIGNERS

1998, Wuran

Standing in our living room, I gasped as I lifted 15-year-old Nigel's shirt. Nasty crimson welts covered his back. It was worse than they had described.

I lowered his shirt and studied his face. His lips were pressed tightly together and he was staring hard at nothing.

Then I looked over at Peter's bandaged forehead. He looked sad and bewildered.

"What happened?" I asked. "I thought you went to a concert."

"Some guys were waiting for us outside after we finished the concert." Nigel spoke in even, controlled syllables.

"Who? Who was waiting for you?"

"We don't know who they were. It was about a dozen guys. They looked homeless."

"A dozen guys attacked you?"

"They ambushed us."

Nigel and two of his American friends had formed a band—Nigel on bass, Butch sang and played electric guitar, and Luke was one mean drummer. They'd had a few gigs at the local universities and a pub, but prestigious Wuran University had invited them to play that night. The university advertised the concert all over campus and thousands attended. I hadn't been able to go because I couldn't take all the cigarette smoke.

"Aren't there always guards at your concerts?" I asked. "I thought they wanted to make sure there would never be incidents like this involving Americans."

"That's the strangest thing," Nigel said. "The concerts are always crawling with guards. But there wasn't even one guard in the auditorium this time!

112

You don't think the university planned this, do you? Or maybe even the government?"

My mind went immediately to our landlord. Could Xing Hui have sent a dozen guys to attack Nigel and Adam? "Tell me from the beginning what happened."

Peter spoke slowly. "Adam and I were standing in the aisle after the concert, waiting for Nigel."

Adam (14) broke in. "And this guy ran up to me, grabbed my head, and slammed it into Peter's."

"He was trying to start a fight," Peter said. "Then he ran outside."

Peter, his Chinese friend Harry, and Adam immediately followed him out.

"I wanted to talk to him," Peter said. "There were girls from the international school there and I didn't want them to get hurt, so I wanted to talk the guy out of having a fight. But when we got outside, a different guy came up to me. He appeared to be in charge and I tried to reason with him. But he was holding a metal pipe and he wouldn't talk with me. Instead, he attacked me. Then a dozen guys came out from behind the trees!"

"They were waiting for us!" Adam's eyes were wide.

Nigel picked up the story here. He and his friend Russ had emerged from the auditorium just in time to see the dozen guys launch their attack. I could feel the anger in Nigel's voice. "Everyone of them had a metal pipe, a club, or a broken bottle. They shouted, '*Da wai guo ren! Da wai guo ren!*' ('Attack the foreigners! Attack the foreigners!')"

"They rushed at us!" Adam said. "Something knocked my glasses off. I couldn't see anything so I stepped back."

Peter's voice broke as he relived the scene. "I tried to get to Nigel but I couldn't. Someone was beating his back with a pipe. I couldn't protect him. I couldn't protect Nigel."

Someone swung a broken bottle at Peter's face. It gashed his right eyebrow. What if it had hit half an inch lower? Peter would have lost his eye! I was almost in tears. How could anyone treat my two sons and Peter like this?

"So how did the fight end?"

Peter looked pleased with himself. "I wanted to get the fight stopped because I was afraid somebody was going to get killed, so I yelled out, '*Liu xue la! Liu xue la!*' ('I'm bleeding! I'm bleeding!') Everybody stopped and stared at me. See, blood was running all down my face. Then they all ran away. It was amazing!"

Nigel started to smile. "You know how fat Russ is? Well, he sat on two of the guys so they couldn't get away!"

Peter, Nigel and Harry took the two guys to the police station. But the cops ignored the attackers and instead interrogated Peter.

"We told them those guys attacked us, that we didn't start the fight. But the police didn't care." Peter sighed.

The police sent Peter to the hospital to get stitched up.

"But when we got back, the guys who started the fight weren't even there," Peter said. "They had let them go. I couldn't believe it! The police told us if we still had a problem we should come back to the station tomorrow morning at 10."

"What are you gonna do?"

"I'm going back. The police need to deal with this!"

The next morning Justin called Peter. "How about if I go with you? I'm afraid the police will hurt you. I don't think that will happen if I'm there."

Peter agreed to think about it. A little while later he called Justin back with his reply: "I talked to my friends. They think the police will take it as a power play if an American comes with me. That won't go well. It's best if just Harry and I go."

When Peter and Harry got to the station, they met with the two policemen from the day before. The officers told them to face the wall in the hallway and squat down. They left them like that for two hours! Peter had also taken a beating in the lower back, in his kidneys. He could hardly squat it was so painful.

The two officers were in the room right next to them, with the door ajar. They kept their voices loud to make sure Peter and Harry could hear them talking back and forth.

"I have a sick relative who needs a kidney transplant."

"Why don't you pick out one of the prisoners to 'donate' a kidney?"

"You can't do that—when the family comes to collect the body, they'll see the scars where the kidneys were removed."

"The family will never know. We'll cremate the body and give them the ashes."

The officers laughed.

"That's why America says we have no human rights."

After two hours, the policemen came back into the hallway where Peter and Harry were. They told them to stand up, and then they said: "We know you have foreign friends. We're warning you not to use them to gain leverage. If we ever hear you speak about the attack again, or if you tell our bosses about it, we will deal with you. Do you have any grievance?"

"No, we have no grievance," Peter said.

I never called or emailed my family or friends in America to tell them what happened to our sons because the police monitored our communications. I never told Chinese or American friends in China what happened, either, because they might tell the wrong person. I was afraid the police would come to take Peter away—and force him to "donate" his kidneys.[1]

---

1. See *The Slaughter*, by Ethan Gutmann, where he documents the harvesting of organs from live prisoners in China.

RESPONSIBILITY

1999, Wuran

Justin and I were weaving our way through the crowds at the night market. Bright red, green, blue, and yellow neon signs, written in Chinese characters, decked the stalls, which sold everything from cheap trinkets to exotic animal parts for Chinese herbal medicine. Vendors shouted out their wares and buyers drove hard bargains, all in the Wuran dialect. The aroma of roasting lamb kabobs, spiced with cumin, filled the air.

The hawkers' stands cluttered the ground, and cars had made a path through the confusion. Drivers honked and shouted for pedestrians to get out of their way.

The December sky was dark, though, and a sheet of ice covered the ground. A young man with one leg sat on the ice on the side of the narrow car lane. He had no coat. His face, hands, and clothes were charcoal, and his hair was matted. By his side lay a short brown stick— his crutch.

His leg was sprawled across the car lane, and a car was coming. His only leg was about to be crushed!

Shoppers raced by, as if the man were invisible. I cried out to Justin, "We need to help him!" We raced over to him, managed to stop the oncoming car, and we helped him up. When I touched him, I realized he was soaking wet. If he didn't find shelter, he may not survive the frigid night. The next car was an empty red taxi; we waved it to a stop and quickly crowded into it with the disabled man before the driver could realize what we were doing.

"Take us to the nearest hotel so we can get a room for this man," we told the driver in Mandarin. There were no homeless shelters in China—our plan was to put him up at a hotel for a few nights until the ground wasn't as frozen. We had taken responsibility for him.

To our surprise the driver said, "No hotel in China would give this man a room!"

We couldn't dump him back out onto the street because he would probably freeze to death before morning. We did the only thing we could think of—we asked the man where he lived. He named a street in the extreme north of Wuran—this huge city with nine million people.

On the long drive, the gray coldness of the night seeped into the unheated taxi. The man was silent. We broke the silence to ask his name. Wang Ping.

Wang Ping directed us to an unlit and desolate road, which ended at a frozen canal. On either side of the road stood one-story cement buildings—a series of small factories, all shuttered for the night with metal gates. There were no houses.

Wang Ping eased himself out of the taxi and hobbled away, leaning on his stick. Justin took off his warm, army green, Russian coat, went up to Wang Ping and put it on him, over his soaked clothes. Then Justin walked with Wang Ping as he headed toward the canal.

I called out to Justin, "He doesn't live here. He's just looking for a place to die." Justin talked him back into the taxi.

Again I asked him where his home was. Wang Ping directed the driver to a factory area on the southeast side of the city, many miles away. That also was not his home. I had suspected from the beginning he had no home.

The taxi driver yelled at Wang Ping, "Why are you saying this place or that place is your home? These are good people. They're trying to help you!" I bristled when he said that. How had this come to be about us?

My mind was spinning. Could we take him to our home? We rented an apartment—did we need the landlord's permission? The police didn't allow Chinese people to live with foreigners because they were afraid we would influence them. If the man came to stay with us, would the police find out? And how would we get him to leave? The whole winter could be icy cold—it was only December.

When had my concern shifted from helping the man to getting rid of him so my life could return to normal?

I turned to the driver. "What should we do?"

"The only place you can take a homeless man is the police station," he replied.

"Please, please, do not take me to the police station! Please!" the man begged us.

We took him to the police station.

Did we have the right to bring the man to the police against his will because we wanted to help him? Or now that we were just trying to get rid of him? He hadn't asked for our help.

The police often beat people in their custody. We were friends with the sister-in-law of a man whom the police beat to death. In addition, China had what they called the *shourong* system, where anyone the police rounded up was to be sent back to their hometown if they didn't have proper identification. But in reality, many of them had to buy their freedom by paying the police. If they couldn't, the police sold them into slave labor. This was a common practice in China.[1]

What the police did to Wang Ping we don't know. How could we have done this to him?

In silence, we took the taxi back home. It took days to wash the filth off my hands.

---

1. Philip P. Pan, *Out of Mao's Shadow: The Struggle for the Soul of a New China* (New York: Simon & Schuster, 2008) 248.

BEGGAR

2002-2003, Wuran

Every Sunday it was the same. "Mom, I'll be leaving right after church to go home." Or, "Hey, I won't be home when you get back from church. I have to go out." Adam (17) was always running out of church, and gone by the time we got home. Always secretive. Always excited.

One Sunday I arrived home early and found him in the dining room with a loaf of bread spread out on the table, slapping peanut butter and jelly onto the slices.

I stared at him. "You're feeding the homeless, aren't you, Adam?"

He looked up at me, startled. "Don't tell Jack, please. Don't tell him that you know." Jack was Adam's classmate.

"What are you guys up to? And why's it a secret?"

"Jack and I feed the beggars outside Liu's Fast Food, but Jack made me promise I wouldn't tell anyone."

"I won't tell."

Adam ran off with a bag of peanut butter and jelly sandwiches.

The summer before, Adam had decided he wanted to learn Mandarin better so he could make local friends and share the gospel. He hired a language tutor 15 hours a week. This homeless ministry was some of the fruit of all that language study.

When Adam returned home, I asked him, "So, Adam, how do you go about feeding the beggars?"

He looked at me, disgusted. "Mom! I don't feed them. That would humiliate them, as if I were better than them. I eat *with* them because they need to feel respected. That's very important."

That was Adam—not just giving them food, but doing it in a way that maintained their dignity.

"So, do you ever have any problems?" I had heard about a couple of foreigners who were kicked out of China for feeding the homeless. Feeding the homeless is an admission that homeless people exist. Communist society was supposed to produce utopia, but utopia doesn't have homeless people or beggars.

Adam's mind went in a different direction. "Well, an old woman beggar stole the sandwich I gave to a girl beggar once. I had already given a sandwich to the old woman, but she wanted more. I made her give it back by telling her I'd never give her food again if she didn't give the sandwich back to the girl. Imagine! Stealing a sandwich from a little girl!"

"That's awful!"

"There's one beggar I really like. His name is Silas. He's in his early 20s and he takes care of a lot of the little kids who are beggars, making sure they don't get hurt. But he's disabled, and I want to see if I can get his disability diagnosed. Maybe he could be cured and get a job."

Adam set to work on his goal. First he talked with a Chinese friend of ours who knew some doctors, and they estimated the cost of getting a diagnosis—about 150 USD. Adam called a Western charity that worked in the area and asked if they'd be interested in funding this need.

He was excited. "Mom, the woman I talked to at the charity said she's interested and she'll call in a week with the answer!" She never called.

"Mom, I called her back. She said she's out of the office for three weeks and she'll call me after she returns." She never called.

"Mom, I called her again and she said they're still deciding."

Week after week Adam called the charity, and every time they delayed giving him an answer.

Finally, Adam came to me quite upset. "Mom, when I called her this time, she yelled at me. She asked me what *I* was doing to raise the money."

"What'd you say?"

"I told her that I was trying to raise the money through *them*. Then she said to me, 'How come you expect *us* to raise the money if *you* aren't even trying to raise it *yourself?*'"

"Adam, she's saying no, but she's doing it in a very mean way. Don't contact her again."

Adam didn't give up. He called another charity and made an appointment with them.

When he came home from the appointment I asked how it went.

"They told me they don't do that kind of ministry. At least they gave me a straight no. I'm really glad about that—they didn't string me along and then blame me."

Adam tried again. He made an appointment with the elders of the international fellowship we attended and presented the need to them. They told him they would consider it. A few weeks later, Adam came to me in church with tears in his eyes. "Mom, the elders just handed me the money to get Silas diagnosed. I can't believe it!"

As a result of Adam's request, the elders of the international fellowship set up the Silas Fund. Members of the fellowship could present a local Chinese person's need, and the Silas Committee would consider it. If approved, they would give the member the funds to help the local. When the elders explained the Silas Fund to the congregation, they said the fund was established because Adam's request for Silas opened their eyes to the need for this kind of assistance. The Silas Fund is a vital part of that international fellowship's ministry to this day.

Silas was diagnosed with a mild case of cerebral palsy, but the Chinese doctors in their white lab coats said that nothing could be done for him.

Adam still pursued it. At the fellowship he found a foreigner who was a physical therapist and one who was an occupational therapist. They agreed to meet with Silas and show him exercises that would increase his mobility and flexibility.

But the therapists weren't wearing white lab coats, so Silas didn't believe them. His doctors had told him there was nothing that could be done, so he refused to do the exercises.

About that time, Silas let Adam into his life as a friend, and took him to the place where he slept at night, next to a stinky canal. Plywood and corrugated metal formed the sides of the little shack, and a sheet of corrugated metal formed the roof. The room was the size of a prone body. Silas had stuffed trash in the cracks in the walls to try to keep the winter cold out. This ramshackle place cost him $1.25 USD a month.

Then Silas told Adam his life story—he had grown up on a farm with a lot of siblings. (Some rural families succeeded in circumventing China's one-child policy.) He did what work he could, and his family loved him. But then one year it rained and rained, so their farm was flooded, and there was no food or work. The siblings all scattered to neighboring provinces to find work, and Silas came to our city to beg.

When Silas visited his family home, about 600 miles away, for Chinese New Year, he called Adam from the one phone in his village to keep up contact.

After Silas returned to Wuran, Adam said, "Mom, I've been thinking about it. Even with his disability, there are still some jobs Silas could do. I want to see if I can find him a job." Jack, Adam's friend who had been feeding the homeless with him, talked his father into hiring Silas to do light cleaning in the office of the company he owned.

"Mom, you won't believe it! Now that Silas has a job, he has so much respect for himself. He holds his head up and doesn't just look at the ground. He's even watching girls!"

So that's a sign of self-respect!

Another day Adam said, "Mom, I bumped into Silas today. He was sound asleep, begging on the stairs of Liu's Fast Food. I woke him and asked why he's still begging since he has a job now. You know what he told me? He said he sends most of his paycheck home to his parents! He gets up at four in the morning so he can beg before he goes to work because he wants to send even more money to his family. He's so happy he can send so much money home now."

We were amazed at Silas' love for his family. That beautiful love is so typical of the Chinese; it comes from the Confucian emphasis on family.

Adam continued. "Then Silas told me that he's a bad beggar—he falls asleep while he's begging, he's so tired. He wants to be a better beggar and stay awake."

Adam and I laughed. We loved Silas and hearing about his goals in life.

Thanksgiving was coming, so I started looking for a turkey. After some research I located a store in a city hours away that catered to foreigners and would sell me a turkey. I ordered one and spent all day on buses with a cooler to pick it up.

Adam invited six of his beggar friends for Thanksgiving, but only two came—Silas and a little eight-year-old girl with a dirty face and matted hair.

I had made the whole Thanksgiving spread from scratch, as close as I could to the real dinner with local ingredients: turkey, dressing, mashed potatoes and gravy, homemade bread, homemade hawberry sauce (in place of cranberry sauce), vegetables, and sweet potato pie (there were no pumpkins). It took me three days to make the meal; I wanted to treat Adam's beggar friends well.

When Silas and the little girl sat down at the table, they looked overwhelmed. They had no idea how to eat the food, and they had never used a knife and fork before. They didn't like the food, but they tried to be polite and eat a bit. The little girl was panting, looking around at the walls and ceiling like a caged animal because she wasn't used to being indoors. As soon as it was polite enough, she ran outside to feel better.

We had all tried so hard.

Adam wanted Silas to learn about the Lord so he invited him to the government church. Although Silas looked out of place there in his filthy, ill-fitting clothes, he tried to act like it was O.K. because his friend, Adam, had brought him. The sermon drew lessons from the lives of Abraham and Moses, but Silas had never heard of these biblical characters. He didn't understand a thing.

I made a suggestion. "Adam, our friend, Layton, is from the same province as Silas. Why don't you invite Layton to share the gospel in the dialect of their province, then Silas might understand."

Adam liked the idea. When Silas and Layton came over to our home, Layton gave a rapid fire, concise presentation of the gospel, without making sure that Silas understood. Silas' head was spinning and it didn't make any sense to him.

Then Adam said, "Mom, Silas needs to learn how to read Chinese so he can read the Bible." Silas had never attended school and no one had ever taught him how to read because he was born disabled. Adam asked one of our Chinese friends to teach Silas how to read.

Then Adam had to leave for the U.S. to go to college.

When he returned a year later to visit us in China, he went to Liu's Fast Food, but Silas wasn't there. He combed the streets of our city hunting for his friend. Neither Silas' workplace, nor the man who agreed to teach him to read, knew where he was anymore. It seems that Silas was no longer living, begging, or working in our city.

Silas, wherever you are, I still pray for you—that you will have what you need and that you will come to know our Lord.

RACHAEL AND THE FORCED ABORTION

1998-2002, Wuran

I was angry.

Half an hour earlier I had left my bicycle for a street-side bike repairman to fix while I went to the market. When I got back, not only had he not even looked at my bike, but there were 10 other bikes lined up in front of it!

How could I have known this was a divine appointment?

In a huff, I sat down on a rattan stool. One of the people waiting, a petite woman in her mid-thirties with short hair, struck up a conversation with me. Rachael was a professor at a local university, and she and her husband had a nine-year-old son. There was nothing special about our conversation, but for some reason my heart was drawn to her.

Our family had recently returned from the vacation to the North Korean border and we were in the middle of the landlord fiasco, so I had trouble trusting Chinese people at that point. If Rachael and I were going to become friends, I would have to give her my phone number, but I didn't want to. I went back and forth in my mind, but finally handed her a slip of paper with my number on it. Two days later she called, and we started taking frequent walks around the neighborhood. She didn't speak a word of English.

Rachael's life was a mess. She was planning to walk away from her family and divorce her husband. She was so suicidal she was afraid to even be in a high-rise for fear she'd jump out the window!

When I was much younger, I had been suicidal, so her desperation was personal for me.

One day in her apartment, she told me her father had died when she was five, and her mother had been paranoid schizophrenic. After her dad's death, her grandma moved in with them so Rachael wouldn't be raised by

124

her mother alone. "When I was a child, my mother often forced me to hide under the bed with her because she imagined intruders were invading. When things got really bad, my mother would attack the neighbors and my grandma had to pull her off them.

"But, you know, my mother believed in Jesus! All the time she quoted her favorite Bible verse—'A bruised reed He will not break.'[1] My mother was the bruised reed." Because her mother was so crazy, Rachael was turned off to the Christian faith.

When I talked to her about the Lord, I felt such a sense of urgency—she needed Jesus fast or she might commit suicide! But she wasn't interested. She wasn't turned off to Christianity simply because of her mother; she herself had become an atheist. She didn't see the point in believing in God.

I couldn't talk with her about God directly, so we talked about life and the difficulties we were facing. When the Lord helped me by answering my prayers, I'd tell her, and she would look at me with longing in her face. "I'd love to be able to pray and get help," she would say. "But I can't because I won't be a hypocrite. I won't pray because I don't believe God exists."

I respected her integrity. "I understand that you can't pray to God when you don't believe in him, but I believe in God, so I can pray for you." When Rachael saw the clear answers to my prayers for her, she took notice, and started to wonder about God. She began to pray to Jesus herself, but at first she kept it a secret from me.

Because I was so anxious for her to come to know the Lord, one day as we were talking, I burst out, "Rachael, the Lord could change your life!" She was livid. "I do not want God changing me!" she said. "My husband is always trying to change me. I don't need God trying to change me, too!"

After several months I gave her a Bible, and she was so interested in it, she read it all the time and had trouble getting anything else done. One afternoon, she said, "Grace, the Bible is true to life. I'd never understood before why women need men so much, but there's the reason right there in the beginning of Genesis."

Then, her husband, Lester, caught her reading the Bible, and he didn't like it. "Why are you reading a book of myths?" he stormed. "I thought you were smarter than that!"

She was hurt by his criticism, but then to her own surprise, she began to defend the Bible to him. The more she defended it, the more she believed it! And the more frightened her husband became that she might become a Christian.

---

1. Matthew 12:20

"My husband told me that he was going to forbid me to see you so you couldn't have any influence on me, and then I wouldn't become a Christian," she said. "But after thinking more about it, he figured you can't speak Mandarin well enough to convince me to become a Christian." She smiled and chuckled. "He doesn't know you."

I think he underestimated the Holy Spirit.

It took nine months, but step by step, she came to faith and was baptized.

It was so joyous! Life became precious to her and she wanted to live. She told me, "It's so ironic. Before, when I wanted to die, I was afraid of death. But now that I believe in Jesus and want to live, I'm not afraid to die anymore!"

Rachael started to love her family. So her husband got his wife back and her son got his mother back. Unfortunately, that still hasn't turned Lester toward Jesus.

Rachael was so happy to believe in God. "Grace, God is amazing!" she told me one day. "When you don't believe in Jesus, nothing in life has any meaning. But after you believe in Jesus, the smallest things are charged with meaning!"

It soon became clear to me, however, that although Rachael looked forward to seeing Jesus when she died, she didn't want to go to heaven. One day when we were visiting, I mentioned to her that she would go to heaven when she dies, and she looked at me, panicked. "No, I don't want to go to heaven! My mother will be there. I can't take any more of her!" I told her that her mother would no longer be mentally ill, so when she sees her in heaven, it will be good.

Rachael was so passionate about reading the Bible, I began teaching her an Old Testament Survey course. After studying Leviticus, she said, "When I can't sleep at night I love reading Leviticus." When we studied Numbers, she told me, "Wow, Numbers is even more interesting than Leviticus!"

Rachael became my closest friend in Wuran.

Rachael's "Forced" Abortion

That was during the time of China's one-child policy. Unless an exception was made, only one child was allowed to be born into each family. China now has a two-child policy, but what happened in this story still happens.

After Rachael came to know the Lord, she and I tried to save the life of her unborn child.

Before Rachael got pregnant, one day while we were walking, she mentioned that she had been fitted with an IUD by a government medical worker. "The government requires every woman of child-bearing age to have an IUD if she's already given birth to one child. But it's really bad. The IUDs are one-size fits all, but my IUD doesn't fit and it's quite painful. Sometimes it falls out and I don't even know it!"

Any personal back-up plan she might use was unreliable because, for example, the condoms were so poorly made they often had holes in them. And Rachael didn't want to get sterilized in case the policy changed and she and her husband could have another child.

Before Rachael came to know the Lord, she had had five unauthorized pregnancies, and the five required abortions. "My husband and I grieved over each abortion because we love children."

One day, about three years after she became a Christian, Rachael called me in a panic. "Grace, I have to see you right away. Let's meet at the semicircle of grass at the entrance to the housing complex."

When we met up, she looked agitated, "I'm pregnant! What do I do?"

After finding out all the details, I asked her, "Do you want to keep the child?" I needed to know where she was starting from, so I would know how to talk with her.

"Of course I do—this baby is my child! But I have to ask you something. In God's eyes is my unborn child a human being? If he is, since I'm a Christian now, I can't abort him even if the government says I have to, isn't that right?"

I pointed her to Psalm 139:15-16: "My frame was not hidden from you when I was made in the secret place, when I was woven together in the depths of the earth. Your eyes saw my unformed body; all the days ordained for me were written in your book before one of them came to be."

"Then my child really is a human being. What am I to do?"

"Rachael, what will happen if you try to keep the child?"

"I might be able to hide the fact that I'm pregnant for a few months, but that'll only work if I don't have morning sickness. If my supervisor at the university suspects I'm having morning sickness, she'll force me to take a pregnancy test. Even if I get through the first few months undetected, I will eventually start to show. Then it's over—they won't stop pressuring me to abort the child."

"Could you wear real baggy clothes?"

"They'd see through that ruse and make me take a pregnancy test."

"Could you just say you're not feeling well and stay home for a few months?"

"My supervisor will suspect I'm hiding a pregnancy, and she'll visit me at home."

"Then the only solution is for you to quit your job."

"They'll still come after me and threaten me, and they'll also come after my husband and threaten him until we abort the child!"

Wow! The government had laid the trap well!

"How will they threaten you?"

"They'll visit me all the time, and they'll threaten me with fines, and maybe even threaten to fire me."

"What if you don't give in?"

"There's no point. If they can't convince me to abort, they'll force me to abort! Since I can't win anyway, why hold out?"

How insidious! The government wanted the mothers to decide to abort their own babies so the blood of the babies would be on the mothers' hands, not the government's. They also wouldn't have as many "forced" abortions on the record. All the while, they planned to force the abortion anyway, if the mother didn't cave in. They would literally capture the woman and inject her with drugs to cause the abortion.

I came up with a plan, and Justin agreed. The next day I proposed to Rachael, "What if you and I disappear together until the baby's born? I would take care of you."

"Like I said, they'll still come after my husband and coerce him into giving up my location."

"Then your husband will have to be on board with the plan, or we can't do it. I hope he'll understand since he's not a Christian. I'm willing to help you by taking you somewhere you won't be found, and I'll stay with you. I know a vet who might be willing to deliver the baby."

We would have to stay away from the hospitals because sometimes even on the delivery table they aborted "unauthorized children."

"Grace, there'll be a fine of two years' salary."

"Can you and your husband come up with half the fine? I'll come up with the other half."

"I believe we can. I'll talk to my husband."

I knew my plan was crazy, but it was one that had been used by many pregnant mothers in China to save their unborn children. If we got caught, I knew the consequences to our family would be bad. But what was at stake was the life of a child. If a mother wants to save her unborn child, what are you willing to do to help her accomplish that?

What I hadn't thought through clearly, though, was that if the child died in delivery, the American vet I was planning to ask would almost certainly be charged with murder by the People's Republic of China.

A few days later Rachael came back with Lester's answer. As much as he wanted to save the child, he didn't think we should go through with it. He wouldn't give us his support.

My heart wept. I couldn't think of any other plan that would work. I knew that Rachael wasn't emotionally strong enough to protect the baby without Lester's support. And she couldn't disappear without telling him where she was hiding. If the State Family Planning Commission came after him, he would probably disclose her location since he wasn't in favor of the plan.

Rachael was willing to give their life savings and sacrifice her job to save her unborn child. I was willing to be imprisoned, and my family was willing to be kicked out of China, but we still couldn't succeed. How could there be no solution? How could we not save the baby?

Before she did something that was terribly wrong, I talked with her about God's forgiveness. At that point I couldn't save the child, but I at least wanted to save the mother's faith. I knew the guilt might make her walk away from the Lord, even though I viewed that the government was responsible for taking the life of this child, not Rachael.

A few days later, the phone rang. I heard a weak voice, "I'll be having the abortion today." I stifled a sob. I didn't know what to say, except, "I'll be praying for you."

I spent the whole day thinking about the child.

It took Rachael months to get over having the abortion. I tried to be there for her. Eventually she drew near to the Lord, and became a vibrant Christian again. She is now helping other Christians grow through her own teaching of the Bible.

ILLUSION OF ICE

1999-2003, Wuran

The little lakes around Wuran always froze over in winter. They were shallow, sandy depressions filled with water, some as big as a football field. We loved ice skating and playing hockey on the frozen surfaces.

There were other lakes at the edge of Wuran. These were deeper and darker, sometimes with a swirl of unnatural greens and blues in the center. A pungent chemical odor exuded from the deep dark lakes in summer; it was hard to bike past them without gagging. We were told they were dumps for sewage and industrial waste. Even on freezing winter days, some of them steamed.

One day in February, Justin and I asked a Japanese classmate, Shiro, to ice skate with us on our favorite shallow lake. When we arrived, we discovered it was already thawing, so we went in search of a lake that was still frozen. We found one, but it was half strewn with garbage and half clear.

I was so excited to skate I ran ahead of the men. Skates slung over my shoulder, I scrambled down the 10-foot embankment and stepped onto the garbage side of the ice in order to walk over to the clear side to skate.

As I went to take a second step, my feet felt sluggish; I couldn't lift them to move forward. I looked down to see that I was sinking in muck—there was no ice! I tried again to lift my left foot to step back onto the bank, but the thick sludge held it tight. It was sucking me in! I was quickly up to my knees. Then my waist. My chest. "Help, help!" I shouted. "I'm going under!"

Shiro ran over, raced down the bank, grasped my hand, and with herculean strength, pulled me out.

We biked home as fast as we could. I was shivering and filthy. Justin turned on the hot water heater to heat water for a shower.

130

I should have taken a shower then, but I was so cold I couldn't bear the thought of the frigid water. I wiped off and bundled in a towel, still shaking, while I waited for two hours for the water to heat.

As I sat on the couch, wrapped up, I didn't know that whatever lived in that lake was creeping into every tiny fissure on my skin. Within a few hours I had an outbreak of infections all over my skin!

I also didn't know about the deeper infection. That took years to show itself.

Over four years later, in the spring of 2003, I developed symptoms of a UTI with a spiking fever. One afternoon I was suddenly so exhausted, I lay down on the couch and could barely get up. Justin hired a taxi to take me several hours to an international hospital in Huangdi.

The German urologist diagnosed a urinary tract infection. After two courses of antibiotics, I still wasn't any better. When I returned to the hospital, the urologist said there was nothing more she could do for me. I was shocked! The doctor had given up on me.

I was scheduled to visit the U.S. in a few weeks, so I could see a doctor there, but I didn't have enough strength to travel.

Desperate, I asked the elders at the international fellowship to pray over me for healing. They gathered around and laid hands on me. A few days later I felt much better and was able to fly back to Seattle, where I was able to see a top-notch urologist.

After testing my urine and reviewing my medical records from China, the doctor just stared at me. "Where on earth did you get this infection?" she asked. "The only way you get this kind of infection is from polluted water! Have you been swimming in polluted water?"

It didn't seem related, but I told her about the ice skating incident.

"There were no other times you were in polluted water?"

"No."

"Then that's where you got this infection."

"But that was four years ago!"

"The bacteria lay dormant for four years."

I was scared. "So what do we do now? How do I get rid of it?"

"Now that's the really strange thing. Your urine test shows you don't have this infection anymore, but the antibiotics the doctor in China gave you wouldn't have touched it! She gave you the wrong antibiotics."

Now it was my turn to stare at her. There could only be one explanation— the elders had prayed over me.

PASSPORT HOLDERS ONLY

1996-2007, Wuran

The Wuran International Fellowship was a conglomerate of about 200 people from every inhabited continent. There was such a variety of nations represented that I had friends from a dozen African countries. I even knew a Manx from the Isle of Man. Everyone was welcome as long as you were a foreign passport holder; your passport was inspected at the door by two young Nepalese men.

In this "church" we had the whole spectrum of Christendom, from Russian Orthodox to Pentecostal. It was such an enriching experience to worship with people from so many different cultures, and it broadened my faith to discuss the Lord with others who knew so much about him in ways I had never been introduced to.

While still holding firmly to the fundamentals, the elders were careful not to allow preaching or practice that would polarize us or alienate a belief set. It was a difficult dance, but they were quite successful. We maintained unity.

We all assumed the Public Security Bureau (PSB), that is, the police, bugged the services. The joke was: "Oh, you missed the service? Well, just get the tape from the PSB!" Those who preached at the service were expected not to ever mention the word missionary, or refer to a mission agency or to any missionary work that was being done.

We had no pastor because we were afraid the police would target him. We had no member list because we didn't want the police to get their hands on it.

Most of the time we were there, the fellowship was technically illegal because it was unregistered, but the police were unconcerned and winked at it. Toward the end of our time in Wuran, however, while Justin and I were temporarily in the States, the PSB convinced the elders to register the group. After that, the PSB interfered constantly. For example, they required the elders to turn over a list of the members, which fortunately, they didn't have. They also required the elders to report their own educational background and work history. They said it was "for our safety," so there would be no bad teaching or cults in the group—as if the atheists at the PSB would know what false teaching was!

Justin had been an elder, but after the group became registered, he refused to continue serving. He couldn't let the PSB see his resume because it included seminary training and church planting. The elders wanted him to continue to make decisions with them, so they made a special office for Justin. He became an "elder adviser." Since his title wasn't "elder," they didn't have to submit his resume to the PSB.

During our time at the Wuran International Fellowship, the Lord called on me to minister to some struggling women in the group. Here are two of their stories.

§§§

"You are so ignorant!" "I need to order food—I'm the only one who could manage that." Niki was a Korean woman in her mid-twenties, and every sentence out of her mouth was a put-down. "You didn't eat all your rice? Well, you sure haven't acculturated to Asia." "You're having trouble with the police? I'm sure you handled things badly, and that's why they've come knocking on your door." After eating lunch with her, I was exhausted and a little depressed. I really couldn't stand her, and I avoided her after that.

A few weeks after I had lunch with her, during my devotions, the Lord impressed on me that he wanted me to be friendly with Niki. I groaned. This was horrible! Now I'd have to talk with her; avoiding her wasn't an option.

The next Sunday at the international fellowship, after I put my purse down, I walked over, greeted her, and asked about her week. Every Sunday, in obedience to the Lord, I tried to be as warm with her as I could tolerate.

Three weeks after I started being friendly with Niki, I walked into the worship service, and she grabbed my arm. "I'm having a problem and I need someone to talk to. Grace, you're the only person who's friendly to me. Could we have lunch together?"

I gulped. I couldn't believe I was the only person who was friendly with her, but I didn't want to go to lunch with her. It was more than I had agreed to do for the Lord. But instead I said, "Yes, I'll go to lunch with you."

We went out for Cantonese dim sum. I sat across the small rectangular table from Niki. We tried to converse in English, but her English was so poor we spoke mostly in Mandarin.

"So, Niki, what's the problem?"

"Some people in the fellowship want me to get baptized, but I was already baptized as an infant. Should I get baptized again?"

I wasn't sure she was a Christian, so I asked her, "Well, before we talk about baptism, tell me about your faith. What's the most important aspect of your relationship with the Lord?"

"I have a standard of behavior that I hold to. This is very important to me."

"What happens if you don't meet the standard?"

"I hate myself and cut myself down."

"What happens if you do meet the standard?"

"I feel so proud!"

Was this the cause of her interpersonal problems? I was surprised she was so honest with me. "Do you require others to meet this standard, too?"

"Of course."

"What if someone doesn't meet the standard?"

"Oh, I think they're a piece of dirt and I want them to know it."

"What if someone meets the standard? How do you feel then?"

"I'm so jealous. I want to bring that person down."

That explained so much. I encouraged her to take the standard down.

"No, I can't do that! It's important to me!"

"Does any good fruit come from your standard, Niki? Look, you either hate yourself or you're proud. You either can't stand others or you're jealous and want to hurt them. Take the standard down!"

She argued with me for a few moments longer, but then she reluctantly agreed.

She became a lovely person. I didn't have to force myself to be friendly and I began to enjoy talking with her. Over time it became obvious that she really did know the Lord.

Eventually she returned to Korea and emailed me that she was attending Bible school. I was glad the Lord had told me to be friendly with her.

§§§

A group of 20-somethings often came to the fellowship drunk after binge-ing all night. They were students at an American university but were intern-ing in China for their MBAs.

One day Justin told me about one of them, a 27-year-old named Isabella, who wanted to be baptized. "But I don't think she's a Christian," he said. "Would you be willing to get to know her and share the gospel with her?"

Isabella met with me at our home, and we talked over tea at our round, wooden dining table. She worked for the U.S. government in D.C. During our conversation, she alluded to all the promiscuous behavior she had been involved in before coming to China.

"In America sin was fun," she said. "People treated each other nicely while we were sinning. But I'm so repulsed by the same sins here in China. It's like my American classmates have no inhibitions in China, and they treat me so crassly here. In China sin has been taken to its logical extent. I hate all this sin now. I want to get free from it and change. I want to get baptized so I'll be a Christian."

My heart went out to her. I had felt the same way when I was 15 years old—repulsed by the sin I was involved in and wanting to get free.

She noticed my sympathetic attitude. "I can't believe this! I've just told you horrible things I've been involved in, but you're not rejecting me! It's amazing—I feel safe with you."

Over the next few months we talked about Jesus, but she was confused about spiritual things. After I told her that Jesus had died and risen from the grave, I asked her why it was so significant that Jesus rose from the dead. She looked at me like I was clueless. "Grace, it shows he could defy gravity—he could rise! Other people can't levitate like that!"

She always thought in business jargon, and it was often quite humorous. When I told her, "Isabella, if you become a Christian, you're going to have to forsake all sin for Jesus. You can't pick and choose." She looked aghast. "Can't we negotiate here?"

I told her about the Holy Spirit, that He would come to live inside her when she became a Christian. First she looked off into the distance, then she looked upset. "The Holy Spirit is holy, and I'm sinful. Grace, the merger won't work!"

Her journey to Jesus took a lot of time. It took me slowly explaining the Scriptures, and it took a lot of deep, open discussion. A few months after we started meeting together, we read Ephesians 2:1-10, which explained the poverty of her life before the merger, what both Christ and she would bring to the table, and how to seal the deal. She finally made her contract with God.

PRISON CAMP

1998-2006, Outside Wuran

"Hey, guys, there's a hole in the wall down here we can crawl through!" Nigel whispered.

Nigel (15), Adam (13), Justin, and I were taking a long family bike ride on the outskirts of Wuran when we noticed a large enclosed area at the side of an orchard.

The four of us stooped down to scramble through the gap in the brick wall that formed the perimeter of the compound. Unmanned guard towers rose above the wall on each corner, so we knew the place would be interesting and worth exploring.

Once inside the compound, we tromped through a dry moat. The burgundied autumn leaves crackled underfoot. The scent of fertile soil and matured fallen leaves filled my nostrils.

On the other side of the moat, buildings were scattered over the area. Some were primitive sleeping quarters. One building looked like a small factory with a large machine in the center. Another had vats of leaking chemicals. I squatted down to read the Chinese label. "Toxic." We ran out.

After our first visit to the compound, I read Harry Wu's book, *Bitter Winds*. Harry Wu was a political prisoner who had been incarcerated in the 1960s and 1970s under horrible conditions, part of the time just outside Wuran. The photograph in the book of the prison camp near Wuran looked like the outside of the compound we explored! Later, a friend confirmed that it was a former prison camp.

When we explored the prison camp, deep in the bowels of one building we saw a large, white femur bone that had been licked clean, lying on the dirt floor! The bone was resting at the edge of strange coffin-sized holes dug into the ground. Harry Wu had written that one of the ways the prison guards tortured him was to bury him alive!

Another building was puzzling. Two steel doors, three inches thick and one at each end of a C-shaped passageway, welcomed anyone who dared enter. The doors had been left open. We entered cautiously. Once past the second door, the inside of the building was completely round, about 12 feet in diameter, and the concrete structure was clad in steel. Above my head, two identical, rectangular holes, each two inches high by one foot long, were hewn out of the walls, one on either side, facing each other.

It felt crazy inside this circular structure. I kept walking round and round. I felt like I was losing my mind. I wondered if that was the purpose—a torture room where just the structure of the room drove the prisoners insane.

We went back as a family three times. The third time we climbed over a wide double-doored metal gate and landed next to more than 100 round, cement Mongolian yurts! Each was built just a few feet from the others. We were baffled when we entered this maze of yurts. What were they here for?

A man ran out to chase us away. We tried to hide, but he caught up to us, and when he realized we didn't mean to harm the yurts, he took us to explore them! He explained why the yurts were there. "A company built these yurts for tourists, but the company ran out of money and never completed the project. I was hired to watch the yurts to make sure no one destroys them."

In the end, those yurts saved me.

After we were caught at the yurt tourist village, Justin didn't want to return to the prison camp to explore anymore because he was afraid if we got caught again, it might not go so well for us. But I hadn't had my fill of fun, so I talked an American friend of mine, Elaine, into biking out there to explore with me. Before we left, just in case we got caught, I called my husband because I'd forgotten the word "yurt" in Mandarin. *Meng gu bao.* It might come in handy.

Elaine didn't speak as much Mandarin as I did, so I told her, "If we get caught, let me do all the talking. Don't say anything!"

We explored the whole prison camp. The last building we entered was the strange circular iron-clad one. Once outside, Elaine poached an old, Chinese army helmet she found among the leaves. Just as she finished hiding it in her backpack, I looked up. An irate, old man was standing directly in front of me, up close, his gnarled finger pointing at me.

"What are you doing here?" he yelled into my face in Mandarin.

"Where are the yurts?" I asked.

Angrily he pointed behind us. "But why are you here?" he barked.

"Can you rent the yurts?"

"Tell me, what are you here for?"

"How much do the yurts cost per night?"

"I don't know. How did you get in here?"

I made a mistake and glanced at the wall where we had climbed over. He saw my glance. His face hardened.

"Where did you get in?"

I swept my hand across a 90-degree radius, inclusive of where we had entered.

He was steaming. "You climbed over the wall!" he accused, stating the obvious. "You need to go to the authorities on the other side!"

Now I was scared! I had read in the news a few months before how two foreign reporters had wandered into a restricted area in China. They were convicted, and were still rotting in a Chinese prison. The reporters said they didn't know it was restricted—there weren't any signs.

Why had I been so stupid and put us in this danger? I knew I shouldn't have let my fun gene get the best of me. I prayed the Lord would get us out of this foolish, risky predicament we were in. The only weapon in my arsenal was to talk about yurts.

The irate, old man pointed to a factory that was still in use at the other end of the prison camp and ordered us to turn ourselves in there. As we marched to our doom, I glanced longingly at the wall where we had climbed over. What if he's not watching us? We could make a run for it and be over the wall before he could catch us. Both Elaine and I were in our early 50s, but in good shape. Before we took off, I glanced over my shoulder to make sure he wasn't watching. He was about 30 feet behind us in a flat-bed tricycle, staring hard at us.

He clicked his lips in disgust when I shot the glance at him. He had been watching us to make sure we didn't make a run for it! He quickly biked up to us, and followed us all the way.

When we arrived at the factory, while Irate parked his three-wheeler and stormed into the building on our left, we waited silently, like lambs to be slaughtered. I wondered if we could avoid prison. If I didn't succeed in talking our way out of this, we might end up in jail, and our families would definitely be expelled from China! And for what? A little fun exploring a restricted prison camp?

A fiery young man stalked out of the building, tailed by Irate. Fiery stood in front of us, wildly waving his arms, yelling and yelling at us, while Irate goaded him on. Fiery was the type to do something rash or call the police. I thought our chances were better if I didn't talk to him. I stayed silent and tried to look repentant.

I was relieved to see a calm, clean-cut, well-dressed man in his 30s come through the door, walking toward us. I could tell he was in charge—he had presence about him. I suspected he was reasonable, and might want to avoid trouble, just like we wanted to avoid trouble. If I could give him a way out, he might not have to admit to the police that they hadn't succeeded in guarding the prison camp from two women in their 50s. Talking about yurts might work with him. I ignored Fiery and focused all my attention on Calm.

Calm asked me in Mandarin, "What are you doing here?"

"Where are the yurts?"

He pointed catty-corner to the factory.

"Can we rent a yurt for the night?"

"No, the yurts aren't for rent."

"Why not?"

"Because the grass has grown up very tall." He held his hand up a couple of feet to show the height of the grass.

I looked disappointed, turned to Elaine and said in English, "We can't rent the yurts because the grass is too tall." I used my hand to show the height of the grass.

If you pretend to translate, but you're actually plotting with your friend instead, an onlooker can spot that right away by your intonation and gestures. Body language goes with what you're actually saying, so I talked to her as if the yurts not being for rent was a real subject.

She played along and kept on the yurt topic.

I turned back to Calm, "That's too bad. If we can't rent the yurts, we'll be on our way then."

Fiery and Irate gesticulated and yelled that we couldn't leave. But Calm waved his hand at them as if to say, I'm in charge and I'm letting them leave.

We turned and walked toward the gate. I was so scared I almost broke into a run, but Elaine warned me, "We're almost home free. If you run now, they'll come after us. Walk slowly!"

The Lord protects the foolish. We escaped from that prison camp, and avoided being charged with a crime and sent to another prison camp!

Did I learn my lesson? I never explored another prison camp in China just for fun, but eventually we were discovered by the Chinese police for another violation. At least that time it was for the sake of the gospel.

CHRISTIANITY THROUGH THE EYES OF A BUDDHIST

1999-2003, Wuran

Sitting in a wooden, cinema-style chair in the government church,[1] I looked around at all the people crowded in the aisles of the 2,000-seat sanctuary. I was excited that my 64-year-old friend, Doris, had come to church with me. She had been a devout Buddhist, but had recently become a Christian. She had even brought her friend Gretchen, who was still a practicing Buddhist.

Everyone hushed as the service started, and after a few words of greeting and prayer, the music began as an old woman plunked out hymns with two fingers, often hitting the wrong notes. But the words of the hymns came alive for me; the beauty of the meaning of every Chinese word I sang made my spirit soar toward God.

We settled back to absorb the sermon, and after about 20 minutes a silent argument broke out between Doris and Gretchen. They scribbled angry notes to each other with fast, jerky movements, then Doris glared at Gretch-

---

1. The government church, which is called the Three-Self Church (self-governing, self-supporting, and self-propagating), is controlled by the Chinese government. Chairman Mao tried to crush Christianity out of existence by outlawing it. When Deng Xiao Ping came into power, he realized that Christianity had just gone underground as a result, so he resurrected the Three-Self Church with the purpose of gaining control over the Christians. Some of the local Three-Self Churches are orthodox and some are not. Many groups of believers have chosen to meet outside the Three-Self Church because they do not want the atheist government controlling their churches. These are known as house churches or unregistered churches. They are illegal, and sometimes the government took action against them but often they turned a blind eye.

en.

Doris was in a huff as we left Gretchen outside the church and boarded the city bus to go home. After we sat down, I turned to her, and asked in Mandarin, "What was that all about?"

She spat out, "Gretchen was trying to find out information about my internal organs!"

"What on earth are you talking about?"

"She never asked my permission, so she stole the information. But I'm not involved in those Buddhist practices anymore. I'm a Christian now."

"Whoa, slow down, Doris. How did she steal information about your organs?" Black magic was going through my mind.

"From practicing Buddhism she has the power to know which of my organs are healthy and which aren't. I used to be able to do that, too, when I was a Buddhist, but I gave up that power to follow Jesus. I don't use Buddhist power anymore and I don't want anyone using it on me."

"But I still don't get it. Why would she want to know about your organs?"

"Well, if she had a diseased organ, say, a bad heart, and she found out that my heart is good, she'd exchange her heart for mine. I'd be left with her sick heart and she would take my healthy heart."

It really was black magic! It seemed like a cruel way to bring about a healing, though—striking someone else's heart with a disease so your heart would be healed.

Doris continued, "Or, if she found out I have a diseased organ, she might have offered to heal it for a fee. She actually did find out that my liver isn't healthy. But she didn't get very far with me because I put a stop to it. She knows I'm a Christian, so she shouldn't have done that to me! She's trying to pull me back into Buddhism."

What I learned from Doris about Buddhism amazed me, as I watched her first encounter Jesus and eventually struggle to become a Christian. The uniqueness of my own Christian faith also became clear to me as I saw it through Doris' eyes.

What made Jesus appealing to this devout Buddhist woman? Why did she eventually give up Buddhism to embrace Jesus when her faith had been so precious to her? Here is the story of how I met Doris, and how she came to place her faith and hope in Jesus.

§§§

Near our apartment, by the "outer ring road," the freeway that circled the city of Wuran, was a patch of grass, flowers, and trees. Not deep enough to be called a green belt, it sheltered the population a little from the heavy traffic circumventing the city. Every day I walked along the road just inside the patch. I tolerated the traffic noise and exhaust fumes because few people walked the road and it provided the verdant beauty I craved.

I was almost finished with my Mandarin language program by now, and I wanted to make friends with some Chinese people. While I walked, I prayed that the Lord would lead me to people who were seeking him, and whose hearts he had prepared to receive the gospel.

On one of my walks I noticed an older woman practicing tai chi alone on the berm. I was drawn to her and asked if she would teach me tai chi, so we arranged to exercise together several times a week. She didn't speak any English. As we practiced tai chi and took walks, I grew to love her.

Doris had taught Chinese literature in high school, and was now retired. Ten years earlier, she had converted to Buddhism, but her Buddhism was different than that of most Chinese I met. Most Buddhists I knew worshiped their ancestors and idols. They had no interest in nirvana or the traditional teachings of Buddhism. But Doris was an orthodox Buddhist; in fact, her grandma had been a bodhisattva—someone who had reached nirvana, but delayed entering it so she could stay on earth and help others reach it, too.

Most orthodox Buddhists I met wore placid, expressionless faces, like masks, because they were aspiring to nirvana. Nirvana is the state of nothingness, reached through having no desires. Doris showed some emotion, mostly frustration or exasperation, but she still looked detached, and rarely smiled.

She had zero interest in God. Whenever I brought up the Lord, she looked bored and talked about something else.

How could I interest her in God? I thought talking about miracles might pique her interest, so I told her about the time God had healed an infection in Adam's brain and saved his life.

She snorted, looked away, and changed the subject. She hadn't seen the miracle herself so she didn't believe it. Besides, she had seen Buddhist miracles, so a Christian miracle was nothing special.

One day, with awe in her voice, she shared the story of her grandmother's death with me. "I was there when my grandma died. There was a piece of wood on the threshold of the door and it just started to spin and spin, all by itself! Then a goat outside rose up to heaven! I was there; I saw it with my own eyes."

I have no idea how the goat rose to heaven, but I asked her, "What was the point, Doris? Why did these things happen?"

She looked at me like I was dense. "To show that my grandma was a good woman, Grace!"

Well, Christian miracles weren't about to impress her. I didn't think the Buddhist miracles she related were as great as Christian healings, though. A goat rising to heaven hadn't helped anybody.

I still didn't know how to interest her in the Lord. The only way I could think of was to talk about Buddhism. She loved talking about Buddhist philosophy and the wisdom it offers for interpersonal relationships. One day we were discussing the value of humility, and she made the statement that only when a person becomes humble is he honored by others.

I didn't think what she said was true because humble people usually aren't highly honored in society. I countered by making another point. "When a person becomes truly humble, he no longer cares if people give him a lot of honor."

She looked at me, startled. What I said went beyond her Buddhist wisdom.

"I learned that from living out what the Bible says," I added. She was impressed, and I was hopeful she would start to see value in the Bible.

In order to more effectively share the gospel with her, I needed to understand her Buddhist faith, so I asked her to explain the principles of what she believed. It seems there are five don'ts Buddhists should adhere to in order to reach nirvana—don't steal, commit adultery, lie, drink alcohol, or kill people or animals (which implies not eating meat). Abstaining from meat was the most difficult for Doris. She kept trying and trying to not eat meat.

Since good karma increases your chances of reaching nirvana, Doris did a lot of good deeds for others. But helping people for the purpose of increasing your own karma seemed pretty self-centered to me. It was hard for her to understand that, as a Christian, my motivation for helping others was love (Matthew 22:39), not accumulating good works for my own benefit.

One day I told Doris about my best friend who lives in New York and is disabled.

"I call her every week," I said.

"That's great!" Doris replied. "Helping a disabled person like that will give you better karma."

"No! You don't get it. I love her. I call her because I love her, not to increase karma."

§§§

One morning Doris introduced me to some of her orthodox Buddhist friends. They were practicing tai chi on the grassy courtyard near her apartment. Their faces were all placid, except for two of the women who had the delighted, nasty, furtive faces of gossips.

After tai chi, one of the placid faces, an 80-year-old man, talked and talked with me about Buddhism, and I told him about Jesus. It finally dawned on me that he was trying to convert me to Buddhism! He offered to lend me a Chinese book on Buddhism, *The Teachings of the Buddha,* which I accepted in my quest to understand their faith. It was simply a book of mental puzzles, like, "What is the sound of one hand clapping?" It was nonsense designed to help the reader realize that nirvana isn't reached through the intellect. In fact, the message was that if a person wants to enter nirvana, then he needs to park his brain.

As soon as I brought the book home and laid it on my desk, a demon attacked me! (This story is related in *Demonic Attack.*) It was horrible! I had suspected that the miraculous power wielded by Buddhists was from Satan, and that demonic attack convinced me even further.

Was I still willing to witness to orthodox Buddhists? It was endangering me spiritually. I loved Doris, so I decided I was willing to risk it, but I needed Jesus' protection.

I continued to try to interest Doris in God, but after two years, she still looked bored whenever I brought up the Lord. Finally, I got irritated at God, "When I asked you to introduce me to someone who was hungry for you, you moved me to get to know Doris, but she is not hungry for you. She doesn't even show the slightest interest in you. Why did you move me to get to know her?"

But the fact that Doris wasn't interested in the Lord didn't mean I wouldn't be her friend. My friendships are real. I don't pretend to be friends just to share the gospel.

I prayed fervently for Doris, that God would draw her to himself and that she would decide to follow Jesus (John 6:44; Joshua 24:15).

Two years after I met Doris, our oldest son was about to enter college in the U.S., so we returned to the States for a year to help him adjust.

When we moved back to Wuran, I called Doris so we could get together. "Grace, I'm very ill. I can't see you." She didn't tell me what her illness was, but she didn't expect to get better. Not only was I concerned for her health, I was crushed that we wouldn't be spending any more time together. Since I was the only Christian she knew, how could she ever come to believe in Jesus?

I prayed, "Lord, I need you to heal Doris. If you don't heal her, how can she become a Christian?" After I prayed, I knew she would be healed.

A few days later, Doris surprised me by calling and asking me to go for a walk. I danced for joy!

At the beginning of our walk, I told her, "Doris, I prayed to Jesus for your healing. Are you healed yet?"

"Yes, I'm healed!" She looked at me strangely as she studied my face. "I didn't know, Grace, that *you* had that power—the power to heal the body."

"No! It wasn't me—it was Jesus! I do not have that power. I can only *ask* Jesus to heal you, and it's up to him whether he heals or not."

It was becoming clear to me that Buddhists think they themselves are the source of the power they wield. That's in sharp contrast to Christian answers to prayer, where the power is God's and we don't control it (II Corinthians 4:7).

I could see the wheels turning in Doris' mind. After that, she seemed to respect Christianity, as if it might be on a par with Buddhism. She also began to suspect that I might know something about God. So a week later she asked me a question that I later learned had been plaguing her for over a decade. *"Grace, I want more than healing. Can God forgive my sins?"*

I was shocked! Where had this come from? We had never discussed sins or forgiveness since I had hardly even been able to bring up the subject of God.

"Doris, God can forgive your sins. But our sins are so bad we deserve to die." I had spoken more strongly than I felt comfortable with.

"Yes, they are that bad," she said. "And I do deserve to die because of them." She hung her head.

"But God loves us. He doesn't want us to have to die."

She looked up at me startled and confused. I had her full attention.

"It cost God everything to pay for our sins. He sent his son, Jesus, to become a man and to die in our place. We need to depend on Jesus having died for us to get rid of our sins."

She gasped. How could God be that good?

Usually I led into the gospel more gradually. But I think the Holy Spirit was prompting me, because later she told me, with a lot of pain written on her face, that during the Cultural Revolution she had betrayed her family to save herself. She knew what she had done was horrible, and she had come to the conclusion that a high price needed to be paid for her sin. If I hadn't explained our situation as so hopeless, and the price God had to pay as so high, I don't think she would have believed me.

Right after I told her about Jesus dying for her sins, she said, *"I have been begging God every day to forgive my sins."*

I stared at her. She *had* been seeking God. "Doris, when did you first start asking God to forgive your sins?"

She thought for a moment, calculating the time. *"Three months before I met you."*

So after she had been praying for three months, God sent me down that road to bump into her. He had moved my heart to ask her to teach me tai chi, all in answer to her prayers! I felt a sense of awe. Still, it had taken three years for her to trust me enough to tell me this, and it had taken the healing to give her hope that God might exist and that I had a connection to God.

The road we were walking on was almost deserted, but it wasn't private enough for Doris. She anxiously looked down the road, then over her shoulder to check the other direction to see if anyone had overheard us. She grabbed my arm and pulled me onto the green patch to make sure no one at all could hear us, then she leaned into me.

"Don't tell anyone that Jesus died for us. This will be our secret."

I couldn't believe my ears. She actually thought that no one but the two of us had ever heard about Jesus' death?

When we resumed our walk, she was silent for a while. Finally she spoke. "I've been doing a lot of good works, hoping that God would notice. Do you think it's because I did so many good works that God sent you to tell me that Jesus died for me?"

"Doris, I think God sent me to you because you were asking him to forgive you. He pays attention when we pray."

Doris thanked and thanked me for telling her how to be forgiven.

"Doris, what are friends for? You teach me tai chi and I teach you about God's forgiveness."

During the three years Doris had prayed for forgiveness, she didn't know who she was praying to. The best concept she had of God was of an impersonal force with no emotions, no personality, and no thoughts or plans.

As a Buddhist, she didn't expect to be forgiven. *Shan you shan bao, e you e bao* was one of her favorite Buddhist sayings. "Good will be rewarded with good, and evil will be rewarded with evil." Doris often told me that, according to Buddhism, there is a celestial scale of justice that metes out good and bad rewards with precision. No grace. No forgiveness.

The God of the Bible is so different than that—he's just, but he aches to show us mercy. Other than the cross, this is most evident in the Old Testament (Lamentations 3:22,23; Isaiah 30:18; Psalm 103:8-14; the whole book of Hosea; the whole book of Jonah …).

Doris told me she had become a Buddhist in order to find forgiveness, but Buddhism just heaped on more guilt with all its rules and condemnation. The better Buddhist she became, the more acutely aware she was that she was a sinner. The Lord was actually using Buddhism to lead her to Christ!

Doris had not become a Christian yet. This was the first time she had heard about Jesus and his sacrifice. She wasn't even sure that God existed.

She wanted forgiveness, but she still had a long journey ahead.

She showed more and more interest in the Lord, but she couldn't understand that God is a person, not an impersonal force. I came to realize from knowing her that someone can't become a Christian if they don't understand that God is a person. No matter how I tried to explain, she couldn't get it. Part of the problem was her Buddhist background, and part of the problem was the Chinese language. Chinese is a more concrete language than English. If you say that God is a person, you're actually saying he's human, but if you try to say "he's personal," it's hard to find a Chinese word to adequately communicate that.

Even though she wasn't ready yet, she was toying with the idea of becoming a Christian, but she was afraid she'd be persecuted if she did. Her family was famous (written up in the history books), so she had been persecuted a lot during the Cultural Revolution and she didn't want to go through that again.

I couldn't believe what Doris did next. She asked a policeman if it was illegal to become a Christian. This was their conversation:

Doris: "I have an American friend who told me about Jesus. Is it legal for me to become a Christian?"

The policeman: "What? No! And it's not legal for her to tell you about Jesus, either!"

After he left, Doris called me in a panic. "Grace, I have to see you right away. Don't come here—it's not safe. I'll meet you at the intersection that leads to the outer ring road."

When we met up, Doris looked scared as she told me about her discussion with the policeman. "Grace, you must not tell anyone about Jesus—it's dangerous for you. Keep telling me about Jesus, though. It's safe to tell me because I won't report you."

I was flabbergasted. Really? She was safe? I know she hadn't meant any harm, but she essentially had just reported me to the police!

When I arrived home, I told Justin, "You're not going to believe what happened. Doris told the police about me." Then I told him the rest of the story.

Justin looked sad. "Grace, I know how much Doris means to you, but you can't meet with her anymore. All of our other ministries could get blown out of the water."

If I continued to meet with Doris, it would be easy for the police to identify her American friend. Justin and I taught the Bible to house church leaders. If the police investigated us, they might discover the house church leaders and the teaching sessions, and there were many more precious Chinese people we might also lead the authorities to. I agreed with him, but the decision made me sad.

I not only stopped contacting Doris, but in case the police had discovered our relationship and we were under surveillance, we temporarily withdrew from some ministries and relocated others. We also kept watching our backs to see if we were being followed.

After nine months of no contact, the Spirit gave me an insatiable desire to see Doris. I talked with Justin, "Dangerous or not, I need to get together with Doris." Justin didn't object.

I went to her home to visit her. After a few minutes, she asked me something she had been pondering for some time. She longed for her family—they were estranged from her because of her betrayal. They had moved to the U.S., and Doris didn't have any of their contact information. Her eyes focused on something in the distance as she asked me, "If I do a lot of good works, do you think God will help me contact my family again?"

Suddenly I felt rage deep inside of me. It felt like a tube of wrath filling the center of my body. I was really confused because I didn't think there was anything to be angry about. I'm not naturally an angry person so to suddenly feel so much anger for no reason scared me. But it didn't feel like I was the one who was angry. Was this the Holy Spirit? Was he angry at what she said?

I knew I was supposed to open my mouth and speak. The idea frightened me, but I did open my mouth, and I yelled at her. I didn't know what I was saying until the words reached my ears. "You use people, Doris! And you think God is just like you—that he uses people, too. But God is not like you. He doesn't use people."

How could I have yelled at my friend like that? I was really shaken. I had never known Doris to use people. What she hated most was people using each other, and here I had accused her of doing just that.

Then it dawned on me. She thought that God wanted to get good works from her before he would be kind to her and give her family back to her, like a barter system.

She hung her head and her whole body slumped. When she finally lifted her head, she said quietly, "Yes, I do use people. *I thought God would be that way because Buddhism is like that. Now I know that believing in Jesus and Buddhism are completely different.*"

Then she pleaded with me, "If I become a Christian, do I really need to go to church? There will definitely be spies in the church, so it's dangerous to attend church." This was the first time she had ever talked directly with me about wanting to become a Christian. She was counting the cost.

We met together the next few days to work out solutions to the problem of going to church safely. Finally she made her decision. "If I follow Buddhism, I don't have to be with other Buddhists, so the government won't find out. But if I become a Christian, I have to have fellowship with other Christians and the government will find out. I will not become a Christian; I will remain a Buddhist."

My heart sank. She had come so close. She didn't look happy rejecting God and the forgiveness she was aching for.

Over the next year (the fourth year) I saw signs of Doris moving toward God. On her own she bought a Bible and started reading it. I could tell she was starting to believe in God. Finally, a year after I had exploded in anger at her, I thought the time had come to show her the *Jesus* film.

She came over to my apartment. I pulled two of our easy chairs close to the TV so we could see clearly.

Often, when Chinese people first hear about Jesus' healings, they think they're just myths. To help Doris realize that all the healings she would see in the film were true, I told her that it was just like when I prayed for her and she was healed.

Doris is a very talkative person, but she was mesmerized by the film and didn't say a word until partway through she commented in a voice filled with awe, "*I see now that Jesus offers forgiveness. Buddhism offers no forgiveness. That's a big difference.*"

Through seeing the person of Jesus Christ in the film, she realized that God is personal. Everything I had struggled in vain to explain was revealed to her through Jesus' life.

At the end of the film, I looked over at her. She was grinning at me, like she had a huge secret to tell. "I prayed the prayer. Now I'm a daughter of God, just like the film said. And I can feel that all the sins are gone. They're really gone—I'm finally free!"

After four years of sharing Christ with her, she had finally become a Christian. I had more joy than I could handle!

After Doris left, I went out for a walk, trying to process everything that had just happened. I bumped into Justin on the street as he was returning home from work, and we walked, talked and laughed together, so happy that Doris had come to know Jesus.

She had carried that load of sins for 30 years. After she came to believe, every time she saw me, her whole face broke into a smile. She didn't say, "Hello. How are you?" Her new greeting to me was, "I was an awful sinner. The guilt was too hard to bear. But Jesus died for me, and now the heavy burden of sin is gone!" I thought her greeting was pretty funny, but it brought home to me that Jesus was the best thing that ever happened to her.

At first she wanted to study the Bible with me in a unique way, a way that she considered safe. We agreed to read the same passage at our homes by ourselves. Then we took walks and discussed the passage from memory. That way no one would know we were studying the Bible.

Then she wanted more. I went to her home three times a week to study the Bible with her. She avidly took notes and asked questions. For me it was grueling though. She misunderstood most of the passages because she looked at them from a Buddhist perspective. I explained and explained the Scripture, but as much as she wanted to grasp it, she understood almost nothing.

But every now and then, when she understood a verse, her face lit up. When we read John 3:16, she gasped. "God *loves* us? He loves us! Wow!" She had never thought that God would love her. She had only hoped for forgiveness. She got so much more from believing in Jesus than she had been searching for.

We looked at Ephesians 2:1, which says, "you were dead in your transgressions and sins." "Yes," she grimaced, "that's exactly what it's like—it feels like you're dead when you have sin." When she read Romans 8:1, "there is now no condemnation for those who are in Christ Jesus," she looked like she wanted to cry, hearing that she was no longer condemned. When we looked at I Peter 2:24, which says, "He himself bore our sins in his body on the cross," she was filled with praise that Jesus had been willing to die for her sins. She understood the basics, but very little else.

Before Doris became a Christian, she often woke up at night in a sweat because of the sins she had committed. She told me, *"I will never ever go back to Buddhism, because if I did, who would forgive my sins?"*

Our studying together at her home was actually dangerous. Her husband was retired from a high-level government position. Every Wednesday he attended a meeting where he was supposed to report any *antirevolutionary activities*, like us studying the Bible together. He was at home when we were studying and he knew what we were doing, but he never reported us.

Doris was afraid of going to church, but I kept encouraging her to attend. "Grace, I can't go to a house church because it's illegal." "I can't go to the government church because then the government will know." Around and around we went.

Spring became summer, and the need to get her into fellowship was becoming urgent. I was her only fellowship, but we were leaving soon to go back to the States for half a year to help our youngest son adjust to college.

"O.K., Grace, I'll go to the government church if the weather's not too hot." But she might as well have said "No, I won't go." Normally Wuran was very hot and humid in the summer, and that summer was exceptionally hot.

It was in the mid to upper 90s and the humidity was close to 100 percent. The pollution made it even more muggy.

I wasn't willing to take no for an answer. "Doris, let's pray that it will cool down Sunday so you can go to church." Every week we prayed and every Sunday the temperature and humidity dropped—the temperature to about 72 degrees! She and I went to the government church together. That summer everyone was talking about how strange the weather was; they had never seen anything like it. What they didn't know was that it was in answer to our prayers!

After this happened a few times, we were walking on the sidewalk near my home one day when she paused, deep in thought, and turned to me, "*I don't know whether this is your power or God's that's making the temperature drop each Sunday.*" I couldn't believe she was saying that. Even as a Christian, she still thought it might be *my* power? It made me sad. I again told her that I had no power—it was all God's power. In so many ways she had trouble extricating herself from her Buddhist thinking.

I began to realize she thought I was a Christian version of a bodhisattva. Not only do bodhisattvas help others reach enlightenment, they also have special powers. I had helped her find Jesus and now she was seeing a display of supernatural power.

The first time she went to the government church, she was amazed that there were so many Chinese Christians. She had thought she was one of the few Christians in China.

But after attending only once, she resolutely told me, "I won't go to church again. I'm ashamed to be there because I'm such a bad sinner. I look around at all those people in church and they are such good people. I don't belong there."

"Doris, all the people in church are bad sinners."

"Really? All those people in church are sinners? Do they all *know* they're sinners?"

"Anyone in church who is a true Christian knows he's a sinner. You can't be a Christian if you don't know you're a sinner."

She thought this over for a few minutes and then commented, "*When a really bad person tries to become a Buddhist, the Buddhists reject him because he isn't good enough. So really bad people have to become Christians!*"

The Lord kept transforming her life. One day, sitting in church before the service, she prayed, "Lord, help me forgive my enemies." When she looked up, there was an enemy sitting in a pew in front of her, a woman who had greatly harmed her in a housing dispute 24 years earlier. Doris immediately went over to the woman and told her that she forgave her. In the succeeding weeks and months, Doris helped her former enemy in any way she could. Doris had become a forgiving person because the Lord had forgiven her. She wasn't just obeying rules or trying to increase her karma. She was responding from the heart in Christian love.

The more she came to know the Lord, the more courageous she became in sharing her faith. All her Buddhist friends told her that her face was so full of peace now and they couldn't understand why. She told them it was because of Jesus.

The former mayor of our city was one of her friends, and one evening Doris was invited to a party at his home. She stood up and announced to all the guests that she had become a Christian. This was a woman who had been afraid to go to church because she didn't want the government to find out that she believed in Jesus. There she was, announcing to the most powerful people in the government of our city that she was a Christian. Surprisingly, the former mayor thought that was great news. He said that whenever he has speaking engagements in the U.S. he goes to church.

Doris talked to her husband about the Lord. He decided that he wanted to become a Christian, too, but was afraid to because he was on a committee that advised the central government on policy. So when Doris returned home from church each Sunday, he asked her to tell him the whole sermon and then he wanted them to pray the congregational prayer together from the bulletin.

Doris was baptized in the government church. The government church asks many questions of the baptismal candidate prior to baptism in order to ferret out who led the person to Christ as well as any unregistered, that is, illegal, Christian fellowships they were attending. When Doris saw me after she filled out the application, she looked pleased with herself. "Don't worry, Grace, I lied on the baptismal application. I didn't tell them that you led me to Christ. Instead I put down the name of my cousin who lives in another city, and I said she led me to Christ. She's not a Christian, so she's safe."

I was not so pleased. I appreciated that she was trying to protect me, but to lie on your baptismal application! It made me sad that Chinese Christians have to face these moral dilemmas. In order to be baptized, she was required to betray me. She refused to betray me, so the only option she thought she had was to lie.

But there are many true Christians in the government church and its local leadership. When Doris went for her baptismal interview, it was a Christian who interviewed her. When the interviewer asked Doris if she attended an unregistered fellowship, the interviewer was supposed to report to the government any illegal fellowships she discovered. But instead, when Doris said that she didn't, the interviewer leaned forward and whispered conspiratorially, "I can recommend a real good one to you!"

I have often thought about what Christianity looked like to Doris. She had looked for forgiveness in Buddhism, but only found rules and condemnation. Jesus was the one who offered her forgiveness and the way to God, not Buddhism.

After I explained Jesus' sacrifice to a couple of other Buddhist friends in China, I asked them, "Since everyone sins and since anyone who comes to God can't have any sin, how on earth does a Buddhist come to God?" They answered, "The only way would be through Jesus!" They also decided to come to God through Jesus.

In America, many have the attitude, "You can believe whatever. It doesn't matter. All roads lead to God." Doris would disagree. She had tried the Buddhist road. It didn't work. When you see Christianity through Doris' eyes, you realize how unique and awesome Christianity is.

DEMONIC ATTACK

1990, 2001-2006, 2013

I've heard some Christians speak flippantly about demons. It's obvious to me they've never encountered one.

One time when we were looking for housing, after we entered the first rental house, the owner smiled at us and pointed to the room on the left. It was a large, almost empty room with red foam mats covering the floor. Against the opposite wall was a wooden table with pictures of gods, in red and gold, all facing the room. Her face full of pride, the owner beamed, "This is our temple."

Oh no, if we rented this house, we would also be renting the temple and the gods!

In every room of the house, a tape recorder intoned a four-syllable Buddhist chant, repeated over and over and over in monotone. But the chant in each room was different, resulting in an irritating cacophony throughout the house. From my experience living in Asia, I assumed demons inhabited that house, and we didn't want to rent a house with demons.

A few days later we were talking with Tim, an American from our international fellowship who had lived in China for many years. Tim loved to talk about methods of expelling demons from an area. Buddhists use mere physical solutions to try to solve serious spiritual problems, such as shooting off firecrackers to scare demons away. Tim's methods also seemed simplistic, almost Buddhist, to me. He advocated that we pour salt into the rivers to rid the city of demons.

Tim asked me about our apartment search. I told him about the first rental we looked at and our decision not to rent it because the house was probably inhabited by demons. Tim looked excited and grinned at me, "If there

154

are demons living in that house, that is no problem at all. Go ahead and rent it. We're stronger than demons because of God!" Was he thinking that demons can never hurt us? Or did he want a showdown? And with our family in the crossfire!

I was horrified. I spoke firmly, "We will not rent that house. We lived in an apartment in Hong Kong that had a demon. When Adam was five years old, one day I saw him sitting on our bed playing and talking with someone I couldn't see. I asked him who he was playing with.

"You know what he told me? He said he was playing with a demon! I took him out of that room and into the kitchen to get him away from the demon. When we entered the kitchen, he looked at the corner of the ceiling and said, 'Hi, Nigel.' When I told him that Nigel wasn't there, he pointed at the ceiling and said, 'Yes, he is.' Adam was dead serious. The demon was impersonating our older son. You have no idea how hard it can be to get rid of a demon. I will not put our family through that again."

What I didn't tell him was this story:

Before my Buddhist friend Doris became a Christian, she introduced me to her orthodox Buddhist friends. One 80-year-old man wanted to convert me to Buddhism, so he lent me a book called *The Teachings of the Buddha*.

As soon as I arrived home with the book, my mind came under severe attack. Doubts about the existence of God crowded my thinking. It felt like these thoughts were forced into my brain.

I had already answered the questions about God's existence when I was in college and in the process of coming to faith. I believe real doubts need to be addressed and answered, but these doubts weren't real questions for me anymore.

All day, no matter whether I was washing dishes, spending time with the Lord, or talking with a friend, doubts pressed in on my mind. Every time I answered one doubt, a completely different reason to question God's existence attacked me. I'd never experienced anything like this, and I was scared—it felt like someone had hijacked my mind. This went on for a whole week. Nothing is more important to me than God, and it felt like I was losing my very soul.

Finally, when Justin and I were taking a walk, I told him about the doubts and that I didn't know what was happening.

"Grace, do the doubts keep changing or is there only one doubt?"

"They keep changing. Every time I answer a question about God's existence, immediately there's another question."

"That's got to be a demon." I had never heard Justin talk like this before.

"I thought I was losing my faith! If it's a demon, then we need to fight the

155

demon."

I returned the Buddhist book, but the attack didn't stop.

A week after the attack started, I confided in a Christian friend and we enlisted her help. After fasting and praying, I was released from the demon's grip. I knew the exact moment the demon left. The doubts stopped and I felt free.

But a week later, the demon returned, this time more subtly. At first I didn't realize it was him again. He wasn't as aggressive and belligerent. Very gentle, prodding thoughts troubled me, always different angles, but the same theme: God could not exist!

We prayed and fasted again, to no avail. That demon plagued me for five years! During those years I endlessly answered questions about God's existence. I felt like a hypocrite being a missionary with all these doubts.

After five years, I cried out to God in anguish, "Show me what to do. Show me how to get free." He did. I stopped countering all the doubts that I already knew the answer to. Instead, standing in our living room, I forcefully shouted my affirmation of faith, "I believe in God! That is where I stand. I do not believe all these doubts!" The demon left at that moment, and he has never returned.

That was a horrible experience for me. I would not be willing to risk a demonic attack except in order to free someone from Satan's grasp, like I did with Doris.

I'm sure if I had understood how to deal with demons, the attack would have been short-lived. But I wouldn't have thought a demon could attack a Christian's mind like this if I hadn't experienced it. Some people say you have to be holding onto sin or have been involved in demonic practices before you can be attacked by a demon. That wasn't my experience. I was attacked because I was serving the Lord—sharing the gospel with people who were using Satan's power.

SARS
(Severe Acute Respiratory Syndrome)

2003, Wuran

"Adam, you mustn't tell anyone, even your friends at school, that Dad has a fever!"

"Why, Mom?"

"Because the government is rounding up anyone who has a fever and putting them in SARS wards in the hospital to make sure SARS doesn't spread. Your dad doesn't have SARS—the symptoms are wrong—but your school may be required to report him to the government if they find out he has a fever. If they put Dad in a ward with everyone else who has SARS, he'll likely get it."

"O.K. I'll be careful. My lips are sealed!" Adam (18) promised.

How do you protect yourself when the government is on a witch hunt to eradicate a disease?

SARS was an acute respiratory disease that was airborne; it could even travel through ventilation ducts to infect adjacent apartments, as it did in Hong Kong. The mortality rate was high—15-20 percent.[1]

Most Westerners don't realize how little Chinese valued human life, or how callous the Chinese government was in its willingness to sacrifice the lives of individuals to protect the country's fragile economic development and the government's power and image.

Early on, our Chinese neighbors didn't know the SARS epidemic was rampant in China because the government censored the news about SARS.

---

1. CNN.com/HEALTH, May 8, 2003, Posted: 11:54 p.m. EDT, and *The Guardian*, May 7, 2009, Posted: 10:29 EDT.

Chinese New Year was approaching and the population would normally spend a lot of money on the celebration and gifts. They would travel all over China to visit their families. If the people knew they might contract SARS, they would have stayed home and China would have lost the economic boost that Chinese New Year always brought to the economy. So, instead, infected holiday travelers further spread SARS all over China.

Furthermore, if the populace knew that SARS was spreading uncontrollably through China, then everyone would know the Chinese government was incapable of controlling SARS and protecting the populace. The government would then lose face. (The Chinese government so badly wanted the people to think they controlled and took care of every aspect of their lives, that once, four years earlier, a Chinese newspaper article had said readers should be grateful to the government for sending them rain during a drought!)

Because Justin had bought encryption for our computers, we had access to international news, so we were aware of the epidemic and knew there were many victims in our city. We urged our Chinese friends to prepare, but they didn't believe us. "Grace, of course the international news says bad things about China—your government feeds lies and propaganda about us to the news all the time."

We had no car, so I biked to the grocery store many times to stock up on supplies. Disposable gloves, 10 bottles of bleach, 20 pounds of rice, 20 pounds of flour, two large bottles of oil, meat for the freezer …

If SARS became too serious, the best prevention was isolation in our apartment; that is, if it didn't come through the pipes from the neighboring apartments.

When the government could no longer deny that SARS was infecting China, they became vigilant in their efforts to stomp it out. All public places, including the stairwell of our apartment building, were daily disinfected.

They put up a chart in our building with everyone's apartment number on it and a place for each of us to write our body temperature every day, so they could forcibly take us to a SARS ward and confine us there if we had a fever. An isolation ward in a Chinese hospital was not like an isolation ward in America. In China it was a place to keep all the SARS patients together, isolated from others, to prevent it from spreading. If you didn't have SARS when you entered the SARS ward, you probably would quickly contract it. My Chinese friends told me how scared they were that they would be taken to a SARS ward.

When I was shopping or in crowds I furtively studied everyone around to see if they looked ill or coughed, or even if their bodies seemed exceptionally hot.

One day when I was shopping, a woman who brushed against me felt like she was burning up with a fever. I rushed home, stripped off my clothes, and shouted to Justin, "Stay away from me! There was a woman who had a high fever. She might have SARS." I threw my clothes in the washer with bleach and jumped in the shower. I scrubbed so hard I almost rubbed myself raw.

We heard rumors that the whole country of China might be quarantined—no flights in or out. Some of our American friends were fleeing, booking flights out while they still could.

One afternoon, Justin, Adam, and I huddled close in the living room to discuss what we should do. We were planning to return to the States anyway in four months to get Adam settled in college. Should we flee right away to save our lives?

Adam spoke first. "I don't want to leave. My Chinese friend, Abel, is on the verge of coming to trust in the Lord. If I leave, I don't think that'll happen. I need more time with him."

Justin took his turn. "I'm teaching eschatology to underground church leaders. But, frankly, teaching eschatology isn't worth dying for."

Then I spoke. "I'm teaching the Bible and witnessing to some friends, but the person I'm most concerned about is Doris. She just became a Christian, but she hasn't gotten into fellowship yet. She's struggling and her faith is weak. I'm afraid if I leave now, she won't continue with the Lord."

Justin said, "We might die if we don't leave. We don't know how bad this epidemic will get. Who thinks we should stay for the sake of Abel and Doris?"

All hands shot up. It's a strange thing to decide as a family what you're willing to die for.

Abel became a Christian, Doris is still walking with the Lord, and none of us came down with SARS.

ROLLER COASTER

2007-2008, All over China, and Seattle

That white guy, he's stalking me! A tall, 60-ish blond guy across the street was walking fast. Staring and smiling at me. Now he's crossing the street to my side!

I looked around for Justin, but he was way ahead, talking excitedly to a potential boss, for a job I now knew Justin wouldn't be able to take. I had been lagging behind, and now I was on my own in this strange city of Zao Gao.

Stalker came alongside me. "So, what are you doing in Zao Gao City?"

How did he know I was a stranger here? Seven million people lived in Zao Gao. Were there so few white faces he could pick out a new one, or had he noticed I was crying?

"My husband," I pointed, "is just ahead of us." I didn't want him trying anything.

Then, without thinking, I poured out our dilemma to Stalker. "We've lived in China for 20 years, but we have to leave." I brushed a tear away, hoping he wouldn't notice. "We really want to stay. We live in Wuran, but the pollution has gotten so bad there I keep getting sick. Someone told us Zao Gao City had clean air, so we flew here to find an English teaching job. But after my husband was offered a job, I realized that the exhaust fumes in Zao Gao are so bad I don't feel well here, either. Since we can't find an English teaching job in a city with clean air, tomorrow we'll fly to Wuran, pack up our stuff, and move back to the U.S. Our time in China is over." I wiped another tear that had escaped.

Stalker said, "Take the five-hour bus to Re Dai. It has clean air and Re Dai University is looking for an English teacher."

I stared at this guy. Who was he? "What is Re Dai? And how do you know this?"

"It's a small town south of here. I'm a headhunter and I place English teachers in China."

Now I was even more shocked. How had this man crossed my path just when we needed him?

"I'm going to tell my husband." I caught up to Justin and first told him that the air of Zao Gao was too polluted, then I told him what Stalker said.

We switched from following the potential employer to following Stalker to his second-floor office, a few blocks away.

Only in the safety of his office was Stalker willing to tell us he was a Christian and his goal was to place *Christians* in English teaching jobs in China. I didn't ask how he knew I was a Christian when he first spotted me.

After discussing the job opportunity, Stalker said, "I know an Australian living in Re Dai who could help you."

He dialed, spoke briefly on the phone, then handed it to Justin.

On the other end Justin heard, "Hello, I'm Rex Balter."

"Rex Balter? I can't believe this! I'm Justin Jacob. We knew each other many years ago in Wuran."

"Justin Jacob? I remember you! Of course, I'll be happy to help. Come along and stay at our home, as long as you need to. I'll introduce you to the head of the English Department at the university so he can interview you. If you want me to introduce you to anyone else, I'll do that, too."

I looked at Justin with a knowing smile. God was leading us.

The next day we hopped onto the 30-seat bus to Re Dai.

The bus wound through verdant fields. Dust breezed in through the windows, covering everything. Occasionally a faint wisp of smoke or exhaust tickled my nose.

We entered lush, tree-covered mountains on a two-lane road that zigzagged in sharp turns around valleys. The driver sped into a hair-pin turn, barely slowing down; and then, with horn blaring, he swerved into the oncoming lane on a curve to pass a long line of cars! I leaned forward, my heart pounding, expecting a head-on collision any moment. After he pulled back into our lane, I sighed in relief and loosened my grip on the handle of the seat in front of me.

Then I looked at the outside edge of the oncoming lane. There were no guardrails between us and the 40-foot drop at the edge of the road! In my fear of colliding with another car, I hadn't noticed that danger. Only later did I find out that buses do tumble off the edge, and on one trip, I even watched as a crane hoisted a bus up from the base of the cliff!

The trip became more peaceful as the land flattened out. We traveled next to watery fields of freshly transplanted rice seedlings, straight rows of corn stalks and the sunshine yellow expanse of rapeseed flowers. Towns appeared—tiny cement houses crowded next to each other with barely an alley between. Each town was a hub in the center of many small farms, like spokes in a wheel.

The road opened up into a wide avenue. Short palm trees and a few flowers for ground cover grew in the center of the road. The closer we approached Re Dai, the prettier the center meridian.

Re Dai was the most beautiful city I had ever seen in China. Large palms and exotic tropical plants and flowers lined wide avenues. The streets were clean of garbage and the buildings white and new. The sky was blue. Very few cities in China have blue sky.

Even though the air looked clean, we wanted to live there for a few months so I could test it. On our first full day there, Justin interviewed for a two-month summer English teaching job at Re Dai University. At the end of the interview the administrator made it clear that he was going to offer Justin the job. The university would inform him in three days.

Rex introduced us to all the foreigners and took us to a house church meeting where I made a few friends. Then Rex asked me to lead a college student to the Lord. "You speak Mandarin, and I want to make sure she understands the gospel." It was easy bringing her to Christ—Rex had already done the work. I was thrilled with the Chinese relationships and opportunities in Re Dai. This was our place.

We hadn't told Rex what job Justin had applied for, and on the morning of our fourth day there, Rex announced, "The university just asked me to teach a two-month summer English course. It's a volunteer position. It's a great opportunity to get to know even more students and share Christ, so I took the job."

Justin and I looked at each other in shock. That was the job Justin had applied for! Justin had told the university they would have to pay him a salary for teaching, so instead they asked Rex to teach for free.

We wouldn't be moving to Re Dai after all.

Justin and I went for a walk to clear our heads. Hadn't it been obvious God was leading us here? What was all that about the Lord sending Stalker and our knowing Rex?

"Justin, we have 24 more hours before we have to leave here for Zao Gao City so we can catch our plane back to Wuran. Remember that American guy we met here a couple of days ago who is living in Wan Zi, just three hours away? He told us he'd introduce us around Wan Zi if we visited. We could take a bus there, spend the night and be back in time to catch the bus to Zao Gao City. Maybe the Lord has a job for us there. It's that or give up now and return to America."

We rode the 20-seat bus to Wan Zi. The seats were sunken springs covered by faded cloth.

Gray limestone cliffs edged the summits of the mountains on the right side of the bus. At the lower elevations, the mountains were covered with terraced rice fields, curving to fit the slopes' contours, as if an artist had created the scene.

Vegetable gardens came right up to the road, and in this spring beauty, the first few leaves of the crops poked up through the brick-red earth.

Cinnamon-brown clay huts with curved, slate-gray, ceramic tile roofs lined the road as we entered the small towns.

The colors in the towns were brilliant. From the bus windows, we could see the women decked in the outfits of their minority groups—strawberry-red skirts bordered in black and blueberry, with sashes of blue and green falling down the front; navy and powder-blue skirts with rose-colored sashes; pleated skirts of chartreuse with baby-blue. Below the skirts, their legs were wound round and round with fabric of sky-blue and cloud-white.

And the tiaras! Red, blue, orange, some reaching a foot above their heads. Many of the women had fastened huge bundles of burlap or sailcloth to their backs. Some carried woven baskets on their backs, full of grain or vegetables.

The men wore duller colors—brown and black. In baggy pants, suit coats and Mao caps, they led hazelnut-brown, bloated-looking water buffalo through the streets by ropes tied to rings in their noses. The buffaloes' large, two-hooved feet grazed the ground in a slow, lazy amble.

Motorcycles, some with covered flatbeds attached, zipped between the cars and small trucks.

The smell of fertilizer, cattle, and diesel wafted in through the windows of the bus as I stared in wonder at the sights before me.

The bus pulled in to Wan Zi, a small compact town set in a valley with tree-covered hills encircling it. The air was clean.

The American we met in Re Dai had referred us to a guest house owned by a British couple. As we sat, waiting, on one of the peach-colored couches in the large community room of the guest house, a serious, thin, blond woman entered—the British wife, Lucy. Without introduction, she stared intently at us. "God told me you are to work for us."

Amazing! God hadn't told us, but it was the answer to our prayers!

"Justin, you will be our guest house manager. Grace, I want you to relieve me. I'm so overworked. And God told me we're to open a bakery, too, so we'll soon have a lot more work."

Why didn't we pick up what was going on? Probably because we were desperate to stay in China.

We discussed with them all the details of Justin's job. We planned to stay in Wuran a few more months until Justin's current job contract was finished. Then we would move back to the States for a year of visiting our supporting churches while the work permit and visa were applied for.

After eating dinner with all the foreigners in Wan Zi, we left the next morning on the bus back to Re Dai, for the return trip to Wuran. The Lord had answered our prayers. We would be able to live in China.

A few months later, while we were in the States, Lucy and her husband applied for a work permit for Justin as the first step in applying for a work visa, but it was denied. They changed the job title and tried again. Denied.

For years I had been excessively tired. While in the States that year I was becoming weaker and weaker, and I struggled just to function in my daily activities. We didn't know what was wrong, and we were concerned about how well I would function when we returned to China.

When we had been in the States 10 months, Lucy and her husband were temporarily visiting Britain, so we called them on our speaker phone to make further arrangements. Lucy, in an accusing voice, targeted me. "I want to know what Grace is going to do. We've only talked about Justin's job. I'm exhausted and I want Grace to relieve me. And we have even more work coming since God told me to open a bakery."

But they weren't even hiring me; Justin was the only one they were hiring. I guess she thought I was trying to wiggle out of a job I hadn't even applied for. I wanted to spend my time doing the ministry the Lord gifted me to do. I didn't mind helping her, but she wouldn't be my boss.

I sagged hearing her implied accusation, trying to figure out how I could ever please her when I found it hard to function.

I knew then that we couldn't work for Lucy and her husband. She had no boundaries, and I suspected she was using "God told me ..." to control others. I hand signaled to Justin that the arrangement wasn't going to work. Justin nodded. He spoke to the British couple, "We've decided we won't be working for you."

Lucy blew up. "We only started this process because we know it's God's will. If you weren't convinced it was God's will, why did you apply for this job? And if it is God's will, you can't give up! We will keep applying for the work permit. You can't quit!"

Justin again spoke firmly, "We will not be working for you. Do not apply for the work permit anymore. Goodbye."

Well, here it was May, almost the end of our year of home assignment and we had nothing again. What was God doing?

Justin called Stalker in China and asked if there were any jobs at the university in Wan Zi. Stalker rode his motorcycle seven hours to Wan Zi, and wined and dined the president of Wan Zi University at our expense. The president offered Justin an English teaching job, sight unseen.

The university sent the paperwork, but when we looked at the application, the year was printed wrong—it said 2009. We contacted the university, but they told us, "The application is correct. We're hiring you a year from now."

We didn't need a job a year from now, we needed a job now. The only thing stable in our lives was that we were being jerked around!

Another international call to Stalker. "Justin and Grace, I have *just* gotten word from Re Dai University that the American who had signed a contract to become their International Student Coordinator *just* informed them that he can't take the job. They're desperately looking for someone to fill the position this fall. This is an administrative job—it's a good job, a lot better than the English teaching jobs."

Since Justin had already interviewed at Re Dai University they hired him immediately. But we had a problem—we had to pass the physicals to be granted the visa. I didn't know if I could pass the physical, or what illness I had.

§§§

I had continued to become weaker. We love hiking, but when we hiked in the Cascade Mountains that year in the States, after only 10 steps, my heart raced at 140 beats per minute and I gasped for breath, sucking in air as hard as I could—I couldn't get enough oxygen. It took 10 minutes of rest before I could walk another 10 paces.

Finally I told Justin, "Hiking is no fun for me anymore. I want to take one last hike to say goodbye to the Cascades." I was heartbroken. To truly experience the alpine lakes and flowers, and the magnificent vistas in the Cascades near Seattle, we had to hike because there were no roads leading to most of the sites. I would never again see that breathtaking grandeur.

I chose Snow Lake for my last hike. Snow Lake is a high-altitude lake tucked near the summit of a mountain with snow hugging one shore, kissing the lake, even in mid-summer. I slogged and gasped for breath for three and a half long hours before we reached the top. In tears I said goodbye to this panorama of beauty and joy in my life.

I was convinced my heart was to blame. When we took the physicals for the visa, I didn't want the doctor to find my heart problem so we could return to China. We were sure God was sending us back to China.

When my physical was over, while I was still lying on the EKG couch, the doctor leaned over me. "You are in great condition, except for one thing—your heart!"

I cringed.

"You really need to see a cardiologist."

"What's wrong with my heart?"

"It's beating too slow. It's in the 40s."

That's all he found? That was nothing. "Can I still go to China?"

"You can. But I think you should see a cardiologist."

I was not going to see a cardiologist. It would take a month or more to get an appointment, and then she would run so many tests it would be months before we could return to China. The job in Re Dai started in a few weeks, and Justin would lose the job if we delayed.

But Justin reasoned with me. "Grace, there aren't going to be any good cardiologists where we're going in China." I relented.

When I called the cardiologist's office, I got an appointment right away, and the cardiologist expedited the tests so within a week all the results were in.

The cardiologist looked at me kindly. "Grace, you need to see a pulmonologist."

"Doctor, I am not going to see a pulmonologist. I can't. We're leaving for China in a couple of weeks."

"Grace, you really do need to see a pulmonologist."

"Would you see a pulmonologist if you were me and you were leaving for China?"

"Yes." I guess I should have known she'd say that.

"O.K., I'm willing to see a pulmonologist if you can get me in right away. Otherwise, I'm going to China."

The pulmonologist came in on her week off to see me, so the very next day my lungs were tested!

"Your lung capacity is 130 percent larger than normal."

"That's great, right?"

"Only if you're an Olympian. You've lacked oxygen for many years, if not decades; you've been breathing so hard trying to get oxygen, your lungs expanded."

And according to the tests, I was only getting 79 percent of the oxygen I needed, even with 130 percent lung capacity!

My diagnosis was IPH—idiopathic pulmonary hypertension. The blood vessels in and around my lungs had become narrow, leading to high blood pressure between my heart and lungs, even though the rest of my body had low blood pressure. My lungs couldn't absorb enough oxygen from the decreased blood passing through them, and my heart had to work harder to pump blood through the narrow blood vessels. *Idiopathic* meant they didn't know the cause. Everything made sense now—the oxygen deprivation, the fatigue, the arrhythmia.

I had felt so poorly that year that I had increased my exercise, thinking that would solve the problem. Instead, the exercise had accelerated the disease because it further increased the high blood pressure between my heart and lungs. It was a rare disease—only two to three people in a million come down with it. At that time it was incurable. And fatal.

I had trouble wrapping my mind around the fact that my life would soon be over. How much time did I have?

I yearned to see the Lord, but what a horrible way to die! I would slowly, very slowly, suffocate to death. Finally, in the Lord's mercy, my heart would give out and put an end to my suffering.

After my diagnosis, every night I kept waking from sobbing in my dreams.

The pulmonologist called and I told her, "I can't even do housework now without huffing and puffing."

"You're getting worse rapidly." She didn't have the best bedside manner.

Wednesday, 9 a.m. The visa the Lord had almost miraculously provided arrived in the mail.

Wednesday, 10 a.m. Appointment with the pulmonologist. "Doctor, can I go to China? We just got our visa today."

"No, you can't go."

What was the Lord doing? It made no sense.

Wednesday afternoon. We wrote a prayer letter asking our friends, supporters, and churches to pray for my healing. Many wrote back that their families, prayer meeting groups, and whole churches were praying for me. Thousands praying for me? Tens of thousands?

Friday morning. I went to my water aerobics class. I hadn't faced that all my exercise was speeding my demise. Water aerobics had become more and more difficult, but I had pressed on. Now I had an extra goal—as I deteriorated, and eventually wouldn't even be able to stand, I at least wanted to enter that time with my muscles in good condition. How dumb! It didn't make any sense.

I eased myself into the pool with all the equipment and started to exercise. My breathing wasn't labored! I pushed myself harder and harder, but it was easy to get air!

After class I raced home. "Justin, I had no trouble breathing in water aerobics! I'm not sure, but the Lord may have healed me!"

We speed walked the hills of Seattle. No problem! We hiked a steep one-mile hill and I had no trouble breathing.

The pulmonologist called to tell me all the tests I needed to undergo.

"Wait, Doctor, just a minute. I need to tell you something. I've been exercising for over two hours now with no symptoms."

"*I have no medical explanation for what you're telling me.* Of course, if you're well, I'm glad, but you still need to have these procedures done."

She didn't believe me. She knew I was a Christian and she thought I was weird, that I was pretending to have been healed so I could return to China.

"Yes, Doctor, I'll do all the procedures you recommend." Bring them on—if I've been healed, let's prove it medically.

Although we suspected I was healed, we weren't sure, so we wanted to test it by climbing to Snow Lake again. Five days later the Seattle rain stopped, and we could hike. Last time it had taken three and a half hours of labored hiking. This time it was an easy one-and-a-quarter-hour climb. I stared into the deep waters of Snow Lake with tears in my eyes. I was now pretty sure the Lord had spared my life.

The next day I had the right-heart catheterization. It's hard to tell a medical professional that something supernatural has happened. I had given it a lot of thought and prayer.

Before the procedure, I spoke to the cardiologist. "I haven't had any symptoms for six days." I was leading into it slowly.

"What did you do, go to a healer or something?" she sneered.

"Something like that."

At the end of the procedure, with awe in her voice, she told me, "You don't have IPH anymore!" After cleaning up, she leaned over me, "So, tell me, what happened?"

I told her the whole story of all the prayers, and the exercise having become so easy. With a big grin on her face, she said, "Grace, go to China! Spread the Word!"

We flew out 10 days later.

Because the Lord had so miraculously opened the door for us to return, there was no doubt in our minds that he wanted us back in China, and he wanted Justin to have that administrative job in Re Dai University. Our four years in Re Dai were the hardest we went through in Mainland China, partly because the police were so opposed to Christianity at that university. As we faced all the difficulties, I often thought about how the Lord repeatedly made our move to Re Dai impossible, and then opened the doors. It encouraged me as I faced all the trials, knowing he led us there.

Our years in Re Dai were also the most fruitful for me, where, not just friends, but many university students placed their trust in Christ.

ONLY ONE LIFE SAVED!

2009, Re Dai

A diagonal scar ran deep across her right cheek, almost slicing off the bottom of her nose, and running shallow on her left cheek. I could see she had once been attractive. Twenty-seven-year-old Rainbow spoke slowly in Mandarin, showing no emotion, as if she were reciting a grocery list. "He lured me into a hotel room. He tried to rape me. I grabbed the lamp and threw it at him and that gave me time to run out the door. A few days later I saw him on the street. He had a broken piece of glass in his hand and he was looking for me. He ran up to me and slashed my face."

I looked away, trying to hold back my tears.

"He told me that he or any other man in my village could do anything they wanted to me because I have no man to protect me—my father is gone. What he said is true." She looked down at her lap.

"Grace, my father used to beat my sister, me, and my mom. Finally, he abandoned us. My mom wants me to find a man—any man—because there's too much work around the farm for us three women. She told me that if I don't find a man, she'll find herself a man. I don't want a husband like she had, or an abusive stepfather, either, for that matter. At first I just ignored what she said, but then I got to thinking that now that I'm a Christian there's a better way. A Christian man wouldn't be like that. There's this guy, Brinley, in our house church who's pretty sweet. He's gentle, too. We started dating."

Brinley was a pomegranate and corn farmer in his early 30s. He owned six pomegranate trees and a tenth of an acre of corn. Somehow he was doing fine financially on such meager produce. He had his own cement home and money to spare.

It's hard for Chinese Christian women to find Christian men to marry, especially outside the big cities, because women fill the churches, and there's only a sprinkling of men. And there are men who lurk around the house churches to pick up sweet Christian women to marry. They pretend to be Christians—wolves in sheep's clothing.

After Rainbow told me about her relationship with Brinley, she asked, "Could I come over to your place a few times a week? I want to handle the relationship with Brinley right, and I sure don't want the advice my mother has to offer. I want Christian advice."

I agreed, and one afternoon, a few months later, when she came over, she was livid. "Brinley tricked me! He said that since we'll be getting married later anyway, why don't we just get the marriage license out of the way. So we went down and signed the papers."

That's a problem in China. Exactly when you're married is a little unclear. Signing the marriage license comes first and is separate from any ceremony you might have. There can be years between signing the license and the wedding. Often when a couple signs the license they mean that they intend to marry, but need to save money to buy an apartment before they get married at the wedding banquet. Are they married when the license is signed or when they have the public wedding, since they're two separate events?

And when do they start living together as husband and wife? Almost all wait until after the wedding banquet. Only a few live together as husband and wife before.

It had never crossed Rainbow's mind that she and Brinley would live together before the public wedding banquet. She didn't think they were married until after the banquet. But Brinley had a flexible definition, depending on what suited him.

Rainbow continued her story. "After we signed the license, he ordered me to live with him and cook his food. Even still, I thought we'd be sleeping in separate rooms until we were married. But when nighttime came, Brinley picked me up and forced me onto the bed. I fought him, but he raped me!

"So I asked him when the wedding feast would be. He's not planning on having it! But that is so humiliating to me—it's like we're not married! If we don't have the feast I will have no honor in my village because everyone will think he doesn't value me." She stared at the floor.

Rainbow kept coming over when she could get away. "Today he accused me of having had a baby before he married me," she said on one visit. "He pointed at my tummy fat and said that's a sure sign that I've been pregnant before."

I listened to her, counseled her, showed her Scriptures, and prayed with her. She really liked being with me because she knew I loved her. I got the impression that my love was sustaining her. I gave her the best advice I could, but it wasn't really very good advice, probably because I didn't realize how badly Brinley was treating her.

One day when she visited, she looked both sad and desperate. "I'm pregnant. And Brinley doesn't believe the baby is his. He accused me of sleeping with another man! I think I'm just going to abort the baby. Maybe that will solve everything."

From knowing her, I knew the baby was Brinley's.

She was so distraught. I talked to her about keeping the baby, and fighting for her marriage. She decided that she needed to stop doing things her way and do what the Lord wanted. She started to depend on the Lord for strength.

The next time she saw me, she'd had a change of heart. With hope in her voice, she said, "Grace, I've decided to keep the baby. Could you name him for me?"

But a few weeks later when she came over, she was desperate again, even more than before. "Brinley told me that it was just a trial marriage. He doesn't like me and doesn't want to be married to me. He said that since we never had the wedding feast, no one knows we're married so it's the same as not being married. He wants me to abort the baby, go back to my mom's to live, and we'll get a divorce. But I can't abort the baby. He's my child!"

My heart ached for her. After we talked about her marriage, I said, "Listen, Rainbow, it's going to be very hard to be pregnant in your village without a husband."

"I thought I had it bad before," she said. "The whole village will be against me now."

"Do you have anyone you could live with outside your village until the baby's born?"

"I have some relatives who live quite a ways away. I'm not sure that would work, though."

I told her, "If you want to live at our home until the birth, you can. We have an extra bedroom you could sleep in, and we'd take care of you. We'll figure out together what to do with the baby. There's only one thing—you would have to stay inside our apartment the whole time you're here. The police can't find out a Chinese person is living here."

"Let me think about it," she said.

The next time she visited she was disconsolate. "Brinley told me I'm worthless and he hates me. I just want to die! If I didn't have this baby, it would be easier. I've decided to kill myself—that's the only solution!"

I had tried so hard to save the baby, but now I was pretty sure I was about to lose both mother and baby. Then I said something to Rainbow that shocked me when I heard myself say it. "It's better to kill one person than two." If she committed suicide, two would die. If she aborted the baby, only one would die. I was afraid she was going to commit suicide as a means of "abortion."

A few days later she called me on the phone. Her voice was flat. "Brinley beat me and threatened to kill me. I fled to my mother's house. I aborted the baby. I'm going to kill myself now. I don't want to live anymore."

"Rainbow, can I come over?"

"No, don't come over."

"I want to see you!"

"No, don't come!"

"Rainbow, I'm coming to see you!"

I needed to get there before she drank the pesticide! But I didn't remember where her home was; I had been there only once, and that was a year ago. It made no sense to ask her where she lived since she didn't want me to come. I was sure I could find her village on the outskirts of the city, but the only thing I remembered about the location of her house was that in the village I had to make a left turn off the main road. There were no street names or house numbers in her village. We didn't have a car, and I couldn't take a taxi because I couldn't remember the name of her village.

As soon as I got off the phone, I called Justin and a friend, quickly explained the situation, and asked them to pray for me.

I took off on my bicycle, pedaling as fast as I could. It took me half an hour to bike to the turn-off that led into her village. A few farm buildings stood at the entrance. One main road went through the village, with lanes branching off to the right and left. All the buildings, including the homes, were block-shaped, gray, cement structures. Most of the homes had cement walls surrounding them with iron gates. Uniform. Non-descript. Difficult to distinguish one from another.

In the middle of the village, a lane on the left looked like hers. *I tried to turn my bike, but my bike wouldn't turn! My bike stayed on the main road!* As I was almost running out of village, I saw a lane on the left that didn't look like hers at all. In fact, I was sure it wasn't hers. *I tried to go straight, but my bike turned there! I couldn't control my bike! It was leading me.*

The second house on the right looked slightly familiar. I got off my bike and walked through the gate. The house itself looked similar to Rainbow's, but everything else was wrong. There were bulls standing in the dirt yard where there had been no bulls a year ago. There were puppies frolicking, but I remembered kittens. I stood there debating what to do. I suspected I was at a stranger's house, and actually inside their wall with their bulls! Chinese bulls are calmer than American bulls, but still.

Just then, a young woman I didn't recognize stepped onto the balcony of the second floor. "Please come in and have dinner with us." I found out later that she had no idea who I was, either. She was just being polite to a stranger who had walked through her gate.

Her friendliness gave me courage, so I decided to try. "I'm looking for Rainbow."

The woman leaned over the balcony railing and pointed to a room on the ground floor. I walked over to the room, opened the door, and there was Rainbow, sobbing on the bed!

The Lord had led me straight to her! (A week later I repeatedly got lost in her village on my way to visit her.)

I put my arms around her and whispered, "Rainbow, the Lord really loves you. I'll tell you how I know. I didn't remember where your home was, but he directed my bike right here. He loves you that much. He doesn't want you to kill yourself." After several hours of talking with her, she decided that she did want to live.

Many people viewed Rainbow as worthless—only to be used and thrown away. She was quite weak, made a lot of bad decisions, and had aborted her child—but, oh, how she was loved by the Lord.

A CHINESE HOSPITAL

2010, Zao Gao

"Here are the results of the blood work for your husband," the nurse at Zhou Memorial Hospital, a Chinese hospital in Zao Gao City, told me in Mandarin. She looked carefully at the results and cringed. "Where is your husband now?" she asked me.

"He's in a hotel room. I came to pick up the results because he was too sick to come. My son's with him."

"He can't be in a hotel room, he needs to be hospitalized right away! He's extremely ill! I'll take you to the doctor."

I was alarmed. I knew Justin was very ill, but I hadn't expected to get that reaction from the nurse.

She led me down the hallway to the doctor. The hall looked scrubbed clean, with all the reassuring pungent, antiseptic smells, not like some Chinese hospitals I had been in. I had heard rumors about how clean Zhou Memorial was. I already knew this was where I wanted Justin to be hospitalized.

The nurse opened the door to a small room where the doctor sat at a metal desk. She said, "Doctor, you need to look at these results right away."

After studying the results briefly, he looked up. "Your husband needs to be hospitalized immediately! He's very ill!"

"How do I get him admitted?"

"No, he absolutely cannot be admitted here. He's too ill."

I was aghast. Too ill to be admitted here? Zhou Memorial wasn't a small hospital. "Where should he go?"

"He has to go to an infectious disease hospital."

I felt fear well up in my chest. I knew what infectious disease hospitals were like in China. They put a group of patients with infectious diseases in one room, regardless of what diseases they had, and regardless of the risk of infecting other patients.

I stumbled out of Zhou Memorial, tears blinding my eyes. "Lord, please help me find a safe, clean hospital for Justin."

Justin had a cyclical fever. About every six hours, within the space of 30 minutes, his temperature rose from normal to almost 105 degrees, while he shook uncontrollably. Doctors call this "the rigors." When he had the rigors, he couldn't function in any way.

We didn't trust the local hospitals, so I rented a taxi to bring Justin and Adam, who was visiting from America for Christmas vacation, the 200 miles from Re Dai to Zao Gao City, a city of seven million. I wanted Justin to be seen at the international clinic in Zao Gao. That clinic was just a minimalist clinic, though, where the doctor could do little more than examine the patient, take his weight and temperature, and refer him to a local hospital, if necessary. But I trusted those doctors because they were trained to American standards.

After examining Justin, the doctor sent us over to Zhou Memorial for tests.

The next day when I stepped out of Zhou Memorial, test results in hand, I returned to the international clinic so the doctor could advise me.

Sitting in the waiting room of the international clinic, I tried to figure out where Justin could safely be hospitalized. The only international hospital in all of China that I knew of was Union Hospital in Huangdi, 1,600 miles away. They had a competent infectious disease doctor, Dr. Casey, who, on more than one occasion, had diagnosed my obscure diseases when I was very ill. I decided that I needed to try to get Justin to Huangdi to be seen by Dr. Casey. It was going to be hard. I would somehow have to get Justin on a plane without the flight attendants realizing how ill he was. I would try. I would go to any length to save Justin. "Lord, please help me get Justin to Union Hospital where he can be seen by Dr. Casey."

I called Union Hospital. "No, Dr. Casey moved back to Canada."

Fear constricted my throat. I struggled to ask, "Do you have any other infectious disease doctors?"

"Only one, but he starts his two-week vacation tomorrow."

I barely had the strength to hang up the phone. I had run out of plans. Justin might die! Tears rolled down my cheeks. I lowered my head so the other patients wouldn't see. I couldn't help it, my shoulders began to shake, my breath caught, as finally I sobbed.

A middle-aged American couple, who were sitting in the waiting room, slipped over to the seats on my left. I didn't see them next to me until they quietly asked, "What's wrong?"

I looked up and told them how sick Justin was, how I had been told to hospitalize him in an infectious disease hospital, and what I feared would happen to him there.

Their faces were full of concern. "We are the owners of this clinic. We'll get you in to see the doctor here immediately. And we'll be praying for your husband."

A little gift from the Lord.

When I showed the doctor the test results in the examining room, he said, "Justin needs to be evacuated to Hong Kong, but he'll need to be hospitalized first until he stabilizes enough for evacuation. Even though Zhou Memorial is a very clean hospital, I wouldn't have advised you to have Justin admitted there. Patients have had very mixed results at Zhou Memorial. Often their treatment plans don't work."

Had the Lord actually saved Justin because Zhou Memorial refused to admit him?

The doctor continued. "I advise you to take Justin to the emergency room of Zao Gao Teaching Hospital. It is the best hospital in Zao Gao City."

Three hours later, I had hired a car and driver and brought Justin to "the best hospital in Zao Gao." After waiting in line at the emergency room for 20 to 30 minutes, Justin was seen briefly by the doctor, who wanted blood tests, urine tests, an x-ray, sonogram, and so on, the same tests he had already taken at Zhou Memorial the day before.

Justin was scared. He was much more sick than yesterday and the rigors were coming more and more frequently. When he had the rigors, he had to be in a prone position, and just try to cope. There was nowhere to lie down in the emergency room, just plastic chairs lining the walls. "Lord, please keep Justin from having the rigors in the emergency room!"

There was no quick or easy way to take all these tests. I stood in line to pay for the first test, then stood in line with proof of payment, then waited in line for the test. I don't know how anyone who is ill does all this. Justin was too weak to do anything but sprawl on a plastic chair in the hallway. I tried to keep an eye on him in case he went into the rigors and needed me, but often I had to stray out of sight to stand in line. When it was finally Justin's turn for a test, I ran over to support him as he walked to the test location, hoping the other patients would hold our place.

After each test, I went through the routine for the next test. It took almost five hours before we returned to the doctor with the results. There was no expedited service or bed for those as ill as Justin, or the dying.

But Justin had no rigors during the hours we spent in the emergency room. "Thank you, Lord!"

When we saw the doctor again and he looked at the test results, he said in Mandarin, "He needs to be hospitalized right away." He solemnly walked us over to the *infectious disease building* of the hospital. With everything I had done to prevent this, he still ended up in a building for infectious disease patients. This is what I had prayed wouldn't happen.

I was past crying. The Lord would have to keep him alive.

Justin leaned heavily against me as we walked into his assigned room that would decide his fate. The tan linoleum floor was scuffed and dirty, and the white tiles on the wall were cracked.

Just as I feared, the beds were packed close together, with only a foot and a half between them. At least his room had only three beds, and for the time being, Justin was the only patient in his room. Later a patient with incurable hepatitis moved into the room.

The beds had metal frames that had originally been white, and they were the filthiest beds I had ever seen, grimy and rusted.

Old wooden night tables between beds, painted white with silver handles, kept patients' personals. They were so smudged with the diseases of previous patients I was afraid to touch them.

A pillow and quilt, both white, covered each bed. They were the only items in the room that looked clean.

There was no heat in the building. I didn't know how Justin could handle this bitter cold room with his fever. The windows were only tied with polypropylene string, and couldn't be closed completely. The golden fabric that acted as curtains billowed over Justin's bed as the frigid December wind blew in.

Could I bring a space heater? I read the Chinese warnings on the inside of the door. "Anyone who plugs in a space heater will be fined." How could they fine us for just trying to survive?

When I opened the smudged pale-yellow door to the bathroom, I reeled back. The squatty potty ceramic hole in the floor, which served as a toilet, was stained with excretions. And there was no sink for the patients to wash their hands. In fact, when I thought about it, I had only seen one sink in the whole hospital for doctors, nurses, or patients. It was in the outpatient bathroom where Justin had collected a sample of his urine.

Then I noticed that the squatty potty was broken. It wouldn't flush! Near the ceiling, a rag fastened a rusty pipe to a hose to fill a bucket for tipping into the toilet to flush it.

Our only hope was that the Lord would save us. Even I was in danger being here.

In the midst of all this filth and disease, the Lord provided a gift, which saved Justin—a short, female doctor, who was sweet, caring, jovial, and most important, she was competent. She felt like a bright light whenever she entered the room.

Justin settled into bed and asked me for water. The tap water in China is undrinkable, so I went to the nurse station, "Where can I get water for Justin to drink?" I asked in Mandarin.

"Down the hall." They pointed left.

I found a large, metal boiling-water dispenser, common on trains in China. But I had no cup.

I returned to the nurse station. "Could you give me a cup?"

"We don't have any cups. You were supposed to bring your own."

Everything in the last two days had been an emergency. I was supposed to have thought to bring a cup? At that point, I didn't think I could cope. How would Justin fare the night with his fever and no water?

It was past midnight. I left Justin and went out into the night in search of water, and finally found a 24-7 kiosk that sold bottled water. "Thank you, Lord!"

I tried to sleep in the empty bed next to Justin so I could care for his needs, but I was so cold I hardly slept.

In the morning Adam came to visit. When he saw the conditions, he spoke lovingly to me,

"Mom, you're not sleeping here again. From now on, I'll stay here for the night shift to take care of Dad." He was another bright light in our darkness.

Hospitals in China don't provide food for patients. Either the patient has to be ambulatory and eat at nearby restaurants, or relatives bring in food.

At lunch Justin spilled soy sauce all over his quilt. I exchanged his dirty quilt for one on another bed. I told the nurses about the dirty quilt, but they refused to change it, even when the hepatitis patient moved into the bed. That was when we realized that they didn't change the linens between infectious disease patients.

When I returned to the hotel I made an Internet call to our home church in Seattle and many people began praying for Justin.

The doctor treated Justin for malaria (we had been in a malaria infected area 100 miles south of where we lived), typhoid (there was an outbreak of typhoid fever on the campus where Justin worked), and kidney infection. The short, jovial doctor eventually determined he had a kidney infection. By the time Justin stabilized, he didn't need to be evacuated. After a week, he had improved greatly and was released from the hospital.

I had prayed for many things during that traumatic week. The Lord often didn't give me what I asked for. But he granted my deepest request, that Justin would live. The Lord gave me my heart's desire.

THE TREE WORSHIPPER

2009-2013, Re Dai

Abby hired a motorcycle, with a covered flatbed, to bring Justin, Adam, and me the 25 miles to her Yi minority[1] farming village. We crowded together on the benches lining the sides of the flatbed. Dust kicked into the open back. Abby was bringing us to her childhood home where her family was cooking a feast to honor me as her friend. I couldn't wait to see where she grew up and meet her family.

As we neared her village, young men in dirty suit coats and collared shirts, the clothes of farm workers, zipped by on scooters and motorcycles, engines snarling. An occasional "tractor," unlike anything I have ever seen in the U.S., sputtered past on the gray dirt roads. The long, narrow engine block, which had no hood cover, extended about 12 feet in front of the driver. The whole contraption looked homemade.

Lush, green crops surrounded cement, block-shaped homes with curved, gray, ceramic-tiled roofs.

I was amazed when I saw the Yi women walk by. They wore thick, embroidered vests of various shades of orange that hung down to their thighs. Their green leggings erupted in a dance of orange stripes over their calves. Orange and gold tiaras rose over half a foot above the crowns of their heads with orange pompoms gyrating at the sides.

When we arrived at Abby's home, I bowed slightly to her mother, and extended my hands with our gift of a box of long-life milk for the family.

---

1. In Mainland China, in addition to the Han Chinese, there are 55 officially recognized minorities, of which the Yi people are one. Each minority has its own culture, language, and dress.

Her mother had elaborately wrapped her head in a green, pink and white flowered towel. That was all she retained of her traditional minority garb. After meeting the extended family, we took a walking tour of the village along pathways through vegetable gardens.

"We worship a tree. Come and see it!"

I expected a leafy tree, full of life and vigor. I jarred up as I lifted my eyes, following the gray bark of this tall tree along its almost barren, gnarled appendages. Its only leaves clung to the tips of the branches. If it could barely keep itself alive, how was it supposed to make the villagers prosper, and how would it be able to answer their whispered prayers?

We strolled on past the tree along the path to the lake at the edge of the village. A pagoda rose up from the waters in the center of the lake. "Our village is so blessed to have this lake," Abby said. It was life-giving, as the source of water for their verdant crops, and the source of the fish they feasted on.

Fishermen stood in the bows of long, narrow skiffs, using bamboo poles several times their height to jab the lake bottom, prodding the boats forward on the way to check their nets.

But when I stared down from the cement ledge where we stood, I recoiled. Not only were debris, garbage, and algae floating on the surface, bloated dead pigs were also floating on the lake!

Eventually I got up the courage, "Abby, why are there dead pigs in the lake?"

"Our village has been hit with swine flu. The farmers didn't want to spread the disease through their farms and to their families, so they dumped the pigs in the lake."

Later, at the feast, Abby smiled and told us, "The fish are so good! They're fresh caught from the lake. Try them!" I poked at the fish, trying to pretend I was eating, and I cringed as Justin and Adam raised fish in their chopsticks with gusto to their mouths.

Abby and I had first met at an English corner, seated around tables in the county library. The library had organized this English corner and it was a gathering of Chinese English speakers who wanted to improve their English through conversation. English corners always welcomed native English speakers to talk with the Chinese who came. Foreign Christians ran many of the English corners and discussed topics that could lead to the gospel, like forgiveness, loving our enemies, our heroes, and life goals.

I attended the English corner at the library that evening because I didn't have any Chinese friends in Re Dai yet and I wanted to make friends. "Our families" was the topic that night. Abby's English was excellent, and as she shared so openly about her family, I wanted to get to know her, because I like open people. At the end of the discussion, I handed her my phone number. Within a few days we started taking walks three evenings a week along the pathways that wound through the tropical foliage of the water park in the center of Re Dai.

Abby was a 39-year-old English teacher, married, with a 14-year-old daughter. Her V-shaped face gave her a beguiling beauty. She had raised herself up from a village where scarce few graduated from primary school; she had moved away, attended high school and college, and now lived in the big town, married to a Han Chinese (a Chinese who is not from a minority group). Abby always dressed with class to accentuate her accomplishments.

As a child and young adult she had been an animist, worshipping their almost dead tree, but lately she had begun to wonder if God might exist. She told me about a couple of serendipitous events in her life, then she said: "I think Someone is orchestrating my life, but I don't know who that Someone is. How can I know if it's the God of the Bible?"

I gave her some ideas, but then for two months she remained silent about the Lord, until one day, while we were walking in the water park, I made an offhand comment that Christians like to help people. When I said it, I thought it was a stupid thing to say.

Her response surprised me. "That's exactly why I want to become a Christian! I've been thinking about whether I should become a Christian or a Buddhist, but recently I watched my mother-in-law praying to Buddha. All she prayed for was her family. That's what Buddhists are like—all they care about is themselves and their families. I'm so turned off to Buddhism. But Christians are completely different. They care for people other than their families, so I'm choosing Christianity, not Buddhism. Could you teach me the Bible?"

How did we get to this point so fast? Obviously, the Holy Spirit had been working in her heart. And he had even used the prayers of a Buddhist to draw her to himself.

The two of us started studying the Bible together, then she began attending the government church with Justin and me. It didn't take long before Abby told her mother she wanted to become a Christian. "No, Abby. I forbid you to become a Christian! You've got to worship the tree or what will happen to our family?"

Abby's face looked pained as she told me, "I can't become a Christian." At 39 years of age, with a family of her own, her mother still dictated her beliefs. Abby avoided me after that, afraid she would give in to the allure of Christianity and so disobey her mother. Abby later told me that during that time her husband tried to get us back together because he had seen such positive changes in Abby as a result of her friendship with me. But Abby refused to see me.

I became depressed. I had lost my only friend, and she was also turning away from the Lord.

After nine months of praying for her, she finally called and asked me to go for a walk the next day. I could hardly sleep I was so excited.

When I saw her at the water park, she grabbed my arm and told me she had spent the last nine months thinking through the issues that had been blocking her from becoming a Christian.

"How will my parents know what I believe in my heart? So I can believe whatever I believe and they can't stop me!

"And there's another thing I've been thinking about. Since I'm a teacher at a government school, I'm afraid I might lose my job if I believe in Jesus. That would be really hard on my family, but I've decided I'm willing to pay that price in order to have Jesus."

I couldn't believe what I was hearing—not only was she still seeking the Lord, she was counting the cost. We studied the Bible together again, but she was fearful about believing in Jesus. "After I become a Christian there'll be all kinds of rules I have to follow, won't there? If I don't obey every single one, God will punish me. I don't know if I can do it—it scares me.

"Also, won't the pastor and church people take advantage of me because I don't know the Bible very well yet? They'll tell me I have to do things that aren't in the Bible and maybe what they tell me to do will even be bad, but I won't know."

We worked through her fears.

She was already sharing what we studied with her family and her friend, Lion, a male English teacher. Lion asked Abby if the three of us could study the Bible together. "No, Lion. We are two women. We have a lot of life issues to talk about while we study the Bible. You're not welcome to study the Bible with us. Go find your own Bible teacher!"

During our times of studying the Bible she was excited, but I was frustrated. Even though she was sharing with others about God, she understood almost nothing. She seemed to have a spiritual block. She wanted badly to become a Christian but no matter how I explained the gospel, it didn't get through. Was it her animist background that was blinding her?

A few days after I realized that she wasn't ready yet, and it would take time and a moving of the Spirit to open her spiritual eyes, she called me. "Grace, can you come over right away? I have great news to tell you."

I biked over and the moment I entered her home, she told me, "I'm getting baptized tomorrow!" She looked elated.

I stared at her in shock. "How did this happen?"

"Jez met with me and asked if I wanted to get baptized and I told her yes."

"What did she tell you about Jesus?"

"Nothing. She didn't tell me anything about Jesus."

"What did she tell you about how to become a Christian?"

"She didn't tell me anything. She just asked if I wanted to be baptized, that's all. Isn't it great?"

Jez was a Canadian missionary. She belonged to a mission agency that required a certain number of conversions a year from each of its missionaries. It was nearing the end of the year, so she needed to plump up her number.

What could I do? I knew I couldn't stop Abby from getting baptized, but she needed to know who Jesus is and understand the gospel to become a Christian. If I didn't lead her to Christ that evening, she would be baptized the next day without knowing the Lord. I've seen what happens to people like that—they gradually conclude Christianity doesn't work because they haven't actually become Christians, and then they lose interest. It's almost impossible to lead them to Christ after that. They're inoculated.

Who knows why, but in that particular town this was such a common occurrence that whenever a local told me she was a Christian, I didn't get excited. Instead, I asked her, "What is a Christian?" and "How do you become a Christian?" If she didn't have a clue, I told her about Jesus and how to believe in him. Then I led her to Christ on the spot; that is, if she hadn't already become apathetic. Later, they often told me it transformed their lives.

That evening with Abby, I did the only thing I could do. I prayed for the Lord to open Abby's spiritual eyes, and I charged in with an explanation of the gospel. By God's grace she became a Christian before she was baptized.

A few days later, I wanted to have a goofy celebration of her new birth, so I made a chocolate angel pudding, stuck candles in it, and brought it over to her apartment. I changed the Happy Birthday song and sang to her in Chinese, "Happy new birth to you, happy new birth to you."

She held my hand all through the new birth celebration, "because now we're sisters."

She loved the celebration, but I was amazed when at the end she asked, "Grace, celebrating the new birth with candles and the birthday song is what we're required to do after someone becomes a Christian, right?" She was trying to figure out all the rules of her new faith.

I continued to study the Bible with her, but now her spiritual eyes were open.

One evening I showed up at her home, only to find her in a lot of pain—her mouth was full of canker sores. I immediately left, biked the half hour home in the dark, ziplock bagged as many stress-B vitamins as I could spare from my stash that I had schlepped from the States, and biked back. I presented my gift to her in the hope that it would heal the sores. She said, "Grace, I am overwhelmed with the love Christians have for each other!"

She had never felt peace in her life before. It took half a year after she became a Christian for her to tell me what she was like before she knew the Lord. Even as a married woman with a child, she had been a hard-partying girl who fooled around with other men. She had also been a few inches short of divorcing her husband. She transformed into someone who loved her husband and daughter, restoring the family. And peace filled her heart.

Then one evening, she called me late at night. Her voice was shaky. "Grace, I need your help right away! I can't meet you at my home, let's meet at the water park."

We sat on a bench in the dark, surrounded by trees that looked like they came from the Garden of Eden. She took my hand. I wasn't expecting what I heard. "My husband's boss from the mine where he works used to call me before I was a Christian. He threatened to fire my husband if I didn't sleep with him. So, of course, I slept with him. I don't know how we'd survive if my husband lost his job. His boss does this to all the wives of the mineworkers."

"Does your husband know?"

"He can't know! My husband would kill him if he knew!"

"His boss hasn't called me since I became a Christian. But he called again tonight. I didn't answer. What do I do? I can't sleep with him now because I'm a Christian. I don't know how to stop him."

With tears streaming down both our faces, we prayed together. I encouraged her to trust the Lord and told her not to answer any of the man's phone calls.

He stopped calling.

In situation after situation, Abby now goes to the Lord for his help. She now worships Someone who can actually help her when she prays—not just an almost dead tree.

YOU ACTUALLY BELIEVE IN GOD?
First University Student Discussion Group, Part 1

2010, Re Dai

Jeanette and I huddled in a restaurant eating mapo tofu. Jeanette was a university student who had been led to the Lord by an American short-term missionary team. "Grace, I've been a Christian for six weeks. I've been telling my friends about Jesus, but not one of them has become a Christian. I can't understand it. Jesus is so good, why don't they want to become Christians, too?"

"Jeanette, I go slow sharing about Jesus. I tell people how God has helped me. Then, sometimes they ask me if Jesus can help them, too."

"Maybe I've been pressuring them too much. I'd like to introduce my friends to you."

The next Friday evening Jeanette brought four of her friends, Carol, Jasmine, Amelia, and Kristen, to our campus apartment. When I opened the door, they shyly greeted me. Then as a tight group they glided over to the white couch in the living room and sat crammed together, arms around each other's shoulders. Same-sex friends in China are very affectionate.

I sat on the floor on the other side of the coffee table, which I had packed with sweet fruit drinks and fresh-baked chocolate chip cookies. I waited to see what Jeanette had planned for the evening; I didn't know why they thought they were meeting me.

Jeanette pulled out her computer to show videos that she hoped would entice them to believe in Jesus. In the first video, dubbed in Chinese, Nick Vujicic, an Australian man who had no arms and legs, told how the Lord had given him so much joy even though he's disabled. His testimony was engaging.

But the women were unimpressed. "Oh, I've seen videos of disabled people before. Big deal."

So Jeanette pulled up a video of someone preaching. Five minutes into the preaching video I stopped her. So this was the pressured evangelism she had already tried. "Jeanette, why don't we just have a discussion."

I turned to the women. "Tell me about your families." "Where did you grow up?" "Do any of you have boyfriends?" "What are you majoring in?"

All of them were first- or second-year English majors, but they could hardly converse in English. We had to switch to Mandarin for deeper discussions.

Then I told them about myself, and how a year and a half earlier, I had been dying of a lung disease, but the Lord miraculously healed me. I thought they would be excited about that, but they didn't look interested at all. Later they told me there had to be some natural explanation because miracles don't happen.

Carol was a stylish, cute, petite girl with a short, blunt haircut. She had the air of being very capable and in charge of herself. At that first meeting, after I tried several times to interest them in God, Carol's eyes suddenly widened and she burst out laughing. Staring at me, she grinned wickedly. "You can't be serious! You actually believe God exists?" Once again she shook with laughter.

"Yes, I do believe in God," I said. "What do you believe in?"

"I believe in life!"

"What do you mean by that?"

"I believe that if you study real hard you'll get the good job."

I started to laugh. "Don't tell me you actually believe life is fair!" I laughed and laughed. I'd never laughed at someone while telling them about the Lord before, but it turned out that was the only way to get Carol's attention and respect.

Actually, I was angry at her belief. My two sons had been unemployed because of the economic crisis. "Carol, many people have studied real hard and have college degrees, but because of the economic downturn, they're unemployed. Life isn't fair, that's for sure."

Carol looked scared. Later she told me she was afraid because she realized that if life isn't fair, she had no control over it.

When Carol laughed at me, I started to like her because I knew she wasn't just telling me what I wanted to hear, like most Chinese people do. Some Chinese will go so far as to pray with you to receive Christ when they don't even believe God exists. Because they want to honor you, they say yes when you ask if they want to believe in Jesus. So whenever I told a Chinese person about Christ, I usually didn't trust their reaction unless they disagreed with me first. Carol had just given me her honest reaction to my faith, so we could talk for real now.

So that is how the first meeting went—the women were either disinterested or laughing at me. I was surprised, then, when they asked to keep meeting with me for a two-hour session each week.

All week I prayed for the next meeting. I felt extremely incompetent.

The second time we met, they invited a couple more friends to join us, so they had to spill from the white couch into the easy chairs.

We read John 8:32 together that night, which says that the truth sets us free. I wanted to expose them to the Bible and start them on the journey of seeking truth. "Is it good to know the truth?" I asked. "Does it set you free?" They were not yet ready to evaluate whether the truth about Jesus would set them free, so we dealt in generalities that night.

Chinese culture doesn't place a high value on telling the truth—rather it values relationships running smoothly. Practically, this means that Chinese people often tell others what they want to hear just to have peace. This comes from the Daoist ideal of avoiding interpersonal conflict. I was pretty sure the verse's emphasis on the importance of truth would be controversial for them and would get them to think.

They came at me with guns blazing. "If you have cancer, you shouldn't be told you're going to die." "If someone hates you, it's best if you don't know because you might hate them back."

I debated with them, "You might need to prepare yourself for death—say your goodbyes, make apologies, get your affairs in order, prepare for the afterlife. If you know someone hates you, then you can try to get the relationship right."

Emma countered, "But some might be too weak to know the truth. It might be too hard for them to know they're dying, or that someone hates them."

"You made a good point." I replied. "I don't know the answer." They were excited that they had stumped me.

During the whole discussion Carol was uncharacteristically somber and withdrawn. Her head hung down, her shoulders slumped. Toward the end she spoke up quietly, "Sometimes a person is happy if they don't know the truth and sad if they do. Let me give an example. *If someone believes life is fair, then they're happy. But when they find out life isn't fair, they're sad.*" My heart ached for her—I could see she was hurting. But she had already started to dismantle some of her false presuppositions in life.

The women told me they had spent all week discussing everything I said in the first session. I couldn't believe it! They had acted so disinterested.

I closed with, "I love truth." They looked at me surprised and repeated "I love truth." It was a new concept to them.

This was the first time they had ever participated in a discussion group where they had been encouraged to think, their opinions were taken seriously, and where truth was the arbiter. They were so proud of being part of the group they often bragged to their friends and American English teachers about it. They invited more friends to come, and told them they would be challenged to think, and they would learn about God.

The third time we met, nine women showed up. In addition to the original five, we now also had Emma, Maria, Del, and Lauri. I was excited the group had grown so much, but I had to tell them not to invite any more friends because we were maxed out for having good discussions. Also, if the group was too big, it might attract the attention of the authorities.

Their Backgrounds

The women had a mishmash of beliefs.

Buddhism had been stamped out by Communism, so I was surprised to find the women had been influenced by orthodox Buddhism, with its denial of pain, suffering, and desire. Orthodox Buddhism has no supreme creator God.

The two *main* influences in their lives, though, were Confucianism and Communism.

The Chinese culture is fundamentally based on Confucianism, which is not a religion, but a socio-political theory. It prescribes the honor and obedience due those in superior positions in society: government, rulers, husband, parents, and older brothers. How the women thought about life, their values, purpose, and what they loved were all guided by Confucianism. It was deep in their psyche.

Their second major influence was Communism. Communism is atheistic, so the teachers and textbooks were required to teach that God and the Bible are myths.

From what I had read about cults, I could see that the Communist indoctrination these women had been exposed to all their lives was similar to the indoctrination of a cult. In fact, when we first moved to Mainland China in 1996, it felt a little like we had been dropped down into the middle of a massive cult group. China was one big closed environment. All sources of information were tightly controlled, and the country was infused with propaganda—from the teaching in schools, to public loudspeakers, billboards, and the news. Most people spouted the government position as their own personal view. In recent years, Communism's stranglehold has been breaking down as the people have been more exposed to the outside world. But these women were fresh out of high school, and into the intense indoctrination of a government university. Their thinking was still narrow.

Between Communism, which doesn't countenance opposition, and Confucianism, where a person must at least outwardly agree with their authorities, these women didn't know how to think. All their views had been given to them secondhand. In the year and a half that we met together, I never knew which belief system would emerge in any given discussion. Sometimes even their own sets of beliefs were contradictory.

One of my initial goals was to teach them how to think—to figure out what they themselves thought was true and why, to recognize their own presuppositions, to be able to defend their points of view, and to evaluate opposing views.

With the exception of Jeanette, the new believer, none of these women had ever been to church. None owned a Bible or had read any of the Bible. None of their family or friends were Christians. They had never read about Christianity, and they had no idea what a Christian believes. Kristen eventually acknowledged that she had never even heard of God before attending university.

Since the majority of them had been told all their lives that God is a myth, they dismissed what I said about him because it didn't make sense to them that I believed in a fable. It was as if I was saying, "I believe in Tinker Bell, and Tinker Bell is more important than anything else in my life. I pray to Tinker Bell, and she answers my prayers and helps me. Tinker Bell loves me. When I die, I'll spend the rest of eternity with Tinker Bell. Would you like to believe in Tinker Bell, too?" God was that incomprehensible to them.

On that campus of 10,000 students, there were probably only about 10 Christian students when our group started.

This was the first evangelistic discussion group for university students that I had ever run.

§§§

At our fourth meeting, I compared the teachings of Confucius and Jesus, so the students would see the beauty of Jesus' teachings.

Confucianism is the main reason for the often beautiful emphasis on family in Asian culture, but there are downsides. For example, Confucianism places more importance on blood relationship than the principles of right and wrong.

I showed the women a diagram I came up with that clarifies how Confucianism affects society, and foreigners in particular.

CIRCLES OF RESPONSIBILITY

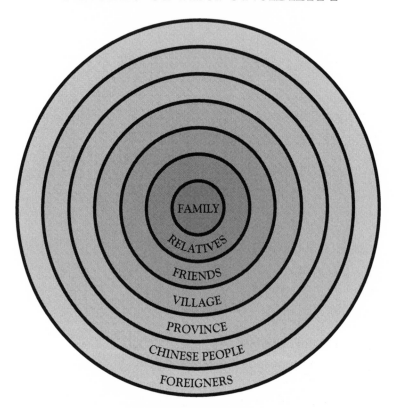

"As a Chinese, you're supposed to help people according to how close they are to the center circle," I said. "Where am I on this diagram?"

"You're on the outer circle."

"So what does that mean practically? When a Chinese person sees another Chinese person hurt or cheat me, he will consider it his duty to stand up for the one who's hurting me, even though I'm the victim. That's merely because they're in the inner circle and I'm not. This has happened to me a lot in China."

We had already looked at Jesus' command to love God first and your neighbor as yourself. I then showed them Luke 10:30-37, where Jesus commended the Samaritan for helping his enemy.

"Jesus calls on us to love those outside our inner circles, even to the point of loving our enemies. How do Confucius' rules of social responsibility compare to Jesus' command to love your neighbor as yourself? Does Confucius teach better ethics? Or Jesus?"

Jasmine, who enjoyed studying Confucian philosophy, piped up, "Wow!

Jesus is even more interesting than Confucius."

§§§

During the discussions, I often shared about my personal life and problems, so they could see how God used the Bible and prayer to help me. One week I had a serious disagreement with Justin. Although I didn't tell them what the disagreement was about, I told them how I prayed and what verses of Scripture helped me to solve the problem.

What makes Christianity convincing to many Chinese people is if it works in their everyday lives. Does it help them solve the problems they face? As they pray and do what the Bible says, does it produce good fruit in their lives, like joy, peace and love? If so, then they're drawn to it, and they wonder if it's true.

As I told them story after story of relationships the Lord was walking me through, they responded, "We want something to guide us through life's problems, like you have."

At one point, Carol made an observation. "*I had always thought that people believed in God in order to avoid problems. But now I'm seeing that God is there to help us face our problems.*"

The more I showed them the gems I've found in the Bible, the more they told me, "We really like reading the Bible."

I had met them in May, and for six weeks until the end of the semester, as we discussed a variety of issues, they became more and more receptive to the idea of God. I couldn't wait for the six-week summer break to be over, so the group could resume.

After the summer they finally trusted me enough to share problems they were having.

Toward the end of one of the sessions, Maria told the group, "I have something I want to share. I am really shy. This is the worst problem in my life, and it hinders me in everything I do. How can I become an English teacher when I'm this shy? Grace, can you help me?" I had noticed how she always hid behind the girl next to her.

"Believe it or not, I used to be shy," I said. They gasped—I came across as so outgoing. I shared some methods I had used to overcome the problem, like preparing a question beforehand to ask a stranger in order to get a conversation going.

Maria tried my suggestions and she started to come out of her shell. Later her English professor talked with me. "Are you the Grace who knows Maria? Well, I asked the class to write about the day that most changed their lives. Maria wrote that someone named Grace told her how to overcome shyness and it was the most important day of her life!"

They shared about painful, broken relationships they had. In each case, they were avoiding their former friends. This is the Chinese way of resolving conflict—avoiding the person who offended you. Again, Daoism.

I directed them to Matthew 18:15. "When we have a serious conflict with someone, if possible, we should talk with them about it. Sometimes we can be reconciled that way."

As I kept talking, Kristen, who had shared about a broken friendship, finally said, "O.K., O.K., I'll do it!"

"Confronting someone is hard to do", I told her. "It's not the way your culture handles strained relationships, and it's just plain hard to confront someone who has offended you, so you're going to need help. How about if you pray to God and ask him for help."

Two of the other women snickered.

Then the group asked for follow-up reports from the women who were going to try to reconcile with their former friends.

The next week the women who had broken relationships told us they prayed to God for help, talked with their ex-friends, and the relationships were restored!

I took it a step further. "You asked God for help and he helped you. It's only right to thank him." They did.

Two amazing things had happened. They were doing what the Bible says and they found it worked. They had also prayed for the first time in their lives and God helped them. They were beginning to believe—just slightly.

If I can get an atheist to pray, she's halfway there!

One day we were looking at verses about forgiving people who have offended us. In response to some things they said, I told the story about the harrowing vacation we took in China, where we were threatened and in a lot of danger. At the end of the story, Carol pointedly asked me, "Have you forgiven the people who did this to you?"

"Well … um … actually, I never thought about forgiving them." Was I ever embarrassed!

Carol said, "Grace, I want you to report to us next week what you did about forgiving them!"

The next week I reported. "I thought a lot about forgiving those enemies, and I finally came to the point where I could forgive them from my heart. But the strangest thing happened. After I forgave them, I couldn't help it, I just kept praying for them."

Kristen burst out, "Maybe God is changing your heart, Grace!"

"Yeah, maybe he is." I grinned.

But Carol wouldn't let it go. "Now that you've forgiven them, you'll return to that place and see those people again."

I cringed. "Forgiving someone doesn't mean you trust them. If someone threatens to kill you and then you forgive them, you don't go back and let them kill you."

"Yeah, I guess you're right."

§§§

In China, most people believe that people are naturally good. So I thought long and hard about how to show the women they were sinners. All the traditional ways hadn't worked.

When I asked if any of them had done bad things or had any bad in their hearts, all but one said, "No! We have never done anything bad, and there is no bad in our hearts."

I prayed about my approach, then I changed the way I talked about sin. Instead of talking about doing bad things, I talked about how I am sometimes disappointed in myself. Since they were so attuned to relationships, I told them about attitudes I had in relationships that I didn't think were right, like seeing people as either black or white. "I want to be different, but it's so hard to change. When I'm disappointed in myself, I ask God's forgiveness and I ask him to help me change. So, what do *you* do when *you're* disappointed in *yourselves*?"

Finally, when I asked them again which ones of them had done any bad or had any bad in their hearts, they all said, "Yes, there's bad in our hearts, and yes, we've done bad things."

§§§

It's common in China to believe there's no absolute truth. In one of the meetings, I brought up an ancient Chinese saying, *Xin zhe you, bu xin ze wu*, which means, "If you believe it, it's true for you." Most of the women said they believed that saying. But when I asked them why, I was flabbergasted at their answer. They brought up superstition! "If you're superstitious, whatever you believe will happen actually will happen to you. But if you aren't superstitious, those things won't happen to you." So your belief system determines reality.

I don't think you can lead someone to Christ if he doesn't believe in absolute truth, because he won't believe God *actually* exists, only that, if he believes, then God exists for him. This doesn't fit with Hebrews 11:6, which says that in order to be able to come to God, we must believe that God exists. We needed to tackle it.

I tried many approaches to the issue, like telling them, "I believe there's a white elephant in the dining area and you don't. Let's test it out." I tried an example of two people seeing a complex murder from different angles. They each have a different version, but regardless of their interpretation, what happened happened. I told them that God's existence doesn't depend on anyone's beliefs. I used myself as an example—I exist whether they believe I do or not. They looked at me like I was an idiot. Nothing I said made sense to them.

If you try to prove something to a Chinese person using Western logic: syllogisms, the law of non-contradiction, and such, you will probably get nowhere. Chinese logic is so much more beautiful and calming to the mind. If you want to prove something, you give a parallel example from life to convince and bring clarity.

Finally, I used a hypothetical example from my marriage. "My husband doesn't lie, and he's faithful to me. Suppose one night he came home at 2 a.m. In reality he's not having an affair, but if I believe he slept with a woman that night, does that mean he did? Does my believing it make it true?"

That did it. "O.K. Now we get it," they said. Most people have been falsely accused of something, so it made sense to them. Believing something doesn't make it true. Believing God exists doesn't make him exist, and believing he doesn't exist doesn't make him not exist. By the end of the discussion, all but one had come to believe in absolute truth. I felt such a sense of awe. Step by step they were coming closer to believing in the Lord.

At the door that evening, Carol turned to me and said, "Thinking through these issues is exhausting, but exhilarating." Later she texted me: "The discussion group is a major highlight of my whole college experience!"

Carol and I started playing ping-pong and badminton together. She told me, "Grace, my parents and teachers have always criticized me for being fun-loving, but you've taught me that it's good to have fun."

When I took Carol out for lunch, during the conversation I referred to her as an atheist. She became defensive. "Hold on. I'm not an atheist anymore. I just don't know if God exists." I couldn't believe what I was hearing and I was excited because that's such a big step up from atheism. Then she nonchalantly added, "But it's irrelevant anyway."

I was taken aback. "How can God not be relevant? He's my whole life!" I could understand not believing God exists since I used to be an atheist myself, but I couldn't at all understand God being irrelevant.

She retorted, "Well, I want to make my own decisions. I want to be the master, not the slave."

"But, Carol, your creator loves you. That's not a master/slave relationship. It's more like a much-loved child obeying her parent.

"And, anyway, Carol, you only have a small box of freedom. You can't have blue eyes. You can't be a man. You can't get into grad school unless you're accepted. You can't become an American citizen unless it's granted. What you actually can decide is very limited."

"Wow, Grace, I've got to put a lot of thought into that!"

The group was becoming more and more excited about God. These were some of their comments and questions:

"God is so good. He's kind. When we ask for help, he helps us!"

"How can we love God when we can't see him?"

"God's will is good for us!"

Then Lauri made an astute observation. "I'm realizing that Buddhism and Christianity are completely different."

"How are they different?" I asked.

She replied, "Christianity is a relationship!"

I was amazed Lauri had figured that out—I had never told them that!

WE REALLY WANT TO STUDY THE BIBLE
First University Student Discussion Group, Part 2

2010-2011, Re Dai

Through the fall, I was still merely baiting the group with the Bible, just reading together passages I thought would interest them. Just after Thanksgiving, they surprised me. In one session, Lauri spoke up. "We have been talking about it and we don't want to only have discussions. We want to study the Bible with you." I was thrilled.

But Carol turned on Lauri, "Shame on you!" she yelled. "The Bible is a foreign book! You should be reading Confucius instead of the Bible."

I looked at Carol. "What have you learned from Confucius?"

"Well … uh… I haven't really read Confucius."

"Shame on you, Carol!" I chided. "You haven't read your own Chinese writings?"

Twenty minutes later, after more discussion, Amelia spoke up. "We really do want to study the Bible with you—not just reading a little here and there."

"But Carol doesn't want to study the Bible," I responded. "I won't turn the discussion group into a Bible study unless everyone wants it." I offered to meet two evenings a week—one for Bible study and one for discussion. That way Carol could come just for the discussion evening and not the Bible study.

Carol quickly responded: "If you're going to study the Bible on another night, I'm coming, too. I want to study the Bible with you!"

That's when we started studying the Bible together in earnest.

By now, the women accepted that they were sinners. They knew that *if* God existed, he was good. They were communicating with God through prayer, and they were getting help from the Lord. They were finding the

198

Bible to be true and practical, but they needed to know God as the creator of the universe.

God doesn't have the same claim on our lives if he isn't our creator. For example, God being the supreme lawgiver and judge only makes sense if he is the creator. As far as I could tell, it had never crossed these women's minds that this world might have been created by someone. They probably thought that if the Christian God existed, although he was very kind, loving and helpful, he was still just one of many gods.

We started our Bible study at Genesis 1 so they could read about God creating the universe. After reading the chapter together, I asked them some questions.

"Did God like his creation? What did he say about it?"

"He said it was good."

"What about people? What did he say about the people he created?"

"He said we're very good!" They were all smiles.

"So what happened? If the people God made were very good when he created them, how is there bad in each of us? Where does the bad come from?"

Lauri looked like she was about to cry. "Something terrible must have happened after Genesis 1!" I tried to suppress a smile—she was leading right into Genesis 3.

But Kristen didn't like where the discussion was going. "The bad comes from having desires." She spoke with defiance. That's classic Buddhist teaching. Evil comes from having desires—any desire, good or bad—and the way to get rid of evil is to stop having any desire whatsoever. If your heart is void of all desire, then you can enter nirvana. It sounds boring to me, but I didn't tell them that.

Instead I challenged them. "So, your desire to eat, marry, and have children, and my desire to be with you—that's where evil comes from?"

They all looked at each other. "No, that can't be." They had just turned away from classical Buddhism's main teaching.

I moved on to discuss the Trinity, using Genesis 1:26, where God said, "Let *us* make man in *our* image."

Carol was dismayed. "Oh no! We have three gods?" My explanation apparently hadn't made any sense. But I did notice she was beginning to consider the God of the Bible to be her God.

We talked about what being made in God's image might mean—all the ways we are different from the animals, who are not made in God's image. I wanted to drive home the point that because we are all made in God's image we're all equal. "I make sure I always greet the sidewalk sweeper and the cleaning lady. They're not inferior to me."

The women gasped. In spite of Communism's purported belief in equality, China is a class-conscious society. It's Christians who actually believe in equality.

"What we see in Genesis 1 is just what we see today," I said. "Animals and plants reproduce their own kind, and man is very different from the animals."

Emma quietly retorted, "But we came from apes."

I had been reading on this subject for months, anticipating this rebuttal. They all believed in Darwinian evolution. (I personally have not found punctuated equilibrium to be intellectually satisfying, so I didn't even deal with it.) I talked in detail about the fact that in the fossil record there are almost no transitional organisms between species, and there certainly are none between the major taxonomic groups. Complex animals appear in the fossil record fully formed, and don't change. Also, the supposed missing links between apes and men are few and don't actually qualify as missing links—they have since been assigned as fully men or fully apes, or a combination of bones from an ape and a man, but not as transitions.

Carol was shocked. I told her I had been shocked, too, when I researched it, because I had also been taught in school that evolution was so obviously true.

Then we read Genesis 2, and Carol asked, "What is this Tree of the Knowledge of Good and Evil, and why did God make it?"

I explained how Adam and Eve had only experienced good because everything God made in the world was good, but if they ate from that tree, evil would enter their lives, and God wanted to spare them from knowing evil.

"God made the Tree because he wanted us to have the ability to choose to obey him or not to obey him," I said. "He didn't want to force us."

Carol took it a step farther. "I'm learning a lot about love from God making the Tree of the Knowledge of Good and Evil," she said. "Love doesn't force people, it gives them freedom!"

But then Emma shouted at me, "Why did God make Adam and Eve so naïve? Did he want them to be like little children who would never mature?"

Laurie joined in. "God was wrong! He should not have made the Tree and given them the freedom to choose when it brought so much evil into the world!"

I said, "Suppose I'm a perfect mother and I tell my little boy not to touch the fire while I'm cooking. What does my boy do?"

"Touch the fire!" they replied in unison.

"And he gets burned. Does that mean I'm not a perfect mother?"

"No. Now we understand. It was O.K. for God to make the Tree of the

Knowledge of Good and Evil."

"I actually wouldn't want to force my boy to do everything the right way all the time or he would never mature."

"Were Adam and Eve basically tied up with rules?" I asked. "They could eat from every tree but one. They were almost entirely free, and had only one rule but they couldn't even obey that one rule."

Carol stayed for a while after everyone left, and she came very close to acknowledging the truth of the Bible. "The Bible is reality. It's tr ..." When she realized what she was saying, she quickly changed the subject.

When we came to the second to last verse of Genesis 2, we tackled the subject of marriage. Verse 2:24 says, "That is why a man leaves his father and mother and is united to his wife and they become one flesh."

These women lived in a very traditional part of China. In fact, several of them told me their marriages would be arranged. In traditional Chinese culture, the parent/child relationship is much more important than the husband/wife relationship. A husband is to love his mother more than his wife. In traditional culture, if the husband's parents order him to divorce his wife, he has to obey them and divorce her. This emphasis on the parent/child relationship over the husband/wife relationship causes a lot of pain in many Chinese families.

After reading the verse, I asked the women, "According to the Bible, which is the more important relationship—parent/child or husband/wife?"

They looked at the Bible, then they looked up at me, confused at first. Then relief started to wash over their faces. "Yes! It's not our culture that's right—it's the Bible that's right! The husband/wife relationship *is* more important than the parent/child relationship." These were young women who were hoping to marry young men who would love them deeply—who would love them more than they loved their mothers. The women longed for what the Bible teaches to be true. It was moments like these in our discussions that convinced them that the Bible really is true.

The very end of chapter 2, just before the first sin of mankind, says that the husband and wife were both naked, but didn't feel any shame. I asked, "What would a world without shame be like?"

Oh, did we ever explore the beauty of this concept—all the things that make them ashamed that wouldn't bother them anymore. They would feel completely good about themselves. I told them that is how God originally made people—without shame because there was no sin. By the time we finished, they were so excited about a world without sin and shame. But it didn't last.

In the next session, I asked a question that had never crossed my mind before; looking back, I think the Lord prompted me to ask it. "Would it be good or bad for Adam and Eve to eat the fruit of the Tree of the Knowledge of Good and Evil?" I could have kicked myself. The answer was so obvious. But I didn't realize that I was presuming that God is good—an assumption they hadn't come to yet.

They shocked me with their answer. All of them agreed that it would be good for Adam and Eve to eat the fruit.

"Why?" I asked.

It turns out it was a core question. Not only were they not assuming that God is good, their training in Communist theory led them in a different direction. "If there were no evil in the world, there would be no struggle, so no one would ever mature or grow. And there would be no competition or class struggle."

In Marxism, which they all had been taught in school, class struggle is how society progresses to a new stage of development: feudalism to capitalism, and then to the final, glorious Communist utopia.

"You can have struggle without evil in the world," I said. "For example, men and women are very different. My husband's comfort zone, like how he converses or deals with stress, sometimes really hurts me. Neither of us has sinned, but we both need to learn to change and love each other in order to get along. There was no evil, but there's struggle, growth, and resolution. So you can grow and struggle in a sinless world."

Carol told me afterward, "What you said really convinced me that there can be struggle without evil, so now I think it's best that they not eat the fruit. But at first I thought you were going to make the case that it would be best if they eat the fruit!"

But at the next session some of the women were still not satisfied. "If there's no evil, then there would be no competition. Competition pushes you to do your best, like at school."

To help them understand, I compared competition *with* evil to competition *without* evil.

"Competition with evil looks like this: when someone else is better than you, you try to bring them down and harm them so they won't be ahead of you. Competition without evil looks different: you try your best to rise above the other person, but you don't try to harm them to do it."

We made some progress, but they weren't completely convinced. "It's an issue of trusting God," I told them. "If Adam and Eve knew that God loved them and that he knew all things, then they wouldn't have eaten the fruit."

"Well, if God told *us* not to do something, we'd be sure to *do* it!"

So I gave them an example of Justin and me. "If Justin told me not to walk

202

on a particular street at night because it's dangerous, I wouldn't walk on that street. Why? Because I know Justin and I know he loves me."

They understood, finally.

Then Carol surprised me. She said, "Please, teach us to pray!"

§§§

Before we moved on from Genesis 2, I wanted them to see how personal Adam and Eve's relationship with God was, so I asked, "What relationship did God have with Adam and Eve?"

"They were friends."

I took it a step farther. "So, what relationship do you have with God?"

Every one of them looked down. Carol finally spoke up, "You've shown us God, but we're still not very clear about him." Then Lauri added, "Grace, you are our bridge to God."

"I hope that eventually you won't need a bridge, that you can go directly to God yourselves. Are you praying?"

Several of them were praying, but only simple prayers, like, "God help me."

"God wants us to tell him what's really going on in our lives. He wants us to be truthful with him and he wants intimacy with us. Every day I tell God what's happened in my life and how I feel—both the good and bad.

"Do any of you want Bibles?" Most of them said yes.

§§§

I introduced Genesis 3, the story of the serpent and the fall of man, with the question, "Why do I look older than you?" I told them, "Because death and aging entered the world as a result of the first sin. If this hadn't happened, I would still look young."

We talked about what God meant by death, when he told Adam and Eve that if they ate of the fruit of the Tree of the Knowledge of Good and Evil, they would die. We talked about the physical consequences and the spiritual separation from God. We discussed how Adam and Eve's relationship with God changed from close friendship to them being afraid of God and hiding from him, how after sinning, they were ashamed for the first time in their lives. We looked at how the husband/wife relationship changed from being so beautiful to one of blaming each other and the husband ruling over the wife, and how because of the sin of the first woman, all women now have pain in childbirth. Even nature was cursed because of Adam and Eve's sin. Maybe that's why we have earthquakes and hurricanes.

When Carol saw how women were punished as a result of Eve's disobedience, she yelled, "Why did God make it that the punishment of the woman was to have pain in childbirth? Many women die in childbirth. A punishment is supposed to help a person. You can't be helped if the punishment is death!"

I met with her one-on-one to explain. "Carol, the punishment of women was not that some would die in childbirth, just that there would be pain in childbirth. Actually, the consequence of people disobeying God already was death. But God, in his kindness, mitigated the punishment and had their bodies die slowly.

"When they ate the fruit, they killed their relationship with God. There was no punishment that could get their relationship with God back. They themselves were fundamentally changed. Although they still had good in their hearts because they were made in the image of God, their hearts were permanently soiled. They couldn't go back.

"Because all of us have sinned, we deserve to die, but Jesus came and died in our place. If we put all our sins on Jesus and let him pay for our sins, then we'll be forgiven and we can get close to God. A lot of the evil is taken out of our hearts then, but it takes a lifetime for God to teach us how to become good."

Carol almost shouted, "I want that! I want my heart to be pure! How do I become a Christian? By reading the Bible?"

"Carol, do you believe God exists?"

"You've shown us evidence. There aren't in-between creatures between apes and men. And I've read that they found Noah's ark. But to be honest, I only partly believe."

"Carol, I'm sorry. You can't become a Christian unless you believe God exists. Why don't you ask God to help you to know he exists?"

"I want to be like you, Grace. I want to be able to speak openly about what's in my heart. I want to live without shame."

"Carol, the reason I can be so open is because God has forgiven my sins. That's why I'm not ashamed. If someone sees something dirty in my heart, it's already forgiven. I'm already accepted by God, and I know I can get help from him to change."

"Grace, every day I'm going to think about what you told me today."

WE NEED SCIENTIFIC EVIDENCE
First University Student Discussion Group, Part 3

2011, Re Dai

During the whole next meeting Jasmine looked like she was thinking deeply. Toward the end of the session she said, "We can't believe this because the Chinese people are Buddhists."

Carol was disgusted, "Open your life, Jasmine! There's a whole new world out there!"

I asked Jasmine, "Are you Buddhist?"

"No, because I think it's superstition. We're afraid this is superstition, too."

I stood up because it was 9 p.m. and the session was over. They all crowded around me. Lauri exclaimed, "We need scientific evidence!"

I asked, "Do you want me to prepare scientific evidence for next week?"

They said yes, they really wanted that. Then one of them added, "This is great! We gave you homework."

When we met a week later, first, Lauri asked me what had convinced me of the existence of God. I outlined my journey from atheism to believing in God. Then I started my presentation.

"There's no scientific proof of God's existence, but there certainly is a lot of evidence. You need to ask yourself what is the most likely explanation for the evidence. Also, are you finding God to be true and helpful when you read the Bible and pray? Ask God to reveal himself to you."

I started with the Big Bang, using a diagram. "Scientists used to believe the universe had no beginning. In the 20th century, astronomers discovered that the universe is expanding, so they realized it had to have a beginning. There was nothing physical before the Big Bang, so the physical universe had to have had a non-physical cause. This matches what the Bible says in

Hebrews 11:3, "what is seen was not made out of what was visible."

I have a biology degree, so science makes sense to me. But none of the women were trained in the sciences, so it was difficult for them.

Then I moved on to the fossil record. "Just about every complex life form arose suddenly, fully formed and fully functional. Doesn't that sound like Genesis 1? When Darwin postulated his theory, he said that the fossil record would prove his theory, but just the opposite has happened. The more fossils that have been discovered, the more evidence there is against Darwinian evolution. There just aren't intermediate organisms between the major groups that Darwin said were necessary for his theory to be true. Scientists who believe in evolution have no good explanation for the fossil record."

After that, I presented the arguments for Intelligent Design. "How do you know if something came about by chance or intelligent planning? There are sciences that deal with this question—forensic science, archaeology, cryptography. If you came across a car in a field, would you think all the parts were assembled by chance, or would you assume an intelligent being designed the car? If something is very complex, and it has meaning or function, then it probably didn't come about by chance because chance doesn't produce meaning. It's not just that there isn't enough evidence for evolution, nature provides evidence that there was a designer.

"Living beings are made up of many 'machines.' Every single part of each of these 'machines' is essential and must function or the whole 'machine' can't function. A system like that cannot be formed by the gradual adding of individual pieces, as required by evolution because the 'machine' won't function until every part is there. There are many, many examples of this in our bodies and nature." We looked at the cell, the eye, bacteria flagellum, and even sex. I told them that sex is even more tricky because two different organisms need to simultaneously evolve in exactly complementary ways—any slight deviation and there's no next generation!

Then I told them about the Anthropic Principle, that the universe in thousands, probably millions of ways—in physics, geology and astronomy—is exactly what is needed for life, and any slight change would doom us all.

I threw in a comment from scientists that there is far more beauty in the universe than there needs to be. Why would this be? Since they wouldn't understand the beauty of the mathematical equations that are the basis of the laws of physics, I instead spoke in concrete terms and gave a minor example, someone they had already met: my beautiful, long-haired, white cat, Snowball. Snowball doesn't need to be that pretty, but she and so much of nature are extraordinarily beautiful. But their beauty is unnecessary—it doesn't improve their functioning.

After presenting the scientific evidence, I showed them historical evidence for Jesus. I concentrated on extra-biblical sources, especially the writings of historians who weren't Christians. Most of the women had actually been taught in school that Jesus never existed!

At the end, Emma commented, "Grace, you really did your homework. We have no refutation for your evidence."

I asked, "So what conclusions have you drawn from the scientific evidence I gave you?"

Everyone but Jasmine said that they now believed in a creator God. Some of them added, "But we don't know who this God is—the God of the Bible, or some other god."

So I asked, "From what we see in creation, what would this creator be like? I want you to keep in mind that a creator can't create something that is fundamentally greater than himself, and what he creates is a reflection of himself."

They each added a characteristic. "He would be intelligent." "He's perfect." "Wise." "He has personality." "Oh, and he loves beauty!" "He's an artist, and a scientist."

That last one, scientist, is especially interesting because in Chinese thinking, science and God are opposites. Science is truth and God is myth. If you asked a Chinese who was not a Christian if they believed in God, they would most likely respond, "No, I don't believe in God because I believe in science." Now the women had come to realize that God is not the opposite of science; in fact, he is the creator of science!

Then they added that he loves us. They had basically come up with the God of the Bible!

I asked, "We can communicate, so can God communicate?"

"Yes." Prior to this group, the women had never conceived of a personal God, so their answer was amazing.

"Does God want to communicate with us?"

"Yes, he does."

Then I said, "We can have relationship with each other. God created that. So can God have relationship?"

"Yes."

"Does he want relationship with us?"

"Yes, he sure does!"

"So what blocks us from having relationship with God?" In answer to this question, I explained the plan of salvation.

Then I asked if any of them wanted a simple version of the Bible, and the women who had previously said they didn't want a Bible grabbed them off the nightstand.

Kristen was so glad to get a simple version of the Bible. I had previously given her an English/Chinese Bible, but the Chinese was written in somewhat classical Chinese. She commented, "Oh, am I glad to get this easier Chinese version of the Bible. The English/Chinese Bible you gave me was useless. The English is too hard for me to understand and the Chinese is nonsense."

Emma, holding a Bible in her hand, said, "I've never been taught how to figure out if something is true. How do I figure out if the Bible is true?"

"How about if you read through Luke during the summer break and write down all the questions you have."

"That's a great idea. I'm going to do that. That should help me figure out if it's true."

Then Amelia said, "I'm going to do that, too!"

Previously, Emma and Amelia had been the most resistant. Now they were the most responsive!

Carol had just come back from one and a half weeks at home and she seemed hardened again. "We're studying Marx. He was a scientist and he was against God. And our top leader [of China] doesn't believe in God, either. I need to follow my leaders."

About this time, Del's boyfriend, who was studying at a distant university, told her he had leukemia. She took a long-distance train to his university to see him, only to find out that he didn't have leukemia. Telling her he was dying was his way of breaking up with her because he had started to date someone else! During the train rides, Del kept reading the Bible. She got so much help from the Lord during that trying time that she came to believe in the God of the Bible. But she told me she wasn't ready to commit her life to Christ yet.

I showed them the *Jesus* film in Chinese. Several of the women were totally absorbed by the film, leaning forward, writing down questions.

At the end Emma said, "I'm really impressed and I'm beginning to believe." Amelia said she also was starting to believe from what she saw of Jesus.

But Carol had a different reaction. She thought the *Jesus* film was hilarious. "It's so funny that Jesus said if someone takes your outer coat, you should give him your inner garments, too."

"What's so funny about that, Carol?"

"Because you'd be naked!"

"That's not what he's advocating, Carol. Unless you have an incredibly expensive coat, who would grab your coat off you? Only someone who is

208

so cold that he resorts to stealing. We often think of being kind and helping people if they're nice to us. But if another person has a need, even if he mistreats us, we should still be kind to him. For example, if I have a loaf of bread and someone steals it from me, it's like Jesus telling me, 'Don't just let him take your bread, give him meat! He needs nutrition. He's starving!'"

Carol was overwhelmed. "Wow!"

Then Carol asked what "turn the other cheek" meant.

To explain, I told a story about someone who was very mean to me. "I confronted the woman. When I confronted her, I was actually turning the other cheek because I thought she might try to hurt me again during the confrontation, which she did. I was willing to be vulnerable again in an attempt to restore the relationship."

Carol laughed. "It's good I only have two cheeks!"

But Jasmine was irate. "All that stuff about Jesus calming the storm—it's hogwash! It didn't happen."

I said, "Since you don't like reading the Bible …"

But Jasmine interrupted me, "Of course I like reading the Bible. It helps me so much. But I've never been taught this stuff and it's too hard to believe."

I used my fingers to form a small box. "A person's background is like this box. It's very small. Much of what you were taught as a child was true, but there are many things each of us didn't learn from our backgrounds. If you stay inside the box of your background, you will be a small person, no matter how good your background was. Am I a broad person?"

They all said, "Yes, you sure are."

"That's because I didn't just stay within the confines of my background and what I was taught as a child. I looked for and embraced truth wherever I found it—inside or outside my upbringing. Don't remain a small person! Embrace truth, even if you weren't taught it as a child!

"There are a couple of other ways you can find out if Jesus is the creator God you now believe in." I showed them Jeremiah 29:13. I said, "If you seek God with all your heart, you'll find him." Then we read John 7:7. I told them, "You will find out if Jesus' teaching is true if you do what he says."

Several of them told me that they planned to obey Jesus to see if he truly is the creator God.

When the group returned after the summer, during the first month some of them were asking me all the questions they had saved up from their summer of reading the Bible.

But then the unexpected happened. A month after the semester started, the university began a smear campaign to try to keep students from becoming Christians. The professors were told to slander Christians, Christianity, and foreigners. The professors told students that one particular foreign Christian teacher was forcing students to become Christians and that he was an extremist. I knew this teacher and neither of these accusations were true. Then the professors told the students, "If you are becoming a Party member and you become a Christian, you are a traitor to your country!" Another professor said, "Foreigners are bad. You can't trust them. They will trick you!"

At first I was able to effectively counter all the accusations by asking a simple question. "Is what they say true?" That question seemed to clear the students' thinking.

But the campaign against Christians continued, so I disbanded the group for six weeks so we wouldn't be discovered and to let things cool down.

When we started meeting again, though, the group had changed. They had been affected by the propaganda campaign and some of them may have been interrogated—they never told me. Many of them had become afraid and apprehensive.

Jasmine seemed determined to turn everyone away from Christianity, even after the rest warmed up a little. When I made a point that impressed the women and they again considered following the Lord, Jasmine hissed at them, "This is foreign religion. You shouldn't believe it!"

The group became untenable and disbanded. I was heartbroken.

Just before all the persecution started, Carol had gone to Thailand as a short-term exchange student, so she missed the slander campaign. Shortly after arriving in Thailand, she met a few Chinese Christians who shared Christ with her and took her to church.

Carol emailed me: "I'm so surprised that I have actually come to believe in God. And I'm dying to tell you why. It's because you, Grace, introduced me to God and all the arguments you gave me about God made me curious and excited. I've come to believe that God is truth and he loves us. I have also been very impressed by your life and the lives of the Christians I have met in Thailand. Your lives are happy and meaningful. You're learning new things from life every day. You also patiently help other people."

From the way she talked about God in her other emails, though, I realized that she didn't actually understand what a Christian is, so I led her to Christ through email. She was baptized in Thailand. I was overwhelmed with joy that this student, who had laughed at me a year and a half earlier for believing in God, had given her life to Christ.

After Carol returned to China, one of the last times I saw her I told her we had to move away from that city because, through another investigation, the police had discovered some of our ministry. I wanted to encourage her to stay firm in the Lord since I couldn't teach her anymore. I showed her Matthew 24:13, which says "the one who stands firm to the end will be saved."

Carol looked disgusted. "I don't need that verse!"

I was upset. "Why?"

"I plan to go deep with Jesus and hold onto him. I don't need that verse telling me what to do!"

Since the investigation was still going on, I said, "Christians will suffer persecution."

"That is our sacrifice for Jesus," was her reply.

The very next week Carol was interrogated and she stood firm! As I write this, she is in Christian fellowship and growing in the Lord.

When I left that city, several of the other women wrote me notes thanking me for introducing them to God and teaching them to pray. I've wondered if they, too, had become Christians.

THE BIBLE IS THE FULFILLMENT OF MY DREAM!

Second University Student Discussion Group

2011-2012, Re Dai

After I had been meeting with the first group for a year—about four months before it disbanded—they introduced me to a group of freshmen so I could start another discussion group. The first group was supposed to have invited them to a general discussion group; that way I could slowly introduce the Bible, as they were willing. But instead they recruited them to a "Bible group."

The new group, made up of five young women who were English majors, were a little nervous when they walked in, but they were comfortable with each other—they were roommates and friends. They could hardly speak any English.

Because they had come for a Bible group, I decided to dive in at the first meeting by asking if any of them had ever read the Bible.

Three of them said they had. Lu spoke first. She had an almost round face, with her hair pulled back in a ponytail. "My aunt and uncle became Christians in America. When they visited, they gave me a Bible. I've read a little."

Then Maria: "I'm Lisu and my father's a pastor. I love the Bible." That was unexpected. The Lisu are a minority group in China who became Christians en masse a century ago as the result of a missionary's witness.

The third girl, whose name was Janna, said she had read a lot of the Bible. "I'm a crazy fan of Jay Chou—you know, the Taiwanese pop singer. He sang a song about Christians. I didn't know what he was singing about, so I looked up the words on the web. He had become a Christian! I'm really interested in Christianity because of him, so I asked a friend to get me a Bible, and I've read a lot of it."

"Do you like the Bible?" I asked.

"Yeah, I like it a lot because it helps me with the problems I face in life."

"Like what?"

"When I have to compromise to get along with people, I think of the queen who was willing to give her life for her people, and then I know what to do."

She had read all the way to Esther? And she was even applying it to her life!

Jane was of the Dai minority, so her family was Buddhist. She had never read the Bible. "But I had a neighbor who was a Christian, and oh, she was kind. I really like Christians because of her."

While everyone else spoke, Lacey kept her head down. I could tell she was embarrassed and didn't want to answer the question. After the other four shared, she looked up at me, and spoke quietly, but with passion. "I've never read it. Four years ago my high school teacher told me the Bible was a great book and I should read it. I've been looking for a Bible ever since! I've searched and searched for one, in libraries and bookstores. For four years I've searched, but I couldn't find a Bible."

I was almost in tears. "Maybe I can help you." I opened the cabinet behind me and pulled out the stack of Bibles I had bought for this group. I held one out to Lacey. "You can have it."

Lacey grabbed the Bible and hugged it to her chest. "This is the fulfillment of my dream!"

After that everyone wanted a Bible. Lacey, especially, started reading her dream book.

It struck me that each of these women had been profoundly impacted by a Christian. These small acts of witness made this group different than any I ever led in China.

For several months before the group started, I had prayed fervently that the Lord would handpick the women for my new group. It was obvious that he had.

Because other people had done some of the preliminary work for me, I didn't have to use most of the pre-evangelism questions I normally asked atheists and Buddhists.

During the first few weeks of reading the Bible together, some of the women's comments were quite humorous. When we read that we are to love our enemies, one of them exclaimed, "I couldn't love my enemies—it's too exhausting to do that!" Another countered, "I've found it's too exhausting to hate my enemies!" When we looked at Matthew 23:11, "The greatest among you will be your servant," one of them commented, "Obama has to serve the American people."

They didn't ask me for evidence of the existence of God like most of the Chinese I worked with. It took only three weeks of discussing life and Bible passages before several of them came to believe in God and were considering becoming Christians! Lacey and Lu said they felt an emptiness inside and wondered if Jesus could satisfy them.

The main questions the group asked were about the cost of being a Christian. I wasn't expecting that, and it was refreshing.

Four of the five were applying for Communist Party membership. They wanted to become members because the best jobs go to Party members. The problem was that you weren't supposed to be a Communist Party member if you believed in God.

They had lots of concerns: "Is it possible to be a Communist Party member and a Christian?" "Even if they don't catch us, wouldn't it be hypocritical to be both?" "In the Party application we'll be asked, 'Do you have a religion?' What should we answer?" "Could we wait until after we join the Party to become Christians? The Party would be less likely to find out then."

The process for joining the Party was stringent. Not only did they have to fill out one or more extensive applications, their lives would be monitored during the application process to find out if they were involved in any anti-revolutionary activities, like attending a Christian fellowship on campus (which was illegal and secret) or participating in my evangelistic discussion group (which was also illegal and secret). Even attending the government church was not allowed for Communist Party applicants because the government didn't want Party members to be Christians.

Applicants were also expected to be involved in leadership roles on campus, and to be civic-minded in the community. The whole process took about a year.

I didn't want to tell them what to do—I just wanted to help them think it through. I discussed with them the problems they would face if they were both Christians and Party members. One thing I was firm about, though. If they became Christians, they could not deny that they believed in Jesus, no matter what happened, no matter what the cost. I showed them Matthew 10:32-33, "Whoever acknowledges me before others, I will also acknowledge before my Father in heaven. But whoever disowns me before others, I will disown before my Father in heaven."

Janna, especially, found this a very difficult decision. She said she would have to think long and hard about it before she could decide whether she would follow Jesus.

Only three weeks after we began meeting, the university started an investigation to try to discover any Christian students or Christian activities on campus. A lot of students were interrogated. The best way to avoid being discovered during an active investigation was to shut down all Christian activities. We discontinued all of our campus ministry and hoped the investigation would pass.

The day we disbanded, I told the women they were not to tell anyone about our meetings. I also told them that if we ever saw each other in public, we had to pretend we didn't know each other. These were our precautions to try to keep from being discovered.

The Lord had moved mightily in the three weeks I was able to meet with them. When we disbanded, they still wanted to find Christ, with or without me, so a few of them started attending the government church by themselves.

In addition to the foreigners' fellowship, Justin and I also attended the government church every week. After the group disbanded, I spotted three of them at church. They lowered their heads and covered their eyes to avoid making eye contact with me. Other students, whom I barely knew, greeted me and hugged me at church. But the ones I knew and loved best had to act like they didn't know me or care to know me!

At the end of the sermon one Sunday, Lacey and Lu went forward at the invitation to receive Christ. The counselor who talked with them, though, told them they weren't ready yet.

After six weeks, it appeared that the investigation had died down, so I restarted the group. I told them that from now on, when we met, they could only come and go to the meetings in ones and twos. I still wanted to make sure we wouldn't be discovered.

We spent the whole first session again discussing the cost of following Jesus. I commented on the fact that on the Party application they would have to sign on the dotted line that they didn't believe in God.

Lacey corrected me, "They'll ask us if we have a religion."

They would also have to write a paper proving that they believe in the Communist Party. "The problem is I don't believe in the Party," Janna said.

That alarmed me. That is something you don't say in China. I had to handle the discussion delicately, because Justin and I were very careful not to criticize the government or political system. Anyone could report us, or someone might just innocently repeat what I said. So I asked Janna why she felt that way.

"Because there are so many problems in this country."

"Well, I believe in democracy, but there are a lot of problems in America."

"No, it's not the same. I think the Party has caused the problems in our country."

I was still walking on eggs. "Oh, that's different. You have to be true to your heart. If you aren't, you'll start down the road of hypocrisy. That's a very bad road because you'll become more and more alienated from who you really are."

At the end of that meeting, Lacey and Janna decided to give their lives to Jesus, right in the group! After Lacey became a Christian, I asked her how she was going to answer the Party's question, "Do you have a religion?" She looked disgusted, "I don't have a religion—I know Jesus! He's not religion. I don't even like religion!"

A couple of weeks later, Lacey told the group, "I've changed so much from knowing Jesus! There was a girl I used to hate; I always got real angry at her. But I've stopped hating her now because of Jesus. Also, I used to lie, especially to my parents. Like, they would tell me I couldn't go out to see my boyfriend, so I would tell them I was going to a girlfriend's house. That way they'd let me go out. Now, I really regret lying to them like that."

Janna said Christ was making her more gentle and kind. "I'm learning to love others and give them second chances. I'm not so anxious anymore, and I'm more outgoing. I also have a sense of quietude in my heart now."

The other three women were paying attention.

"Because Janna has changed so much since becoming a Christian, I'm really attracted to Jesus," Jane said after one meeting.

I started seeing the women one-on-one in addition to the group meetings, so I could talk with them more personally, and they would open up to me.

I sensed that Janna, the "crazy fan" of Jay Chou, wasn't growing as a Christian, in spite of the fact that she had changed so much. I suspected I knew why. I asked her during one of our private sessions, "Who is more important to you—your Creator or Jay Chou?"

"It's a toss-up! You see, Jay Chou introduced me to Jesus, so Jay Chou came first! Jay Chou's more important to me."

I didn't say any more, but the question plagued Janna for weeks afterward. She knew her answer wasn't right, and she finally came up with the answer herself, using her own logic. "God sent Jay Chou to introduce me to himself, so God came first! He's most important." She paused and then added, "You know, Jay Chou used to be my god." I had guessed that. After that Janna started to grow as a Christian.

When I met with Lacey, she told me she wanted to tell her dad that she had become a Christian, but she was really scared. She felt close to her dad, but she thought he would be angry that she now believed in Jesus. As we discussed it, she decided that she first wanted him to see the changes Christ had made in her life. After he was attracted to the new Lacey, she would tell him the reason for the changes.

But Lacey was so excited about having become a Christian she couldn't wait. When she was on the phone with him she said, "Dad, I've changed."

Her dad sneered, "That's impossible! I don't believe you! I don't believe you could be a good person!"

After telling him some of the ways she had changed, she added, "I believe in God now, Dad."

Her father burst out laughing. "Why on earth would you do something as stupid as that? Why would you ever believe in God?"

Lacey replied, "That's my secret!" She meant me, that I was her secret, because she wasn't to tell anyone about me!

As they talked more, he began to realize that his daughter actually had changed. He closed the conversation with, "Well, if something can get you to change, I'm in favor of it, whatever it is."

When Lacey went home for the Chinese New Year break, she stayed up late each night to wait for her father to come home from work so she could share with him about the Lord. Finally, her father began asking her to read the Bible to him.

When she returned, she told me, "I'm so excited. My dad told me he is O.K. with me being a Christian. He had only one request. He doesn't want me to be public about my faith or get baptized until after I become a Party member next semester. That way I won't jeopardize my application to the Party."

Surprisingly, it was Lacey's boyfriend who opposed her coming to believe in Christ—so she broke up with him over that vacation. She was incensed as she told me, "He tried to force me to stop believing in Jesus! He wouldn't stop arguing with me. Our perspectives in life are completely different." I talked with her about what it's like to be married to a Christian man. She was quite excited about the idea.

At one of the group sessions, I showed them the *Jesus* film. Lu asked, "So, Jesus is God?"

Maria, the one whose father was a pastor, replied, "No, he isn't."

I quietly corrected, "Yes, he is."

A little farther into the film Lu again asked, "Is Jesus God?"

Maria again responded. "No, he isn't God. He's God's Son."

I again quietly contradicted her, "Jesus is God."

Afterward, I asked to meet with Maria. I had wondered even before the film if she really did know the Lord, and I wanted to talk with her about it.

As soon as Maria walked into our apartment, before I could say anything, she asked, "Who is Jesus?"

All it took was showing her John 1:1-3, 14. Then she commented, "Oh, so Jesus is God!"

"Maria, what is a Christian?" That question and "How does a person become a Christian?" are the most effective questions I ask people who profess to be Christians when I suspect they aren't.

She replied, "Someone who obeys every law in the Bible." I jarred up, but I tried to hide my reaction. She paused, then said, "But that's the problem. There are so many laws in the Bible, I have trouble following all of them! I've been trying, but some of them I don't even understand. Could you help me so I can follow every law?"

Instead, I showed her Romans 3:20 and Galatians 3:10-11, which say that no one is righteous by obeying the law. She was stunned. After that I showed her from Scripture how a person does become righteous before God. She finally came to faith and her life was revolutionized.

Later she said, "I have never understood sermons or the Bible before. My eyes have been opened. It all makes sense to me now."

I began studying the Bible every week with her. We studied topics like the plan of salvation, the Holy Spirit ("He's an angel, right?"), Satan, temptation, an overview of the Old Testament and its significance. She read Galatians and was totally confused by it, so I went over Paul's arguments against legalism in Galatians. She finally understood.

Then she asked me to teach her how to share the gospel. She had told some people about Jesus dying for them but it hadn't meant anything to them.

"Don't start with Jesus' death, Maria. First find out what your friends' felt needs are. Also, find out what they believe so you know where they're coming from."

The next week I added another idea for how to witness. "Open up your life and share both the good and the bad that you've experienced. Show them how you are finding solutions to life's problems through prayer and the Bible. That way they'll see from your life how God can help a person. You need to match what God has done in your life with their felt needs. Tell them about Jesus' death later.

"You can also tell them you're praying for them when they tell you a struggle they're having. Many people will see that as an expression of love. It's a good starter. Tell me, what's the most precious thing God has given you?"

She immediately replied, "Jesus died for me."

"How does that help you personally? Like, how does it affect you emotionally?"

She drew a complete blank.

I explained how it affects me emotionally. "I feel clean because of what Jesus did. It also makes me feel free. I'm not ashamed. I'm able to be open and honest, because I've been forgiven. I'm courageous in moral dilemmas because if I make the wrong decision, he'll still forgive me. And, oh, I know how much I'm loved!"

After that she was able to respond from her heart how Jesus' death affected her.

"They need to see your emotions. It's rare that a person would respond to a detached, emotionless, intellectual presentation about God or the gospel."

She started to become more effective at sharing her faith.

Then she told me that she had a friend who was going to Bible school, and she was teaching him everything I taught her!

In the end she told me that she wants to become an evangelist and Bible teacher to her own people. "My people, the Lisu, are completely confused about their faith. They hardly understand anything, even if they're going to Bible school. I want to help them know the Christian faith. And when I teach them or share the gospel with them, I'm going to do it the way you taught me—by asking them questions. Whenever you asked me a question, I became so curious and was dying to know the answer."

When I met with Jane alone, she told me about her family. They were stonecutters. Her brother's eye was injured when a sliver of stone had flown into it. They didn't have money to buy goggles.

Her mother was illiterate. Jane was of the Dai minority, which, at least in her community, didn't value educating their daughters. Instead, they often married them off young. (There were minority women in that area, already married with a child or two by age 14!) Jane's parents didn't force her into an early marriage, and were willing to sacrifice financially to put her through high school. She applied herself to her studies and was accepted at college, so her parents continued to sacrifice for her college education. Clearly, they loved their daughter.

One evening Jane called me. "Is it possible to see you tonight? I really need to talk to you." I biked the half hour to our apartment at the university. When I saw Jane, she cried and cried. "I just found out my father is a heroin addict. Many of the men in the area I come from are heroin addicts. But I hadn't known that my dad was also. He has severe stomach pain all the time, and he said he started taking heroin to dull the pain."

I cried with her, comforted her, and prayed with her for her father. There weren't any drug rehab centers where her family lived, and with so many men in the area addicted, it would be hard to break the habit and stay away from drugs.

I told her that she could pray to Jesus for her father's healing, and I also told her how Jesus had healed my lung disease. She said she would pray, and I assured her that I would pray for him, too.

I also tried to get medical help for her father's stomach disease.

Then she told me, "I really, really want to become a Christian. My mother is Buddhist. When I go home for vacation, I'll ask her if it's O.K. for me to become a Christian. If she doesn't object, I will."

When Jane returned from vacation, she had some good news. "My father's taking less and less heroin, and my family's becoming more unified because he's taking less drugs. I'm so excited!"

"Why do you think your father is taking less drugs?"

"Well, of course, it's because I've been praying to Jesus for him."

I grinned.

"So, what was your mother's response to you wanting to become a Christian?"

"She said it could jeopardize my Party membership, so I've decided to become a Party member and not a Christian."

She looked so unhappy. I followed it up. I wanted her to see her own heart's desires. "Tell me, Jane, why do you want to become a Christian?"

"I know a woman from a poor family who's a Christian. She told me how God helps her cope and be happy in her situation. God gives her peace. That's so attractive to me. Also, I myself have changed a lot because of Jesus. Now I'm friendly, courageous, and self-confident. When I'm afraid of the dark and I pray, Jesus helps me not be afraid. I'm happy now." I had seen her transformation from being sad all the time to glowing with joy. It was a light that couldn't be hidden. She continued, "Furthermore, I've seen the changes in the others in the group after they became Christians, and I really like it."

"So, why do you want to become a Party member?"

Her face fell. "To tell you the truth, I don't. It's just that my mother wants me to, and it'll help me get a good job. My mother and I don't think I have much potential, so Party membership would really help me land a good job."

"It's important to honor your mother, Jane, because she's your parent, but God is your greater parent—he created you. In fact, he created your mother, so he's even the father of your mother. You need to obey God even more than your mother."

220

I asked if she believed God could help her get a job. She said yes.

"Even if you aren't a Party member?"

"Yes, he can."

I shared with her about the learning disability my youngest son had had, and how, after fasting and praying, he passed his medical training. Jane cried.

I had started to suspect that Jane already was a Christian, but she just didn't know it. The next week I told the group, "Some people are telling you that you cannot believe in Jesus. But how can someone tell you that you don't believe what you believe? If you believe in Jesus, you believe in him!"

I turned to Jane. "Do you believe in Jesus?"

"Yes."

"Do you believe Jesus is the creator God, that he died for your sins and rose again?"

"Yes, I do."

"Have you confessed your sins to Jesus and asked him to forgive you?"

"Yes, I have."

"Do you want to obey Jesus?"

"Yes."

"Jane, you already are a Christian!"

Jane jarred up. Things hadn't happened the way she planned. She had accidentally become a Christian!

The whole culture of Jane's people group, the Dai, is based on Buddhism and Buddhist rituals.

A week after Jane realized she was a Christian, she told me she had called her mom and told her the news. Her mom told her that becoming a Christian was really a bad idea. "She said that as a Christian, I won't be able to participate in the Buddhist rituals," Jane said. "And when the old women in the village realize I've become a Christian and won't participate in the rituals, I will be cast out of the village and ostracized."

Jane looked dejected.

I waited a few weeks to let Jane think about what her mother said. I wanted to give her a chance to reconsider her commitment to the Lord. If she didn't want to be a Christian, I wanted her to be able to walk away from Jesus.

I asked her, "Knowing that you will be rejected by your village and the Dai people for being a Christian, is this a price you are willing to pay? Do you really want to be a Christian?"

She replied simply: "I will follow Jesus."

"How are you going to handle this?"

"I won't be able to live at home for any length of time."

"How do you feel about that?"

"I'm so sad. I love my people and my culture."

"Do you know any other Dai people who are Christians?"

"No, I don't think there are any besides me."

"If you won't be returning home to live, how are your people going to find out about Jesus?"

"I've been worried about that, too."

"Maybe when you're stronger as a Christian, you can go back and share with them."

On her next visit home, Jane did just that. She shared with her people about Jesus. But then the village started persecuting Jane's parents because of her belief in Jesus! Jane told me that was harder for her to bear than if she were being persecuted herself. But her parents loved her so much they told her that they were willing to be ostracized so Jane could be a Christian if that was what she really wanted.

Of the five women in the group, Lu was the only one who had not become a Christian. She had told me privately, a few weeks before Jane realized she was a Christian, that she wasn't ready to take that step. A week later, as a group, we studied John 4, which is about the woman at the well. As we discussed what "living water" meant, I showed them John 7:38-39, that the living water is the Spirit of God living in us, that when we're Christians, life wells up in our spirits and overflows. Lu spent the whole next week thinking about the living water. She wanted that for herself.

Then, at the meeting where Jane discovered she was already a Christian, we discussed some basic questions about the gospel. Lu's answers were the clearest.

I joked, "Lu is the only one who hasn't come to believe in Jesus, but she's the one with the clearest grasp of the gospel."

Lu got mad. "Why do you refer to me as the only one who doesn't believe?"

"Because a few weeks ago you told me you weren't ready to believe in Jesus."

"But I do believe in Jesus!" she shouted. I was overwhelmed with joy, but I also looked over at the window, hoping no one outside had heard.

I asked her the questions I had asked Jane, and I realized that Lu had already become a Christian, too!

When Lu and I met that week, I asked her about a speech she had recently given.

"Grace, I don't want to talk about that. I want to talk about how bad I feel about myself. Everyone else in the group has so much to contribute to

222

society—Jane is trying to build a home for homeless children in her village, Lacey was elected student council president and is writing and organizing plays at the university … But I have no skills and no contributions. All I do is study."

I showed her I Corinthians 12, which is about the different gifts in the church. "All of us are needed for what we can add because everyone's gifts are not only different, they're complementary. Even though this Scripture is about the church, this principle applies in society, too. You, Lu, have unique contributions because of your personality, experience, and gifts. You should not try to duplicate what others are doing. That's not needed. What's needed is what only you can offer."

After looking at I Corinthians 12, Lu began to blossom. She stopped comparing herself to others, and discovered her own unique gifting and contributions. She discovered that she's a great actress. It was beautiful to see.

I Corinthians 12 had set her life on a new course. She was also hooked on reading the Bible. During one of the group sessions, she hugged her Bible and said, "I love this book! It's changing my life!"

In a group meeting a few months after everyone had become Christians, Lacey told us a story that should have alerted us, but we didn't realize the significance of it at the time. "I was told by my teacher that I had to meet with two men instead of going to class. My teacher said they wanted to talk with me because I'm the class monitor."

When she showed up for the meeting, the two men said they were graduate students at a university in another province, and they were doing research on the religions of minority students.

"But something wasn't right. The students they were interviewing were English majors. It was obvious they were conducting these interviews because they thought English majors would most likely be influenced by Christianity. So they weren't researching minority religions at all. They were trying to find if any students had become Christians. I knew right then they were fakes.

"The teacher had given the men the class roster, which includes each student's minority group and dorm room number. They questioned me for a whole hour!"

This is the transcript I wrote from Lacey's report of the interview-cum-interrogation:

Two men: "Do you like religion?"

Lacey: "I'm not interested in religion."

Two men: "Are there any religious groups on campus?"

Lacey: "That doesn't interest me."

Two men: "Do you belong to a religious group?"

Lacey: "Like I said, I'm not interested in religion."

Two men: (Maria and Jane were Lacey's minority roommates.) "Maria is Lisu. Is she a Christian?" Even the government considers the Lisu people to be a Christian people group.

Lacey: "Yes."

Two men: "Is she open about her Christianity?"

Lacey: "Why are you asking me this stuff?"

Two men: "We would like to talk to Maria. Call her on the phone!"

Lacey: "Maria is in class right now so you can't talk to her."

Two men: "Call her on the phone, we said! She can leave class."

Lacey: "She's in class. I won't call her."

Two men: "Jane is of the Dai minority. Is Jane Buddhist?" The Dai people are known as a Buddhist people group. This was an explosive question because Jane, a Buddhist, had become a Christian. The two men really wanted to find out this kind of information. Lacey didn't know how to respond.

Lacey: "I don't like Jane." This was probably not true.

Lacey said to the group, "I knew they weren't graduate students doing research. Every time religion came up they leaned forward and got excited. They also didn't have the humility of researchers. They thought they could boss me around. This was a trick and a trap!

"I was so angry! Afterward, I told my teacher not to ever do that to me again. She asked me why. I told her that they were just tricksters!

"After it was all over, I felt so bad that I had lied. I keep begging the Lord for forgiveness. I lied to protect all of you."

Turning to Maria, Lacey said, "I'm so sorry I told them you're a Christian." Lacey felt like she had betrayed Maria.

Maria smiled and replied, "I don't mind. I used to be afraid of people knowing I was a Christian. In the past it was a secret, but that was when I didn't understand my faith. Now I understand what I believe, so I'm glad to have people know I'm a Christian."

When this happened, we thought it was a one-time attempt to investigate/intimidate the Christians on campus, so we didn't take it seriously. We carried on as usual, with our security cautions in place, until the bombshell came four months later.

The two men had continued interrogating students, but now they claimed to be professors of that same university. They were actually the Chinese FBI. When they interrogated one student, she betrayed us, as you will read in the story *To Betray or Not to Betray*. Right after we were discovered by the Chinese FBI, I called Maria and said I needed to see her away from campus.

When she got off the bus, I didn't approach her. Instead, I hand-signaled for her to follow me. We walked about 20 feet apart so no one would know we were together. Only after we entered the restaurant did we talk.

I told her that the Chinese FBI had discovered some of our campus ministry and that we would be moving from Re Dai in a few months. We wouldn't be able to meet anymore. I asked her to tell the others. I was so sad. I couldn't help all these new Christians become stabilized in their faith.

After the summer I met with the group one more time, a long way from campus. Once again, we maintained pretenses in public, as if we didn't know each other. We were together for 10 hours—dumplings for lunch, duck hot pot for dinner. This was our farewell.

The Holy Spirit had still been working greatly after I was removed. They were excited to tell me how much they had shared the gospel over the summer. I counted about 60 people these five women had shared Christ with during their summer break! They asked me for more Bibles to give their friends who were interested. I could hardly dig up enough Bibles to satisfy the need!

Maria taught Bible stories to children, using the methods I had taught her.

Jane had thought it would be useless to share the gospel with her father because he would just defer to her mother and her mother's Buddhism. I had suggested she tell him just a few sentences about what the Lord had done for her. She did. She was elated that he was interested in what she had to say.

Janna told me, "My mother saw me praying and she didn't object! I also told my good friend about Jesus and she responded well!"

Then Janna said, "I've been thinking about it all summer, and I've decided to be baptized. My decision to become a Christian is a decision for my whole life, so it's obvious I should be baptized. Can you help me get baptized? But don't wait too long. I want to do it soon!" A week later Janna was baptized by a house church leader in our bathtub. Justin and I didn't baptize people unless there was no other option because one of the questions the police would ask Christians was: "Have you been baptized?" and the follow-up question was, "Who baptized you?" It was better for all involved if the answer to the second question led to a local instead of a foreigner.

At our farewell meeting, Lacey told us that she taught English to a class of 22 students for her summer job. "The text brought up Jesus." (It probably said he was a myth.) "Since the text mentioned Jesus, so could I. So I told them all about Jesus and that he is God. The students said that what I was saying was crazy. So I changed my tack. I told them that if they have a problem, they can pray to Jesus and he'll help them. In the end, 10 of them were interested in Jesus, and one even wanted a Bible!"

"So, did you give him your Bible?" I asked.

"Are you kidding? There is no way I would give my Bible away—then I wouldn't have a Bible!"

Lu had put a lot of thought into how to share the gospel with her friends. "I picked out 12 of my friends to share with. I decided I could bring up Jesus by asking them the questions I had before becoming a Christian, like, 'Do you believe in evolution?' I was really surprised. Ten of them wanted to talk with me about Jesus!"

Then Lu said, "I had to share Jesus with them. What would have ever happened to me if no one had told me about Jesus?"

TO BETRAY OR NOT TO BETRAY?

2011-2012, Re Dai

After meeting with students all afternoon and late into the evening, I would usually get up a little late the next morning and stay in my nightgown for a few hours while I slowly woke up, got dressed, and had a lazy time of devotions with the Lord. Not now! Every morning as soon as I came to, I bolted upright, rushed out of bed, and tried to put some order into the mop of brown curls on my head. I dressed a little better than usual, put on my makeup, and sat stiffly on the edge of our couch, waiting for the police to arrive. Besides fretfully waiting, I didn't seem capable of doing anything but the bare essentials.

The police had discovered our college student Bible study, and not just the police, but the Chinese version of the FBI! I was afraid they would come to my home and start interrogating me. What better way to extract information than to question me alone while Justin was at work.

Over the weeks of waiting, a lot of the curls on top of my head fell out, handful by handful. Stress. I usually have an excellent memory for conversations, but I kept embarrassing myself by not remembering what was said to me just a few days before.

My mind constantly raced, playing over and over the anticipated interrogation that I dreaded and what I would say to the police to protect my Chinese friends. An American friend of ours had been interrogated for 48 hours straight before he was kicked out of China for spreading the gospel. I knew that if I didn't handle the interrogation well, my Chinese friends could lose what freedom they had, or maybe even their lives because of police brutality.

My hope was that, since the police hadn't caught us in the act of teaching the Bible or sharing the gospel with a group, they wouldn't take action. Before the police kicked our American friend out, they had barged in on him in the middle of a meeting, but we had shut down all of our Christian activities with the locals as soon as we knew the police were on to us, so there was nothing to barge in on.

As I sat on the edge of the sofa day after day and planned how to answer the police, the Lord reminded me of Matthew 10:19-20, that I didn't need to worry what I would say to the police because the Lord would give me the words to say. When I realized I could trust the Lord with the interrogation, I stopped sitting on the edge of the couch every day. My hair still kept falling out and my memory was still spotty, though. (Later both came back.)

When did all these problems start? It's hard to know. In early October, nine months earlier, Chrystal, a Chinese co-worker of Justin's, came into his office and asked to talk with him for a few minutes on the lawn in front of the administration building so no one could eavesdrop. Chrystal was a Christian who worked in the administration, a floor above Justin.

"I overheard my co-workers talking," she said. "The police told them they have pictures of Mel [an Australian missionary] reading the Bible with Chinese students in his English training center. They are now investigating both him and any other possible Christian activities going on with the university students." Chrystal had put herself at risk to warn Justin.

Justin immediately called me. He talked in code. "Tommy has pictures of Mel with the 66 and Penners. Tommy wants to find out what other Kie things are going on at Penn." Tommy meant police. Mel is a pseudonym. 66 is Bible. Penners meant university students. Kie meant Christian, and Penn meant university.

I shut my eyes to take in the seriousness of the situation, then I responded. "We have to let all the other foreigners know. I'll tell the foreigners who are in the city and you tell the foreigners who are on campus."

Since we didn't have code set up with the other foreigners, we had to make personal visits so the police wouldn't hear anything suspicious on the phone.

I spent the next half day informing Mel and his wife, and the rest of the Christian foreigners in town, so they could decide for themselves whether or not to shut down their ministries until the storm passed. Everyone put their ministries on pause.

What happened next took us by surprise and was very painful. Jez, a Canadian missionary from the foreigners' fellowship, the one who had tried to baptize Abby without introducing her to Christ first, was away on vacation with her family when all of this went down.

Jez always pumped us for information about our ministries, while lying to us to hide the most mundane facts of her own life. When the foreigners' fellowship would meet at our home, as soon as Jez walked in the door, she would race down the hall to my private study where my appointment calendar was hanging and examine it to find out who I was meeting with, what time and where! When I realized what she was doing, I started to code my own personal calendar. I used pseudonyms, and altered the time and date so only I could decipher it. Then Jez, herself, bragged that she had advised the police how to expel one of the foreigners who had lived in Re Dai! We always noticed she had no fear of the police and could function freely as a missionary. We wondered if the police told her that she could do her missionary work without hindrance if she would rat out the rest of us.

When Chrystal told Justin about the police investigation, although we were wary of Jez, we kept giving her the benefit of the doubt. It's hard to convince yourself that someone you're fellowshipping with is out to destroy you. But Jez eventually made it very clear.

When she and her family returned from vacation, we told her about the police having pictures of Mel with university students and how they were investigating other Christian activities with students.

The next Sunday, during the foreigners' fellowship, at the end of snack time when no one was around, Jez pulled me aside in the dining room of the home we were meeting in. She leaned in and spoke secretively, "Grace, the police know about Justin's Christian work on campus!"

I stared at her, a chill running down my spine. "No, Jez, they didn't discover Justin, it was Mel they discovered."

Did she know something I didn't know? Had we been discovered? We were very careful—small meetings, quiet.

After the fellowship was over, Jez grabbed my arm. "I need to talk with you, Grace." She led me into the storage room.

"Grace, let me tell you what happened. A policeman walked into the administration office and told them about the Christian work Justin is doing with the university students."

"Who told you this?"

"Chrystal."

Now I was sure she was lying. The best lie has some truth in it. Her story bore some resemblance to what had happened. But I knew the police had not actually entered Chrystal's office, because Chrystal had told us clearly that the police had not been there, and Justin had questioned Chrystal to make sure no other foreigners, including us, had been mentioned.

I didn't respond to Jez. She didn't realize we were close to Chrystal. Chrystal had told Justin everything, and we trusted her.

But just in case there was some mix-up, we wanted to confirm with Chrystal before we confronted Jez. I wrote out exactly what Jez told me and the next day Justin called Chrystal out to the lawn in front of the administration building, where all secrets were told. He showed her what I had written and asked if that is what happened.

"No! Not at all! Not only is that not what happened, but I never said that to Jez." Chrystal was angry.

The next day we asked Jez and her husband to come to our home. We confronted Jez with her insidious lie—telling us the police were after us when they weren't! Jez was totally still, hardly moving a muscle, as liars are when they don't want their body language to betray them. Then she made the most telling comment. "Since so many foreigners get booted out of Re Dai, they may think that I'm responsible, that I ratted them out." What a strange thing to say! After she said that I was sure she was a rat.

Then Jez's husband yelled at us for the next 55 minutes. "Are you calling my wife a liar?" "You have no right to treat her that way!" The best defense for heinous behavior is to blame the victim.

Unfortunately I was intimidated by his pretense at outrage, which was just what he wanted.

We quit the foreigners' fellowship because we couldn't fellowship with anyone who would tell us the police were after us when they weren't.

I have had many lonely times in China, but that was the worst. We no longer had any Christian fellowship and I was avoiding my local friends so the police wouldn't discover them.

It was six weeks before we felt like we could resume our local ministries. Then, five months later, in early March, Lacey told us about the two men posing as research students from Ren Min University, who were investigating Christian conversions on campus, as you read about in *The Bible is the Fulfillment of My Dream!*

We thought that was just a passing little problem, especially since we didn't hear anything else about the two men for four months. Then, late one afternoon at the end of June, while I was discipling Jane one-on-one, my phone rang. Two women, Brave and Faith, were on the line. They were the strongest Christians from the Bible study we led for Christian students. "Grace, we need to see you immediately. Something's happened!" Faith told me in Mandarin.

After Jane left, Justin, Brave and Faith met me in the apartment. We sat at the dining table.

Faith spoke first. "I was interrogated by two men posing as professors from Ren Min University from Chao Shi Province."

230

I sneered, "Yeah, a few months ago they said they were research students from the same university."

"They were very mean! They asked if I'm a Christian, what other Christian students I know, and they wanted to know if there are any Christian student gatherings on campus.

"I told them I was willing to tell them about myself and all about my commitment to Christ, but I wouldn't talk about anyone else."

Her face looked pained. "They laughed in my face and said, 'You think you're so smart! We already know everything anyway so you might as well tell us.' Then they told me that they know the names of the pastors at the government church."

I couldn't help myself. "Well that's stupid! That's public information! It's the government church, for crying out loud—it's not a secret!"

"Yeah, but that was only the beginning. They told me they know that Justin leads a Bible study for the students on campus at 6:30 every Sunday evening. And they told me the Bible study guide we used to use."

I became very still. I felt my throat constricting. This is what we had feared ever since we came to Mainland China. I said, "We used that study guide seven months ago, last November, so their information is old. And do you know who told them?"

Faith continued, "The two men said they had talked with May and she told them."

I turned to Justin, "Who is May?"

"She came only once to the Bible study last November."

"Faith," I asked, "what accent did the two men have? Are they from this province?" Every province, and even every city has its own dialect or accent.

"They were not from this province."

I said, "Then they were probably sent by Beijing, and they are the Chinese FBI. They have been here for months investigating Christian activity on campus." The three locations that had authority over us were the local police, the capital of the province, and Beijing. If they were sent from the local police or the capital of the province, they would have had the accent of this province.

Later they did clearly identify themselves as the Chinese FBI, when they showed up at the home of a house church pastor friend of ours named Ranger.

That week Faith talked to May and found out what happened. "May was called in by two men who said they were professors of Ren Min University from Chao Shi Province, but, of course, they were the Chinese FBI. They asked her about Christian meetings on campus, but she didn't want to tell them, so they told her, 'You can trust us. We won't tell anyone.' She felt she had to give up someone. Since she always attends Ranger's meetings, she's close to him and didn't want to rat him out. She only attended your Bible study once, so she doesn't feel close to you. She decided to betray you instead. May is really stupid!"

Justin and I knew we had to shut down all of our ministries immediately, and if the police didn't kick us out of China, we needed to move to another city. If we stayed on in Re Dai, the police would keep such a close eye on us we wouldn't be able to do any ministry. Moving was the best scenario we could hope for. It doesn't make sense, but in China, after you've been discovered by the police, you often can just move and start afresh.

But Justin would never be able to get another job in China if he didn't finish out his work contract, which wouldn't terminate until the end of October, so we decided to try to last until then. Four long months!

That's when I was waiting, with my hair falling out, for the police to visit, but by God's grace, they never came.

It was so confusing. I had never led so many people to the Lord as I had in the previous two years, and I had arranged for evangelistic student discussion groups to introduce me to new students for new discussion groups. My ministry would keep perpetuating itself if I stayed in Re Dai. But now we would have to move.

And what about all the new Christians that I hadn't had the opportunity to adequately disciple or place into fellowship? I would have to trust them to the Lord's care. I felt like the apostle Paul, when he was persecuted and had to flee, but didn't know if the new converts would make it (I Thessalonians 2:17–3:10).

That summer, Justin and I traveled the province in search of a job. Justin landed an English teaching job in another city to start a year from then, so we could return to the States for a year to visit our supporting churches.

The last couple of months in Re Dai we met secretly with Brave and Faith several times to train them to continue the work with the Christian students. We discovered a restaurant in town with an upstairs dining room that was rarely used. The waitresses were lazy, so they rarely entered the room to replenish our tea or serve us beyond the bare minimum. Lazy waitresses are ideal for secret Christian training.

We taught Brave and Faith how to lead discussion Bible studies. Then each of them prepared a Bible study, with us as participants. They had come surprisingly far in their ability to lead a study in just three sessions of training. They took over the leadership of the Christian student group after we left. If we hadn't been leaving, they wouldn't have had the opportunity to

232

take the leadership.

In the last session of training, though, before Justin and I could even get started, Faith, who always had it all together, burst into tears. Between sobs she told us, "The FBI have been interrogating me over and over. They won't let up! Every few days I have to go to another interrogation. They keep asking me questions that could only lead to the two of you. I keep trying to divert the conversation, so I won't have to talk about you, but it's so hard! I know that if I would just give you guys up, they would lay off and stop interrogating me. It's you they're after. But I'll never betray you two, no matter what happens!"

The police were looking for more incriminating evidence so they could close the trap on Justin and me. There was nothing current since we had shut down all our ministries. If Faith had told them what they wanted to find out, we suspect they would have kicked us out of China.

Faith spent an hour telling us about the interrogations. If you've never been interrogated by Chinese police, you have no idea how horrible the experience is. I was interrogated once for a minor incident, so I have a little idea what she went through.

At the end of our meeting, I hugged her, and through my tears, I whispered in her ear, "Thank you. If you had betrayed us, we wouldn't be able to do any more ministry in China. From now on, any work we do for the Lord, or anyone I lead to Christ in China, will only be because you were willing to suffer through the interrogations and protect us."

She was only 19 years old.

Because of her, we successfully moved to Kao Shan and continued our ministry in China.

After we moved, the FBI left her alone and she was accepted into grad school.

EMOTIONAL ANGLE

2015, Kao Shan

"Are you going to write about us in your book, Grace?" Rock and Amos, two college seniors asked me in English after I told them I was writing this book.

"Only if you tell me what you really think and feel, then I might write about you. But if you just tell me superficial things, I definitely won't write about you!"

I had met Rock and Amos for the first time that evening when I went to meet college students at a hangout owned by American Christians. The two of them looked like brothers, and except for their smiles, they could have passed for members of a Triad with their large square faces and massive, solid chests.

Amos didn't have a care in the world, and everywhere he went, he turned it into a party. Deep thoughts were banned from his jovial face. But Rock was pensive and a little sad—he couldn't help but try to solve the problems of his country. I couldn't understand how these two guys were close friends.

The women who ran the hangout told me that Rock was quiet and not very open, and that neither of them was interested in Jesus.

Rock, Amos, and I talked about our lives. Rock and Amos were both artistic, emotional, and sensitive. Amos was a musician and Rock wrote moving poetry. As they talked I listened closely to see what areas of life were important to them and how the gospel would appeal to them. Since all three of us were into the creative arts, I wondered if I could use emotions to make a case for the gospel. I had never done that before.

When I asked them to tell me the three things that were most important to them, family relationships dominated. When it was my turn, I told them

God was most important to me. They ignored my answer; God meant nothing to them.

Then Rock suddenly opened up to me, like a fire hydrant gushing. "My home province has so much corruption it's impossible to live without a lot of money. You can't see the doctor without giving him a bribe, you have to pass money under the table to get a driver's license, and you can't even drive down the road without a policeman stopping to give you a ticket unless you pay him off. It's horrible. I hate my province! How can I make enough money to bribe doctors, policemen, and officials so my parents and future wife can live? I love my parents and I want to take good care of them, but it takes so much money to bribe."

Amos sneered, "Rock just loves money, that's all."

"Amos, that's not what Rock's saying," I said. "What's important to him is taking care of the people he loves, it's just that he can't do that without a lot of money for bribes."

Rock looked relieved that I understood him and as a result, his deepest longings burst out. "I have such an emptiness inside," he said. "I don't know how to fill it. I'm desperate! I'm searching for the answer to life." I couldn't believe he was saying this to me—we had known each other only 20 minutes.

Amos looked listlessly over at a table full of card players.

My heart went out to Rock. "I know what you're talking about. I used to feel that emptiness, too. I searched and searched, and then I found." I was baiting him.

Rock was on the edge of his seat. "What did you find? Tell me! What's the answer? I need to know."

"I'll tell you later, but first I want to hear about your search. What have you been doing to search?" I didn't know Rock well enough; I didn't know what part of my search he could relate to.

"I read Confucius, the Bible, and I went to church."

I was surprised because he had shown no interest in God. "So what did you learn from Confucius?" I wanted to slowly lead into talking about the Lord, but Rock thought I said "church," instead of "Confucius."

His eyes looked off into the distance and a little smile played on his face. "The people had such pure hearts. They were happy. I felt happy being with them. They are good people."

"Those people are what you want to be."

"Yeah, they are."

"They're so different from what you grew up with."

"They're completely opposite."

"Has it ever occurred to you that you may have started to find what you're searching for? I mean, you went to church and it was so satisfying to your heart."

Amos started to fidget.

Rock was thinking deeply. "Yeah, whenever I have anything to do with God, the emptiness seems a little gone."

I wanted to break his fixation on money before I continued talking about the search for meaning. "You talk a lot about money. Money is important because you need enough to live, but sometimes things happen that you can't control—like you lose your job or become ill, and then you don't have the money you need. My husband and I pray for God to help us because we can't protect ourselves from all possible disasters. As important as money is, God is more important."

I let that sink in.

"You also equate money and love—you think that only if you have enough money to provide for someone's needs do you love them. I understand your thinking, but I don't completely agree. My husband wants to provide for me financially because he loves me—so love and money are related here. But even if he loses his job and can't provide for me, he still loves me deeply and that means a lot to me."

Rock was moved by what I said.

"I'll tell you about my search now. I couldn't find any meaning in life, and I didn't think life was worth living if there was no meaning. I was really difficult to be around. All I wanted to do was find the answer to life, nothing else was worth my time. So when I met someone new, the first question I asked them was if they believed in God. If they said yes, I asked why. If they said no, I asked why. If they couldn't give me a good answer, I just walked away from them—I didn't think they were worth talking to.

"I read all the religious scriptures from every religion I could find. There was some good stuff in them, but they all seemed like they were just written by men. But when I read the Bible, it was completely different. It seemed greater than what a person could write.

"Through my search I eventually found God, and he was the answer to my search. He's the greatest thing I have ever found. That was 39 years ago, and I have been getting to know him better and better ever since."

My story fascinated both of them. Amos asked, "You actually walked away from people if they couldn't tell you why they did or didn't believe in God?" We joked about how sassy and unreasonable I used to be.

Then I asked, "We really want life to have meaning, don't you think?"

Amos got up to play the piano. I had lost him.

"That's the whole point," Rock replied.

236

"If God created everything, then everything would have meaning because of him."

"Yes, he would give everything meaning."

"But if everything came about by evolution, then there's no meaning because it would have all come about by chance. But that is not how we experience life. We experience life as having meaning. Your relationship with your parents, your friends, your future wife, it all has meaning. We can feel there's meaning. We know it."

"Yeah, that's true."

I had never used this emotional argument for God and against evolution before, but it made sense to Rock because emotions were so important to him.

I continued, "Everything in the world is full of meaning for me." I pointed out the window. "Take that tree out there. It's just a tree, but it's full of meaning for me because I know its creator.

"If God created everything, then we know a lot about him. From the tree we see that he loves beauty, he's a scientist, an artist, and he's creative.

"And God actually loves that tree. I know that because he gave it everything it needs—soil, water, sun. It's the same with us. He gave us oxygen to breathe, and all the things we need for life because he loves us."

Rock was thinking deeply. "When I had an exam that I wasn't going to do well on, I prayed. I ended up doing really well. I told everybody that God helped me on the exam, but they thought I was proud and wouldn't listen to me. But God loves me, that's why he helped me!" This was a new thought for him. "I've been studying the Bible with Matt, my Chinese friend."

I was shocked. I hadn't realized that Rock had had some significant Christian input. He hadn't acted like it.

"So what did Matt tell you about Jesus and what he did for us?"

Rock's face brightened, but he sounded like a tape recorder with the volume turned up, "The Father, Son, and Holy Spirit!"

I jarred up. Of all the great things about Jesus, his takeaway was something he probably couldn't even understand? But the fact that Rock had been studying the Bible with Matt encouraged me to press forward.

I told Rock how amazing Jesus is. Then I asked him if he knew how to get close to God. He didn't. I told him that the bad things we do separate us from God because God is completely good.

Rock objected. "But we get forced to do bad things because of corruption. We can't be good enough for God."

"Let's put that issue aside for the time being. What about the bad things we do that we're not forced to do. Like, sometimes I hate someone, or I hurt other people, and sometimes I don't forgive others. Do you have any bad in your heart, or have you done bad things?"

"Yeah." He looked down.

"Well, that stops us from getting completely close to God."

"But God answered my prayer."

"Yes, he's very kind to us because he loves us so much, so he's willing to come a little close and answer our prayers. But he can't get real close to us unless the bad in us is gotten rid of." Then I told him about Jesus dying for us, how we can be forgiven and get close to God. I asked him if he wanted that.

"Yes, that's what I want!"

He prayed with me for forgiveness and to turn his life over to God.

Right then Amos returned from partying through the rest of the hangout. I turned to him. "Would you like to get close to God?"

"I don't feel any emptiness inside and I don't believe in God."

"Next time I come I want you to tell me why you don't believe in God. And you better have a good answer!"

Rock laughed. "Or you won't talk to him just like you wouldn't talk to those other people who couldn't tell you why they didn't believe in God."

As I waved goodbye and took the late bus home, I felt a sense of awe, but I was also puzzled. Why did Rock open up to me so quickly? And why were the emotional arguments so meaningful to him? I had been hesitant to use them because they never would have convinced me. And God loves a tree? What was that about?

A GOD BEYOND IMAGINATION

2015, Kao Shan

The next week Rock brought his good friend, Lisa, to meet me at the hangout. Lisa had shoulder-length hair and a thin, guarded face. She couldn't speak a word of English so all the rest of our conversations were in Mandarin.

Lisa and I both majored in biology, so first we talked about what we enjoyed about biology. Then I asked Lisa, "Have you ever read the Bible?"

"I've read some of the Bible, and I really like it because it makes me feel so peaceful."

"That's great! Do you believe in God, Lisa?"

"No."

"Why not?"

"Because of evolution."

"So why do you believe in evolution?"

"Because I've been taught it all my life."

"That's not a good enough reason to believe anything."

Rock looked over at her and put his hand on her shoulder. "Lisa, if evolution is true there's no meaning in life. We all know there's meaning, so evolution isn't true."

Lisa glared at him.

Rock laughed.

Since Lisa was studying the sciences, she needed a more scientific approach. I talked about the fact that there are almost no intermediates in the fossil record, and I told her about intelligent design. "Lisa, evolution doesn't select creatures because they're intelligent; rather, it selects organisms that produce a lot of babies. Bacteria are evolutionarily the fittest organisms because they produce the most babies and furthermore they are the most adaptable. So why would bacteria have evolved into organisms, like us, that are less fit according to evolution?"

Lisa tensed up.

Since I suspected she was quite conservative morally, I concluded, "I read in a science magazine about evolutionary ethics. Because of evolution men want to have a lot of offspring, so they sleep with as many women as they can. Women, on the other hand, bear the babies, so they want the man to stay around to help support the kids. That's the ethics evolution leads to."

"That can't be right. Evolution teaches us morality. That's where our morals come from."

"How is that?"

She didn't say anything and looked confused.

Then Amos sauntered in, two hours late, with an announcement. "I don't believe in God and I don't know why."

After Amos realized we had been discussing evolution, he blurted out with a big smile on his face, "That's why I don't believe in God—because of evolution!"

We arranged to meet at my home to watch two movies in Mandarin. The movies would explain some of the flaws in evolution.

The next week, the four of us huddled around the TV in my study to watch. I had to press pause frequently because they asked me so many questions. Our discussions and watching these movies were the first times they had ever heard about the weaknesses in the evolutionary theory.

Lisa and Amos had completely different responses. Lisa calmly said, "I can now accept that the arguments against evolution are valid." But Amos looked alarmed. "If evolution isn't true, then what's the point of life?"

Lisa was starting to consider believing in God, but she wanted to make sure she wasn't believing a myth. She commented, "We've always been taught that God is just wishful thinking, that man imagined God."

I responded, "Falling in love, where you only imagine what the person is like, now that's wishful thinking. You think the person is just what you imagined him to be, but you're not actually connecting with a real person.

"Really knowing someone is completely different—he won't be just what you imagined, and there will be things you don't like about him. Also, the relationship can grow deeper.

"My relationship with God is a real relationship. How do I know? He's not exactly what I imagined he would be. He's way beyond what I imagined. Also, I keep getting to know him more deeply. That doesn't happen with an imagined relationship.

240

"In fact, although most things about God I really like, there are some things I don't like about him and the Bible. If God came out of my imagination, I would like everything about him. So God is not just wishful thinking."

Lisa responded, "Oh. Now, I understand."

"And anyway, your teachers don't know God, that's why they say that. If they knew him, they'd think differently. Actually, I think Communism is just wishful thinking!" I grinned.

The last time we met, before they graduated, I invited the three of them out for a goodbye dinner. It was only the fourth time I had been able to meet with Lisa.

She told me, "I've been thinking a lot about God and evolution. I really want to find out if God exists and if evolution is not true. Now I need to do my own research."

"That's a great idea! I also researched before I came to believe in God. If you come to believe in God, it has to be because you, yourself, are convinced. No one can force you. What is really important, though, is that you base your life on what is true. If you believe things that aren't true, it messes up your life. But if what you believe is true, your life becomes fuller, richer, more free, and full of peace and joy. So you have to be careful. You really want to believe what is true."

"Yes, I definitely want to know the truth and base my life on it."

She asked me for a copy of the movies about evolution so she could watch them again. And I gave her a going away gift—a book written by a Chinese biologist, telling what convinced him to become a Christian. "I am definitely going to read this and it will be part of my research. I am so excited that I'm going to find out the truth about God!"

Two months earlier Lisa had had no interest in God. All that was needed was for someone to ask her why she didn't believe in God, and to help her explore the reasons.

WHO IS ANSWERING MY PRAYERS?

2014-2015, Kao Shan

Professor Li smiled as she looked intently at me from across the table in the restaurant. "Grace, about 60 of my students are interested in spiritual things. I've shared with them a little about the Lord, but since I'm a professor at a state university, I can only do so much. Could I introduce them to you to see if you can lead them to Christ?"

I could hardly sit still in my seat. I had been hoping and praying for an opportunity like this for the nine months we had lived in Kao Shan. "It will work best if I start a discussion group with about six students. Let me begin with one group, then I can start more groups after that."

"That sounds great! After I make introductions, I can't meet with the group, though. It's important that I maintain my distance from sharing the gospel."

After I arrived home, I was singing and dancing and praising the Lord. I had been making a few relationships with Christian and non-Christian locals in Kao Shan, but this was my breakthrough.

Professor Li invited five women and me out for dinner. One of the women, Fatima Bao, was very picky about the food. "I can't eat pork. In fact, I can't eat any of the food you eat—it might not have been prepared properly." I looked at Fatima confused. She said, "I'm Muslim."[1]

I gulped. I was going to have a Muslim in the group? I had only once

---

1. There are over 20 million Muslims living in China. Fatima was a Hui Muslim. The Hui are the descendants of Silk Road travelers, and of Middle Eastern Muslims who were brought to China by the Mongols (who ruled the Yuan Dynasty) to act as administrators. These Muslim men married local Chinese women. Their descendants are the Hui Muslims, who are scattered through much of China.

witnessed to a Muslim—that was in Malaysia where I just said several sentences about Jesus to a Muslim woman I had become friends with. I really didn't have a clue how to witness to a Muslim. Why had Professor Li invited a Muslim?

I went home and ordered five e-books on how to witness to Muslims. I would do the best I could. "Lord, help me!"

The first day the women came to my home, I decided to discuss something neutral—What are you looking for in a husband? They went around the group giving their thoughts: handsome, funny, outgoing …

They had already seen the beauty of Justin's character when he served us coffee. I told them about aspects of marriage they hadn't thought about—how to fight, how to forgive, how to solve problems. I told them about the love letters Justin and I write to each other, how Justin roots for me in all my endeavors, and the role our faith plays in our marriage.

They were mesmerized. Fatima cornered me afterward. "What you told us about marriage was really helpful. Our parents don't talk to us about life issues."

After the discussion, I taught Sherry, Tammy, and Roz guitar while Fatima and Eileen banged out a percussion beat on my djumba drum to the blasting of Chinese pop music on Fatima's phone.

The next week the women brought another friend, June. At that meeting, Sherry, who was an extraordinarily beautiful girl, told us her deepest pain soon after we all sat down at my round, wooden dining table. "My family didn't want me. They already had a son and two daughters. Because I'm a girl, they farmed me out to another family, but that family didn't love me either. I don't feel very good about myself and I don't have a foundation in life."

I looked at Sherry's almost round face, her hair cut blunt just below her shoulders and colored with a little henna, and wondered how a young woman that beautiful could feel so bad about herself. I sympathized with her and told her about some of my struggles. I tried to help her see that her parents may have loved her; sending her away may have been their best option.

Next, we talked about forgiveness. I had prepared a handout with Scripture verses. Fatima looked sour all through the Bible discussion. Whenever I said something, like, "We can't hope for God's forgiveness if we refuse to forgive others," Fatima evaluated what I said, then announced, "Yes, that is true. That is what our Muslim doctrine teaches."

I was so frustrated. Usually these group discussions were organic and energetic, but not this one. How were the women going to grapple with Scripture, evaluate if it was true to life, and try it out by applying it to their lives, when Fatima kept deadening the discussion by applying her doctrinal checklist? Was Fatima going to be able to learn anything about the Lord from the discussions when all that motivated her was fear of going against her Muslim doctrine? Could the group move forward with Fatima attending?

Then I made a huge botch. Eileen asked me, "Is Jesus God?" I stared at her, silent, afraid of offending Fatima. I had planned on talking about Jesus' identity, but not this fast—not in the second session. Eileen couldn't figure out why I wouldn't answer her. She rephrased her question. "According to Christianity, is Jesus God?" I finally whispered yes, hoping Fatima hadn't heard. I'm sure Eileen concluded that I was ashamed of Christ.

I didn't think there was any future for the group. If they had all been Muslims, I would have styled the group for Muslims, but I couldn't do that with only one Muslim.

That evening, after they left, I felt bad. I was debating ending the group because it wasn't workable. While I was licking my wounds, Sherry unexpectedly texted me, "Thank you for letting me see that my parents loved me. Maybe I should find God. I believe he can help me in my troubles. You made me realize it. I'm looking forward to next time because I want to find out more about God."

I could hardly believe it! I decided not to shut down the group.

After an hour of discussion about life and the Bible each week, the second hour we usually played games. I taught them Pit, and once they understood the game, I couldn't shake them from it—that was the only game they wanted to play. The second hour was full of shrieks and laughter as we outwitted each other at Pit.

Then one day Eileen said to me, "We've all been talking about it. Do you know why we like coming here? It's because you love us so much. Also, you're so full of joy. We all feel happy just being around you."

Because of a school activity, one evening, only June and Tammy were able to come over.

"What would you like to discuss?" I asked.

June was fuming. "I want to talk about anger! Someone was mean to me and I've been so angry lately!"

I showed them Ephesians 4:26 and Psalm 4:4. "It's O.K. to be angry." As soon as I said that, June visibly calmed down. "God gave us anger so we could protect ourselves from being mistreated. But you can't stay angry; you need to forgive. If your anger is an over-reaction, there is probably unresolved anger from your past, like against your family for mistreating you or maybe people looked down on you because you're a woman. If you resolve anger from your past by forgiving those people, you'll find you don't over-re-act to current offenses."

June and Tammy were thinking deeply. June said, "What you're saying is very helpful."

Tammy then read the verses before and after the ones we had read together. She looked up at me. "I'm confused. What the Bible says and what Confucius says are similar. Both tell us how to live. I don't understand because there's overlap between the two—shouldn't one be true and one be false?"

"Well, truth is truth, wherever you find it!"

She looked off into the distance for a minute, then broke into a smile, "I see."

"A lot of what Confucius said was true, but not everything," I said. "I do believe everything in the Bible is true, though. But, wherever you find truth, it's true! Now, tell me, what's the main difference between Confucianism and Christianity?"

"If you're a Confucianist you don't have to believe and follow everything Confucius said, but if you're a Christian, you must believe and follow everything in the Bible."

I laughed. "That's true, but the main difference is that the Bible talks about a creator God, but any god Confucius believed in, he didn't consider important or relevant. So, what's the core of Christianity?"

They drew a blank.

"God wants relationship with us!" I thought that was all they could take, so I stopped there.

Two months after we first started meeting, the day before Sherry was to take the 2,000-mile train ride home to see her biological parents for the summer vacation, she called. "Can I come over? I really want to see you."

When she arrived, she said, "Grace, recently I've been talking to God all the time, telling him the good and bad things that are happening in my life, and he's helping me! He's been telling me what to do to solve the problems I have!"

"Do you know who you're talking to, Sherry?"

"No. Who is it that's helping me? Who am I talking to? I want to know who he is!" Sherry put her faith in Christ that night.

Her smile was so wide after coming to know Jesus, her face hurt!

The next day Sherry rode the train home, and told her parents about her faith. They were angry! They know some people, whom Sherry described as fake Christians, and her parents find their faith ugly. They thought Sherry's new faith was the same as the fake Christians.

Six weeks later, when Sherry saw me again, she yelled she was so mad. "My parents are wrong!"

Sherry started attending a Christian fellowship, spending whole days in Bible training, and telling her friends about Jesus. Her joy was so evident, the rest of the women told me, "We all see how happy Sherry is because of Jesus." I looked around at their faces. They looked envious of her joy and her faith in the Lord.

Sherry told me privately that they were all considering believing in Jesus.

Shortly after Sherry returned from summer vacation, only she and Fatima were able to visit one evening. Sherry was bubbling over, talking about the Lord. I also wanted to give Fatima a chance to talk about her faith, so I turned to her. "What do you believe, Fatima?"

"I believe in the true God." Oh, that settles it! "I have Muslim brothers and sisters and I enjoy them. My parents are Muslim and I was born into Islam. I love it and it makes me very happy." That's it?

Sherry piped up, "Well, I'm very happy because of Jesus!"

I joined in, "And I have Christian brothers and sisters I love."

Fatima was shaken. After they left, the two of them walked back to the dorm instead of taking the bus so they could talk. As they strolled along the lake for two hours, Fatima emphasized to Sherry that Christians and Muslims believe essentially the same things. Really?

Later, the women told me that Fatima was very attracted to Jesus, but she was afraid she'd start to believe in him, and she wanted to make sure that didn't happen.

The first couple months we met as a group, Fatima often told us how excited she was to attend two-week sessions where she studied Islam. But after Jesus became attractive to her, she kept finding excuses so she wouldn't have to attend the Islamic study sessions. "It's too cold there. I don't want to go!"

After months of Pit, guitar lessons, learning to make chocolate chip cookies (where Fatima abstained in case any of the ingredients were verboten), discussions about life and the Bible (while Fatima looked upset), and decorating our Christmas tree, shortly before Easter I asked them what they wanted to talk about.

Fatima spoke up, "I feel such a hollowness inside. What do I do?"

What a question! But how far could I take it since she was still making faces and looking irritated whenever we discussed Jesus or the Bible?

I showed them Luke 12:13-21, the parable of the rich fool who built barns to store all his wealth, and then he died. "What was he living for?" "Was that worthwhile to live for?" "What does 'life does not consist in an abundance of possessions' mean?" I told them how I used to feel empty inside, but after I found Jesus I stopped feeling empty.

Roz asked, "Grace, do you really feel no emptiness inside whatsoever?"

"Well, I feel a small emptiness because some of my relationships are not as satisfying as they should be, but I don't feel the big emptiness I used to feel before Jesus."

They went around and all told whether they felt a big emptiness or a small emptiness. What a strange but honest discussion! Unexpectedly, two weeks later, it resulted in beautiful fruit.

After our discussion about emptiness, I asked, "Do you want Bibles of your own?"

Everyone, including Fatima, was excited to get a Bible. They actually stroked the Bibles I gave them! "The Bible is so interesting! We're definitely going to read it."

I dug out American Christmas wrapping paper from our storage shelves, and they wrapped their new Bibles in glittering golds, greens, and reds, so no one would know what book they were reading.

The next week was Easter. We decorated Easter eggs together, but when Fatima found out the significance of Easter eggs is new life, she opted out.

After that we watched the *Jesus* film. Except for Fatima and her best friend, Eileen, the women were on the edge of their seats watching it. Eileen spent the whole time comforting Fatima since she knew that such a beautiful depiction of Jesus' life would be upsetting to her. Fatima was trying so hard to hold on to her Muslim faith.

When the movie was over, Tammy looked shaken.

A week later Sherry texted me. "Grace, I have good news. Tammy wants to know Jesus!" I hadn't seen it coming. I raced into Justin's office to tell him.

They took a bus to my home as soon as possible. After we sat down at the dining table, I asked, "So, Tammy, why do you want to become a Christian?"

"I couldn't stop thinking about the discussion we had two weeks ago about feeling empty inside, and then the film about Jesus shook me up! I decided right then that I would follow Jesus, but I still wanted to think about it for a few days because it's such a big decision."

"Before you make this decision to follow Jesus, do you have any questions you'd like to ask?"

"In the film Jesus said that we need to take up our cross. How do I take up my cross?"

Her question brought tears to my eyes. I replied, "Everyone has a different cross to bear for Jesus—some are persecuted or put in prison, some are rejected by their parents, some lose their jobs. Your cross will be different than mine or Sherry's, but we must be willing to make whatever sacrifice for Jesus we're called upon to make." Then I told her about the cross of rejection I have borne for the Lord, and we talked about Sherry's parents' reaction to her faith.

After Tammy committed her life to Christ, we discussed baptism. I said, "Your heart just got baptized, and your body and heart have to be in sync, so your body also needs to be baptized." Up until then, Sherry had resisted getting baptized. Sherry said, "Looking at it from that perspective, I want to be baptized, too." (The responsibility to baptize them I turned over to a house church pastor.)

Every now and then, the others were tied up with required school activities, and just Sherry and Tammy were able to come over. Each time, with a huge grin on her face, Sherry downed about 15 chocolate chip cookies, the whole batch except for the paltry two Tammy ate. After that, all I could get out of my mouth was, "Do you want to read …" and the two of them whooped with joy that we were going to study the Bible together.

A couple of weeks before they all left for their final internship before graduation, Tammy told me, "I hate to read, but the Bible, well, that's different. When I became a Christian you told me to read the Bible 10 minutes a day, so I set a timer. But I get annoyed when the timer goes off because I want to keep reading, so I set it for another 10 minutes. I keep doing that until finally I turn the timer off completely and read the Bible to my heart's content! And the longer I believe in Jesus, the more joy I have!"

A FEW THOUGHTS ON EVANGELISM

2014-2015, Kao Shan

My 29 years of living in Hong Kong and Mainland China taught me many lessons about sharing the gospel. I couldn't start from my way of thinking and expect *them* to make the transition—almost definitely they wouldn't. *I* had to make the switch and think like they did. In order to do this I had to listen closely to everything they said and sometimes I had to read about their beliefs. When I talked with them, I used their presuppositions, not mine.

Sometimes how I tried to share with them about the Lord didn't work, so I changed my approach midstream.

When we lived in Kao Shan, a veiled Muslim friend, Noor, visited me once a week. She hadn't been veiled when we first met. Then one day she came over wearing a beautiful black embroidered and sequined veil. When I asked her about it, she told me in Mandarin, "The imam in our village is now requiring all the women to be veiled." The Chinese government was persecuting the Muslims at that time, so I guess the veiling was in solidarity with their persecuted brothers and sisters.

Before she was veiled, I had hinted that I believe in Jesus. Then one morning she asked me, "What is it you believe?"

I was excited to have the opportunity to talk with a Muslim about Jesus, so I poured out a concise explanation of the gospel: Jesus is God. He died for our sins and rose again.

She stared at me with no comprehension or interest.

I was so frustrated. It motivated me to read more of the books I had bought about how to share the gospel with Muslims. I began to understand what she believed and how to start with the overlap in our beliefs.

About a month or two after she started wearing the veil, she came over looking very sad. She said, "I just aborted my baby. I had accidentally become pregnant, but I was taking medicine that could damage the baby. I wanted to keep the baby, but my husband and son said that I should abort her. See, if I kept the baby we would have to pay a very expensive fine. My husband and son told me that we have enough money to pay the fine for a healthy baby, but why pay it for a damaged child? If we paid the money for the damaged child, we wouldn't have money to later pay for a healthy baby if I became pregnant again. They talked me into aborting my child."

We cried together.

Then Noor said, "According to Islam I've sinned because I had an abortion."

"As a Muslim, is there any forgiveness for you?" I asked.

"I would have to go to Mecca, if I could, to be forgiven. But I can't go to Mecca."

"Noor, I will pray to the prophet Jesus that he will forgive you. Prophet Jesus' special task is forgiving sins." (Muslims believe that Jesus is one of the prophets and that each prophet has a special task.)

Noor was overwhelmed. "Thank you! Thank you!"

I was beginning at her starting point and trying to take her step by step toward Jesus.

Several months later Noor had some more bad news: "My son was ambushed and beaten up by two other students. He's only 13 years old." Her breath caught. "I took him to the doctor and they're not sure if he'll ever be able to father a child when he grows up. He looks horrible down there—he's all black and blue—and he's in a lot of pain." A tear slipped down her cheek.

That would have been terrible for any parent, but with the one-child policy, it was especially heart-wrenching.

"Noor, I will fervently pray to Jesus for your son."

She looked amazed and grateful. "Wow! You depend on Jesus just like we depend on the *true God*!" Then, surprisingly, she corrected herself and changed "true God" to "Allah." Muslims tend to be in your face that they are the ones who serve the *true God*. Was she wondering if Jesus might be the true God?

Later when I told her I would be returning to the States, she asked me what I would do in America. I told her I would be writing this book. She said, "Jesus will help you write the book."

I had researched what she believed so I could find common ground. I tried to think the way she thought, and be gentle and non-confrontational, starting with her felt needs.

§§§

A group of eight college students had studied the Bible in English once a week for a few years with an American woman, Angie. It meant free English lessons, and they liked Angie. As far as I knew, Angie had never asked them if they wanted to become Christians.

One evening I was introduced to the group so I could lead a discussion with them. I anticipated that some of them were on the verge of believing in Christ because they had studied the Bible for so long—the hard work had already been done and they just needed someone to ask them if they wanted to believe. I used a combination of English and Mandarin with them.

To find out which ones were close to trusting Christ I asked, "Do you pray?"

"Yes, we pray," most of them answered.

"Who do you pray to?" I don't assume anything.

Each student had a different answer. "Everyone I can think of." "No one." "Just in my heart. I pray to myself." "Buddha." "The sacred mountain."

My heart sank. They certainly weren't on the verge of believing in Jesus, so I went a different direction. "Whoever you pray to *has to be real* for him to answer you. *If you pray to someone who isn't there, no one's listening!*"

I looked around at their faces. They looked surprised. I don't think it had ever crossed their minds that they needed to be sure the one they were praying to really existed. I realized then that they didn't believe in absolute truth.

I continued. "If you're going to get the help you need when you pray, there are four things that must be true about the one you're praying to: One, he must exist. Two, the one you're praying to must be listening to you. Three, he must love you, or he won't bother to help you. And four, he must be powerful, or he *can't* help you."

They all talked about how to find out if those they were praying to exist. They decided that if he answered their prayers, then he exists. Some of them even decided to find out if the God of the Bible exists by praying to him to see what would happen.

When I realized that I had completely misjudged where they were, I switched my approach on the spot. Then I started where they were, and tried to gently provoke them to think seriously about their gods, and put their gods to the test.

Sharing the gospel didn't just change the lives of those who were hearing the gospel, it changed my life as well. It taught me to listen and respect others' beliefs, while at the same time gently challenging their belief systems. It also taught me to pray and depend on the Lord to show me where to take conversations.

CHINA, THE LAND OF MY HEART

2015, Kao Shan to USA

Professor Li was introducing me to more and more students, faster than I could form discussion groups. Leading four student groups was exciting, but I was finding it harder and harder to run the groups. After 29 years of breathing polluted air, I was repeatedly coming down with sinus infections and bronchitis. I struggled to keep appointments, and I had to cancel more discussion groups and evangelistic appointments than I could keep. I also was hardly able to teach English at the private school, the job Justin and I shared for our work visas, because I was too sick. That meant that Justin wasn't free to teach Chinese church pastors.

We wrote our prayer supporters an email, asking them to pray for my healing so we could continue our work in China. Every other time we had needed a miracle so we could remain in China, the Lord had granted it. Not this time—he didn't heal me. The Lord closed the door for us to work in China, and he used my illness to do it.

A year earlier, the Lord had lined up our visas, rental agreement, and job contract to all terminate July 1. It hadn't made sense to us at the time—all the other parties had asked us to change the terms of the contracts, to *their* detriment. When I became so ill, we understood why it happened. The Lord had been planning our departure long before it had ever crossed our minds.

With tears, we packed up and gave away decades of possessions in a month. Then Justin and I headed to different airports so he could accompany the luggage; I would fly to Justin's airport.

My taxi drove away from the mountain that overlooked Kao Shan, the last city in China I loved. We rode along the lake where fishermen were casting nets from their long skiffs. On the right were the colorful, distinctively

Chinese, curved ceramic tile roofs.

I was so blessed to have been able to spend 29 years of my life in Hong Kong and Mainland China, making Chinese friends, and speaking the dialects of their hearts. They opened up to me, and I opened my heart to them.

My Chinese friends taught me about love and committed friendship. They taught me the graciousness of gift-giving, lavish hospitality, and the importance of properly saying goodbye to the ones you love.

My Chinese Christian friends showed me how to suffer for my faith.

I came to their land, which is now my land, as fully American—I left as part Chinese.

In the great land of China, I came to know my God. Seeing him through the eyes of Buddhists, idol worshippers, atheists, Muslims, and an animist gave me an awe for the beauty of the God I worship. Living in the crucible of China, I came to know his great love for us and the power he uses on our behalf. Being stripped of the safety zones in life, I learned to pray and to trust the Lord; being stripped of pat answers, I came to know his Word.

My taxi driver interrupted my thoughts. He turned to me and asked if he could show me where he and his wife were buying a condo. He drove up a hill near the lake. "Look at the beautiful view of the mountain and the lake!" His family finally had the money to buy a home and he wanted to share his joy with me. Then he took me the back way into the airport to make sure I wouldn't miss my plane after our excursion.

When our Chinese friends all around China found out we were moving back to the States, they asked if they could fly or take trains to our home to spend time with us before we left. Because I wasn't well and we were packing, we had to turn them down, so they flocked from around the country to the airports along our route to see us. Some of them traveled hundreds of miles to the airports to say goodbye to us. Many of them, by God's grace, I had led to the Lord.

Peter, who had been persecuted as a young man, was now middle-aged with a family. He still lived in Wuran, a city we hadn't lived in for years. He told us, "Even though you haven't lived in my city for a long time, it has always felt good that you at least lived in the same country as me. You living in a different country is going to take some getting used to."

You are very important to the success
of *Dragon Ride*.

If you enjoyed the book,
please tell your friends,
write an Amazon review,
and post it on your favorite social media.

Thank you so much.

I would also love to hear from you at:
hisfragrancespreader@gmail.com

ACKNOWLEDGEMENTS

My thanks go, first of all, to Justin, my husband and my friend. Without his daily encouragement and occasional criticism, this work would not have been possible. He believed in me so I kept going.

I am grateful for the insights of my son, Adam. He sparked ideas for complete revisions of a few of the stories.

Dr. Kevin Haley (author of an awesome book, *The Extraordinary Ordinary Egg*) formatted the book. His help was invaluable.

Many friends and acquaintances read *Dragon Ride* while it was in process. I greatly appreciate all of your feedback.

And, finally, I would like to thank Evangeline Boston (age 7), who helped me choose the cover.

NOTES

47159977R00167

Made in the USA
Columbia, SC
28 December 2018